Tricks
of the

eBay®

Business
Masters

Michael Miller

qUe®

800 East 96th Street,
Indianapolis, Indiana 46240 USA

Tricks of the eBay® Business Masters

ISBN-13: 978-0-7897-3699-4
ISBN-10: 0-7897-3699-3

Library of Congress Cataloging-in-Publication Data:

Miller, Michael, 1958-
   Tricks of the eBay business masters / Michael Miller. — 1st ed.
      p. cm.
   ISBN 0-7897-3699-3
   1. eBay (Firm) 2. Internet auctions. I. Title.
   HF5478.M556 2008
   658.8'7—dc22

                                    2007026050

Printed in the United States on America

First Printing: August 2007

Trademarks

All terms mentioned in this book that are known to be trademarks or service marks have been appropriately capitalized. Que Publishing cannot attest to the accuracy of this information. Use of a term in this book should not be regarded as affecting the validity of any trademark or service mark.

Warning and Disclaimer

Every effort has been made to make this book as complete and as accurate as possible, but no warranty or fitness is implied. The information provided is on an "as is" basis. The author and the publisher shall have neither liability nor responsibility to any person or entity with respect to any loss or damages arising from the information contained in this book.

Bulk Sales

Que Publishing offers excellent discounts on this book when ordered in quantity for bulk purchases or special sales. For more information, please contact

   U.S. Corporate and Government Sales
   1-800-382-3419
   corpsales@pearsontechgroup.com

For sales outside the United States, please contact

   International Sales
   international@pearsoned.com

Associate Publisher
Greg Wiegand

Acquisitions Editor
Michelle Newcomb

Development Editor
Kevin Howard

Managing Editor
Gina Kanouse

Project Editor
George E. Nedeff

Copy Editor
Mike Henry

Indexer
Erika Millen

Proofreader
Debbie Williams

Technical Editor
Jenna Lloyd

Publishing Coordinator
Cindy Teeters

Book Designer
Anne Jones

Composition
Fastpages

This Book Is Safari Enabled

The Safari® Enabled icon on the cover of your favorite technology book means the book is available through Safari Bookshelf.

When you buy this book, you get free access to the online edition for 45 days.

Safari Bookshelf is an electronic reference library that lets you easily search thousands of technical books, find code samples, download chapters,and access technical information whenever and wherever you need it.

To gain 45-day Safari Enabled access to this book:

- Go to http://www.quepublishing.com/safarienabled
- Complete the brief registration form
- Enter the coupon code 4KLT-N2DM-2KYW-2JM4-UWZ3

If you have difficulty registering on Safari Bookshelf or accessing the online edition, please email customer service@safaribooksonline.com.

Contents at a Glance

Table of Contents

About the Author

Michael Miller is an eBay master who has written more than 75 nonfiction books over the past two decades, including Que Publishing's *Absolute Beginner's Guide to eBay, Easy eBay, eBay Auction Templates Starter Kit, Making a Living from Your eBay Business,* and *Tricks of the eBay Masters.* He also writes about digital lifestyle topics for a number of websites.

Mr. Miller has established a reputation for clearly explaining technical topics to nontechnical readers, and for offering useful real-world advice about complicated topics. More information can be found at the author's website, located at www.molehillgroup.com.

Dedication

To Sherry, who there's no trick to at all.

Acknowledgments

Thanks to the usual suspects at Que Publishing, including but not limited to Greg Wiegand, Michelle Newcomb, Kevin Howard, and George Nedeff. Thanks also to technical editor Jenna Lloyd, who has worked on several of my previous eBay books; she helps to make these books more accurate than they would have been otherwise.

We Want to Hear from You!

As the reader of this book, *you* are our most important critic and commentator. We value your opinion and want to know what we're doing right, what we could do better, what areas you'd like to see us publish in, and any other words of wisdom you're willing to pass our way.

As an associate publisher for Que Publishing, I welcome your comments. You can email or write me directly to let me know what you did or didn't like about this book—as well as what we can do to make our books better.

Please note that I cannot help you with technical problems related to the topic of this book. We do have a User Services group, however, where I will forward specific technical questions related to the book.

When you write, please be sure to include this book's title and author as well as your name, email address, and phone number. I will carefully review your comments and share them with the author and editors who worked on the book.

Email: feedback@quepublishing.com

Mail: Greg Wiegand
         Associate Publisher
         Que Publishing
         800 East 96th Street
         Indianapolis, IN 46240 USA

Reader Services

Visit our website and register this book at www.quepublishing.com/register for convenient access to any updates, downloads, or errata that might be available for this book.

Introduction

Want to be your own boss? Want to make a decent living selling online? Want to build your own successful eBay business?

Others have done it. Others have turned simple eBay selling into a profitable business. Others have figured out how to run a profitable business on eBay.

What do these sellers know that you don't? You'd be surprised; there are a lot of tricks involved in building a successful eBay business.

One hundred and one of those tricks are presented in this book, *Tricks of the eBay Business Masters*. One hundred and one tricks that show you how to sell profitably and successfully on eBay. One hundred and one tricks that show you how to grow your business into one that provides a full- or part-time income for you and your family.

What kinds of tricks am I talking about? Well, you'll have to read the book to find out, but in general these are tricks that help you plan for growth, locate and purchase inventory to sell, create effective auction listings, pack and ship efficiently, and manage your business and business growth.

Want to know what products to sell? That trick is in the book. Want to find out the best service to use for shipping your products? That trick's here, also. Want to learn how to increase your profit on every item you sell? That's here, too.

Where do these tricks come from? I've garnered these tricks from years of personal selling on eBay, and from observing hundreds of successful eBay sellers over those years. The tricks come from those who've learned how to do it themselves—the eBay business masters who run their own successful eBay businesses.

You can use the tricks in this book as a step-by-step guide to planning and building your eBay business—or, if you're already selling, you can use these tricks to help you sell more and more profitably. Whether you're a big or a small seller, you'll find more than a few tricks in this book that will help you become more successful.

How This Book Is Organized

Tricks of the eBay Business Masters contains 101 tricks for building a more successful eBay business. These tricks are organized into 11 chapters, each focused on a particular aspect of eBay selling:

1. Tricks for Managing Your eBay Business
2. Tricks for Deciding What to Sell
3. Tricks for Purchasing and Managing Your Inventory
4. Tricks for Creating More Effective Listings
5. Tricks for Setting Prices and Handling Payments
6. Tricks for Packing and Shipping
7. Tricks for Promoting Your eBay Business
8. Tricks for Running a Successful Trading Assistant Business
9. Tricks for Cutting Costs—And Increasing Profits
10. Tricks for Expanding Your eBay Business
11. The Ultimate Trick for eBay Business Success

At the end of each chapter you'll find a profile of a particular eBay business. These eBay business masters share their advice and expertise about selling on eBay; they're examples of how it works in the real world. Read and learn from them.

Conventions Used in This Book

I hope that this book is easy enough to figure out on its own, without requiring its own instruction manual. As you read through the pages, however, it helps to know precisely how I've presented specific types of information.

As you read through this book you'll note several special elements, presented in what we in the publishing business call *margin notes*. There are different types of margin notes for different types of information, as you see here.

note

This is a note that presents some interesting but not necessarily essential information about a topic discussed in the surrounding text.

tip

This is a tip that might prove useful for whatever you're in the process of doing.

caution

This is a caution about something that could prove harmful to your business—so take care!

There's More on the Web

Now that you know how to use this book, it's time to get to the heart of the matter. But when you're ready to take a break from setting up your new wireless network, you might also want to check out my personal website, located at www.molehillgroup.com. Here you'll find more information about all the other books I've written and am in the process of writing. I'll also post any updates or corrections to this book, in the inevitable event that an error or two creeps into this text. (Hey, nobody's perfect!)

In addition, know that I love to hear from readers of my books. If you want to contact me, feel free to email me at businesstricks@molehillgroup.com. I can't promise that I'll answer every message, but I do promise that I'll read each one!

But enough with the preliminaries. Turn the page and start planning your eBay business!

1

Tricks for Managing Your eBay Business

The eBay business masters know that one of the most important parts of establishing a successful business is to effectively manage that business. Business management starts with the planning of the business, includes the formal creation of the business and all its operations, and continues through the day-to-day running of the business. After all, the selling of items on eBay is just part of what you do in your business. You also have to manage those auctions, communicate with your customers, pay your bills, calculate and file your taxes, generate a profit and loss statement and other accounting reports, and on and on and on.

For a really big eBay business, all these backoffice functions can be quite time-consuming—and vitally important. How you manage these operations goes a long way in determining how successful your business will become.

Trick #1: Create a Business Plan—And Stick to It

You're already selling items on eBay. You think you're profitably doing so. Why in the world do you need to create a business plan?

Why You Need a Business Plan

It's relatively easy to stumble into short-term success, or at least what appears to be success, especially on eBay. It's much harder to take that short-term success and make it a long-term proposition.

To create a solid, long-term success, you need to plan for it—and then follow through on that plan. Luck will take you only so far.

Every successful business that I know, large or small, has become successful because its owners had a plan of some sort—formal or informal. That plan describes what they want the business to be, where they want it to go, and how they intend to get there. The plan is like a roadmap to success; follow the instructions in the plan and you'll get to where you want to go.

That's not to say that a business plan is totally set in stone. If so, a business would have no flexibility, no capability to jump on trends or jump out of fading markets. No, a business plan is a guideline but not necessarily a hard and fast rulebook; it's a living document that points you in the right direction, but also allows for timely and profitable diversions when they make sense.

Without such a plan, your eBay business has no direction. You don't know what your business will look like a year from now; you don't know what you'll be selling, or how much you'll be selling. Without this direction, you can't prepare your business for the future. If you don't know what your business will look like next month or next year, how can you invest for growth? Should you rent warehouse space, hire employees, or sign up for a third-party credit card service? You can't answer any of those questions unless you know where your business is going.

With a plan, growth becomes easier, more predictable, more manageable. If you plan to increase sales 100% in the next six months, you know what that means, and can plan for it. You can find more space for your inventory, search for lower-priced suppliers, hire part-time help, sign up with a new shipping service—whatever it is you need to do to manage your expected growth.

A good business plan tells you not only where you expect your business to be in terms of sales, but also how you expect to get there. It's not enough to say that you want to double your sales; you need to know exactly how you plan to achieve that doubling. Will you sell twice as many items, or items that sell for twice as much? Will all your growth come from traditional eBay auctions, or from sales in eBay stores, or from sales outside the eBay site? What do you have to do to reach the sales level you want to achieve? That's what a business plan is for.

Writing a Business Plan—For New eBay Sellers

It doesn't matter whether you've been selling on eBay six weeks or six years, a business plan is essential if you want to grow your sales into a profitable business. That said, there are differences in the type of business plan you might write; a plan for a new business is a bit different from that for an established one.

When you're creating a plan for a new business, you have to detail exactly how you'll get that business off the ground. You have to define what it is that you do, how you do it, and how well you plan to do it.

If this sounds very business-school-like and complicated, it doesn't need to be. A business plan doesn't have to be a formal document, full of business-speak and charts and graphs and such. A business plan can be a simple one-page declaration of your business goals and expectations. In fact, I like to think of a business plan as a conversation between you and anyone interested in your business. You write your plan just as you would describe your business to a friend.

If a friend asked you about your planned eBay business, what would you tell him? Imagine yourself sitting down for a cup of coffee, and you have five minutes to describe your business to your friend. Here's what you'd probably mention:

- **Why you're in business**—In a corporate business plan, this part would be called the *vision*, although that sounds terribly formal. Let's make it simple. In a sentence or two, describe why it is you want to start this particular type of eBay business, as opposed to spending your time and money doing something else. Maybe you're selling a particular type of collectible on eBay because you have a love for the hobby. Maybe you're selling holiday gift baskets because you know there's a demand for them and no one else is selling them. Or maybe you see a big market for digital photography supplies and know you can get a share of that market and make some easy money. Answer honestly—why do you want to do this?

- **What you sell**—This seems pretty basic, but you need to think it through. You can't just say "I plan to sell merchandise on eBay." That's not very detailed. You have to determine what type of merchandise you want to sell—in as much detail as possible. It's not enough to say you want to sell "collectibles," you should determine what *type* of collectibles you want to sell. Maybe you want to sell "vintage toys"; or, more precisely, "vintage toys from the 1960s," "vintage science fiction toys," or "collectible Major Matt Mason action figures and accessories." The more precisely you can describe your product, the easier it will be for you to follow through on your plans—and to stay on the prescribed path.

- **Who you want to sell it to**—You have to know your customer. Saying that you want to sell gift baskets won't help you sell them; you have to know who is the potential customer for those baskets. After you know your customer, you'll know a lot more about how you can generate sales—what types of items the customers want, what they're willing to pay for them, where and when they'll buy them, you name it. The better you know your customers, the more effective you'll be at selling to them.

- **How much you sell it for**—Now we get into the quantitative part of the plan. If you know what you're selling and to whom, you'll have a pretty good idea as to how you should price it. Certain customers will pay a high price for an item that's well-made or somehow distinctive; other customers are always looking for the lowest price. You should also do some research, specifically looking at eBay sales of similar items. What was the average selling price for items similar to what you intend to sell? You probably can't price your item much higher than the going rate. It's also good to examine ongoing trends, to see if prices are rising or falling, and then plan accordingly.

- **What you'll have to pay for it**—Hand in hand with the price you charge is the price you have to pay for each item. If you're selling $20 gift baskets, how much do you have to pay to purchase or build each item? Subtract the cost from the selling price and you get your rough profit per item, which is the money you put in your pocket after each sale. (Well, not really; you still have to pay your eBay and PayPal fees, which we'll get to in a minute.)

- **Where you'll get them**—Similarly, you need to think about where you'll obtain the items you intend to sell. Is it something you make yourself—and if so, what is your reasonable output per week? If it's something you have to purchase, do you have a list of suppliers in mind? How many do you have to buy at a time? If you have to buy in large quantities, where will you store the extras until they sell? Or maybe you want to think about drop shipping, where you don't have to hold the inventory? Finding a reliable but low-cost supplier is one of the chief challenges to any business, online or otherwise; give this one a lot of thought before you get too deeply involved.

- **How many you expect to sell**—Given the type of item you'll be selling and the price you can charge, how many items per week do you think you can sell? Again, research on past eBay sales can be helpful; how many similar items have sold on eBay over the past month or so? That's only a start, however; maybe there's an untapped market and you can well exceed the current sales rate, or maybe you can expect to get only a fraction of the existing sales. The better you know your customer and your market, the better you can predict how many units you can expect to sell. Then you can take your expected unit sales, multiply by your rough profit per item, and get a general idea of the gross profit you hope to generate (before fees, of course).

- **How you're going to sell it**—Notice that each step of this plan gets a bit more detailed. In this section, you should think about the process of selling an item on eBay—what you need to do to create and post an auction listing, what type of listing you need to create, how many days in each auction, whether to offer the Buy It Now option, whether it's an auction or a listing in an eBay Store, that sort of thing. Maybe it's as simple as saying you'll use "traditional seven-day eBay auctions," but consider any complications beyond that.

- **How you're going to manage the sales**—Here's even more detail. How much work will it take to prepare all those items for auction, to create all those auction listings, to communicate with all your winning buyers, and to pack and ship all the items you sell? Unfortunately, this is one part of the plan that not enough people think through. You don't have to get too detailed, but you need to know upfront whether you can do what you need to do in an hour after work each day or whether you'll need to quit your job and work full-time on your eBay sales—or, for that matter, whether you need to hire someone to help you out. This is also where you consider using an auction management program or service; yes, that can be part of your plan.

- **How much money you'll have to spend**—You'll spend more than time to run your eBay business; you'll also have a variety of business expenses. Start with your eBay fees (both listing and final value), add in expected PayPal or credit card fees, and then keep adding things—such as packing boxes, bubble wrap, envelopes, packing tape, postal scale, new computer, monthly Internet bill, new shelving to hold your inventory, boxes to store your old records, and on and on and on. Break down your expenses into fixed (rent, computer hardware, shelving, anything that you have to pay for even if you don't generate any sales) and variable (eBay and PayPal fees, packing supplies, postage, any expense that varies with the number of sales you do). Then work out a monthly expense budget, based on the number of sales you expect each month.

- **How much money you expect to make**—We're talking profit here, not revenues. So, it's not enough to say you expect to sell $10,000 per month; that's your gross revenue number, and ultimately not that important. What's important is how much profit you generate—your gross revenue less the cost of merchandise less all your other fixed and variable expenses (including but not limited to eBay and PayPal fees). It's sad but true that many eBay sellers don't do the math and don't realize until too late that even though they're racking up big sales numbers, they're losing money on the entire endeavor. Know upfront whether you'll make money or not, and how much.

- **How you expect the business to grow**—This is the last paragraph in your plan, but it's very important if you intend to build a successful eBay business. You'll start out selling at a certain level, but want to increase your sales over time. How much do you want to grow, and over what period of time? Even more important, *how* do you expect to achieve that growth—by selling more of what you currently sell (and how?) or by expanding the number of products that you offer? Think a year or two out and imagine what you want your business to look like; this is the long-term goal to set.

Sound like a lot of stuff to think about and ultimately write down in a plan? It is, and it isn't. Yes, it's a tad more involved than just placing a few more listings on the eBay site. But thinking through each and every step of your operation is essential if you want to build a successful (that is, profitable and growing) business.

And, as I mentioned, the plan doesn't have to be that long. If you're talking through your business with a friend, you can talk through all these points in 5 or (at most) 10 minutes. On paper, that translates into a paragraph or so per point—no more than two pages total. You can write in bullet points if you want, or just talk it through into a tape recorder and transcribe what you say. Formality isn't essential; thinking through what you need to do is what matters.

By the way, don't be surprised if you get to a particular section of the plan and find out that things aren't really as you imagined. One of the reasons to do a plan is to discover roadblocks that might stand in the way of your eventual success. Think of these as challenges, and then find a way to work around the challenges. This is a plan, after all; when you find an obstacle, you have to plan your way around it.

Writing a Business Plan—For Established eBay Businesses

If you've read this far, it's possible that you already have some form of business up and running on eBay, and want to grow that business. Planning is essential for existing businesses, too, especially when you want to grow.

We'll assume, at this point, that you already know what kind of business you have, and why you have it. Your focus is now on taking what you have and making more of it—growing your sales and profits to whatever degree you decide.

You need a plan to grow your business reliably. You need to know how much you want to grow, how you expect to achieve that growth, how much you have to spend to make all that extra money, and how you expect to manage the increased number of sales. That sounds a lot like a traditional business plan—because it is.

Again, imagine yourself sitting down with a friend for coffee and describing the next phase of your business. Here's what you're likely to discuss:

- **What you've accomplished so far**—This is the "overview" section. It can be as simple as "Last year I sold $40,000 worth of baseball cards on eBay" or as detailed as listing your gross sales, net sales, expenses, profits, and so on. You need to establish where you're at before you move on from here.

- **How much you want to grow**—Here is where you set your financial goals. Say you want to double your business, or increase sales to $20,000 per month, or something similar. Try to be realistic; it might pay to do a little research to determine what other similar businesses are doing. In other words, don't overstate your upside—be optimistic but realistic.

- **How you expect to achieve that growth**—This is the nuts and bolts part of the plan. Just how do you expect to double or triple your sales? Will you just try to sell more of what you're currently selling—and if so, how? Do you intend to expand your product mix? Raise your prices? Open an eBay Store? Sell on a website outside of eBay? Just what do you have to do to meet your sales goals?

- **How much you have to invest to achieve that growth**—When you know how you want to increase your sales, you have to figure out what you have to spend—in both money and time—to achieve that sales increase. If you plan on doubling the number of auctions you list each week, how much extra cost and effort is involved? If you plan on setting up your own non-eBay website, how much will that cost you? If you plan on selling additional products, where will you obtain those products—and how much will you pay for them?

- **How you'll need to expand your operations to manage that growth**—Sell twice as many items as you are currently, and you'll have to pack and ship twice as many items, too. How will you manage that additional activity? This is where reality comes in; a larger business takes more effort to manage, and you need to plan for that.

- **How much money you'll make from the larger business**—This final section "bottom lines" everything. Take how much more revenue you intend to generate, subtract the cost for all that product, and then subtract the necessary expenses and any additional investment. What's left over is how much profit you'll make from your new, larger business—and, ultimately, it's the bottom line that matters.

Again, you want to think of this short little business plan as your roadmap for growth. Write as detailed a plan as necessary to get you started, and to guide the way.

Updating Your Plan

As I wrote previously, a business plan is a living thing. Six months later, it's unlikely that the world will be exactly the same as it was when you first wrote your plan. Be prepared to reexamine your intentions and your suggestions, and then make any adjustments necessary for changed market conditions or updated information. Let's face it: You'll be a lot smarter about a lot of things six months from now, and you should use that increased knowledge to adjust or fine-tune your plan.

That said, you shouldn't abandon your plan in mid-stream. If the plan adequately described your goals and intentions, it should be followed—to some degree. It also needs to be used as a gauge, something to be measured against, which means comparing what you've achieved with what you said you'd achieve. Set up milestones, either monthly or quarterly, and compare your progress to plan at each step. Are you doing better or worse than you anticipated—and why? What's changed since you put together the initial plan? How do you need to adapt your plan to better meet your goals?

Worse comes to worst, you discover that your initial plan was totally unrealistic. Don't worry; it happens. Use this new knowledge to create a new plan, based on the new realities, that more accurately describes what you can achieve, and how. It's okay to adjust your plan mid-stream—especially when the ship isn't getting to the other side.

Even a successful business plan needs to be evaluated at ongoing intervals. Maybe there are more opportunities than what you recognized at the beginning. Maybe the costs are higher than you anticipated. Maybe you've discovered it's more work than you want to do. Whatever has changed, take that into account and put together a revised plan, something to guide you forward another six months to a year.

Making Use of Your Plan

A business plan may be a continually evolving roadmap, but it's a roadmap nonetheless. Without such a guide, your eBay business will float aimlessly, without direction. With a well thought-out business plan, your business stands a better chance of achieving success—assuming, that is, you take the plan seriously and follow your own direction.

How, then, do you use your business plan to guide the growth of your eBay business?

Using your business plan requires that two aspects of your plan were properly presented: the steps necessary to accomplish your goals, and the goals themselves—presented as either monthly or quarterly sales targets. Let's examine each.

The most obvious way to make use of your business plan is to follow the steps you set forth in the plan. If your plan involved buying a pallet of a particular type of item, renting warehouse space, and then placing 100 eBay listings each week, it's pretty easy to follow those steps—or note if you haven't. The more precise the instructions in your plan, the easier it will be for you to follow them.

Equally important are the financial or sales goals you set forth in the plan. You want frequent and measurable goals so that you can track your progress to plan. If your goal was to achieve $20,000 in monthly sales by the sixth month of operation, you can compare your actual sales to the projected sales and easily see where you stand.

Ultimately, you want to meet or exceed the goals put forth in your business plan. If you fall behind, you want to figure out why—and then adjust your operations accordingly.

Trick #2: Arrange the Necessary Funding—Without Going Broke

As they say, it takes money to make money. That is especially true for eBay businesses—and particularly so for growing ones.

When you put together your business plan, you should detail how much money you need to start things in motion. If you're just starting out, you have some initial expenses to consider: a computer, packing supplies and equipment, and that sort of thing. But even established businesses on a growth path have new expenses to worry about.

Paying for Inventory—Before You Sell It

Possibly the biggest upfront expense for a growing eBay business is the cost of inventory. That's because you need to purchase your merchandise before you can sell it on eBay. That means spending money in advance of receiving money from your customers—in some instances, well in advance.

Imagine that you sell consumer electronics products on eBay. Your primary supplier sells merchandise with a minimum order requirement, or perhaps offers volume discounts that kick in at a certain quantity level. Whatever the case, you find that you have to buy a 100-lot quantity of DVD players, and that quantity will last you about a month and a half.

Now, keeping 45 days of inventory isn't that big a thing; depending on how tight you run your business, you probably want to keep anywhere from 30 to 60 days worth of inventory on hand. The bigger issue, assuming that you have enough space to store 100 DVD players, is paying for these items. At $20 per unit, for example, you'll have to outlay $2,000 for six weeks of inventory.

Or consider the plight of the collectibles seller. To sell collectibles, you have to buy collectibles. Maybe you purchase new items at conventions or hobbyist shows. Maybe you purchase large lots of items at garage sales or estate sales. Maybe you buy entire collections from individuals. In any case, you need to make large cash outlays at relatively regular intervals to build your inventory of merchandise to sell on eBay.

So, no matter what you sell, you need to spend money on inventory before the first dollar of sales arrives in your mailbox.

Other Reasons for Needing Financing

Growing an eBay business takes money—and not just for inventory. Sometimes you have to finance the place where you store all that inventory. Obviously, storing a thousand baseball cards won't take a lot of space, but storing a thousand plasma TVs will. When your garage gets to be too small to hold your growing inventory, you need to start looking at warehousing space. And warehousing space doesn't come cheap.

In addition to your monthly rent (and probably some upfront payment—such as your first and last rent amount), you'll probably need to invest in shelving of some sort, maybe a table or two to use for packing, maybe some storage boxes, whatever it takes to hold and move your inventory. Few warehouses come thus equipped; you'll need to spend money to make your new space usable.

Or maybe you're enhancing your eBay sales with your own e-commerce website. You have to pay a web-hosting service, pay for your new domain name, pay a design firm to design your site, pay for the software necessary for your site's shopping cart and checkout system, and so forth and so on. It might be $1,000, it might be $10,000, but expanding into a new sales channel costs money.

Ways to Finance Your Business

Unless you're independently wealthy (and if so, what are you doing mucking about on eBay), you'll have to find some way to finance this investment in your business. What are your choices?

- **Savings**—Okay, you don't have to be independently wealthy to have a little cash saved up in your savings account. The least-costly way to finance business growth is to pay for it yourself—no borrowing, no loans, no floats. Spend as much money as you have and can afford to spend; you won't pay a cent in interest charges.

- **Credit card loan**—This is one of the worst ways to finance business growth, but also one of the most popular. If you have a credit line of $5,000, you write yourself a credit card check for that amount and "self-finance" your investment. The benefit of this method is how easy it is; no one to consult, no applications to fill out. The downside, however, is the cost; a credit card loan is one of the most expensive types of loans you can make, in terms of interest rates. Check your credit card statement—chances are, the interest rate is at least 18% per year. (Although sometimes you can find promotional rates for using your credit checks.) That means if you borrow $5,000 against your credit card, you'll pay in the neighborhood of $900 in interest fees if you don't pay it off within the first year. Can your business afford an extra $900 expenditure?

caution

The interest fee isn't the only fee you'll pay if you write a credit card check. Most credit card companies charge some sort of cash advance fee, typically in the 2%–4% range.

- **Second mortgage or home equity line**—This approach borrows money from the equity you have in your house. (Assuming that you own a home, that is; renters need not apply.) Instead of the 18%+ interest rate you'll get by borrowing against your credit card, home equity lines and second mortgages typically come with rates in the 6%–8% range. Using our $5,000 example again, we're now talking yearly interest fees in the $350 range—a considerable savings over what you'd pay in credit card interest.

- **Business loan**—If you're running a real business, you can always go to a bank and apply for a traditional business loan. You might not get it (not all banks consider eBay businesses real businesses), but you can apply. (Most banks look for a minimum $10,000 for most business loans.) If you qualify, expect to pay prime plus a few points (currently in the 8%–9% range) in terms of interest—in the same area as what you'll pay for a home equity loan, but without having to reduce the equity in your house.

tip

If you're interested in a small business loan, check with the Small Business Administration (www.sba.gov), which exists to help small businesses like your own.

- **Friends and family**—If you don't have the cash, maybe someone you know does. Borrowing five grand from mom and dad or Uncle Fred might not sound appealing to you (let's not go into the personal stress of borrowing from friends and family), but if they're willing, you might get the cash sans interest or at a low payback rate.

- **Investors**—If your business is big enough and shows enough growth potential, you might be able to attract potential investors to pony up the cash you need. Know, however, that taking on an investor is essentially giving up co-ownership of your business—which is a whole other can of worms.

So, of these methods of financing, which do the eBay business masters recommend? First on the list is the first on the list: borrowing from your own savings. Some business masters would say if you can't self-finance your growth, you shouldn't be growing.

Other business masters, however, say that to achieve fast growth, you need outside financing. The best form of outside financing comes from either a small business loan or borrowing against your home's equity. You get relatively low interest rates (typically 8% or so) with relatively little hassle.

tip

If you go the business loan route, investigate establishing a business revolving credit line. This lets you borrow against the credit line as you need it—which is perfect for when you need to finance large inventory purchases.

The worst form of financing? That would be credit card borrowing. At 18% interest rates, it's a horrible way to obtain funds. Simply horrible. The monthly interest payments will kill you, let alone trying to pay back the principal. Avoid this method at all costs; if you have to use your credit card to obtain funds, you should think about delaying your investment.

As to the length of the loan, go as short as you can afford. If you're using the loan to pay for inventory, the loan should be paid off when the inventory is sold; stretching it out further would mean you're using the money for something other than that inventory. If you're financing capital improvements, try for a one-year loan. Remember, the longer the loan period, the more money you pay in interest!

Trick #3: Establish a Legal Business

A real eBay business isn't a hobby. A real eBay business is a real business—and you need to establish it as such.

This means setting up your eBay business as an official legal entity. (It also means keeping records accurate enough to satisfy the government and other interested legal beagles, if it ever amounts to that.)

note

I am not a lawyer, nor am I an accountant; I just write books. For that reason, you should take the information in this chapter as general in nature, and consult an appropriate professional for more specific legal and tax-related advice.

Choosing a Type of Business

When you're setting up your eBay business as an official business, you first have to decide what type of structure you want your business to have. The different types of businesses each have their pros and cons, and you should seriously evaluate which structure is best for your individual situation. These types of business include but are not limited to the following:

- **Sole proprietorship**—This is the most common type of business entity used by eBay businesses. It's the easiest type of business to form, and the easiest to manage on an ongoing basis; you don't have to file any papers of incorporation, nor do you need to withhold and pay monthly payroll taxes and the like. You file income tax for the business under your own name, using your Social Security number as your tax identification number. You'll file and pay this tax in quarterly estimates, but the paperwork burden is minimal, compared to other forms of businesses. On the downside, the owner of a sole proprietorship is personally responsible for the debts and legal obligations of the business—which means if the business owes money, you're personally on the hook for it.

- **Partnership**—A partnership is the two- or more person version of the sole proprietorship, and the way to go if you're in this business with a partner. You and your partner have to contractually agree as to who is responsible for what, and how to share the business's profits or losses. You'll definitely want to draw up formal partnership papers, which means bringing in a lawyer. Legal registration is similar to that of a sole proprietorship, although the partnership must obtain a federal Employer Identification Number (EIN). The individual partners report the company's income on their personal tax returns.

caution

In a partnership, all partners are personally liable for losses and other obligations. This also means that one partner is liable for the other's actions—so you can be sued for something your partner did.

- **Corporation**—A corporation establishes a legal entity separate from you personally. As such, the corporation's money isn't your money; the corporation pays you a salary, as well as stock dividends This typically produces some amount of personal tax savings because you can shield some of your personal income from employment tax by having the corporation pay you a dividend rather than a salary.

(Dividends don't have employment tax attached; salaries do.) Additionally, your personal liability is reduced if the business ever falls into debt or gets sued. Potentially offsetting these benefits is the fact that the corporation itself has to pay taxes on its profits, and you'll pay increased fees to your accountant to manage all the official forms and filings that come with corporate status. At the very least, a corporation must have a federal EIN and withhold and pay monthly employment taxes for each of its employees.

tip

If you have investors in your business besides yourself, you might want to consider filing as a *limited liability corporation (LLC)*. In an LLC, the business's income and losses are shared by all investors, although investors are subject to limited liability (hence the name) for the corporation's debts and obligations.

So what type of legal business entity is best for your eBay business? When you're first starting out, there's nothing simpler than a sole proprietorship. But as your business grows, the tax advantages of a corporation become more appealing—even as they come with more paperwork and such. Ask your attorney and accountant for advice, but I recommend considering the corporate route when your business profits exceed the $100,000 yearly level. Obviously, your accountant and attorney will prepare all the papers you need to register as whatever type of business you decide.

Filing and Registering

Whatever type of business you decide to create, you'll probably have to register that business with your local government. The rules differ from state to state (and sometimes from county to county!), but a good attorney or accountant can fill you in on what specifically you need to do where you live. You should also check with the staff at your county clerk's office or chamber of commerce, or on your state's official website; they'll tell you what you need to do.

note

For a state-by-state list showing where to obtain business licenses, check out the Where to Obtain Business Licenses page on the SBA website (www.sba.gov/hotlist/license.html).

Many states, counties, and cities require that you register any new business with them. Some locales require you to obtain a permit or license for your activity; you should also check to see if your location is zoned for the type of business you plan to conduct. You'll also need to register with the feds and the state to collect and pay sales tax; we'll discuss the tax issue in more depth later in this chapter.

You might also have to obtain a sales permit or reseller license from your local government. Your sales tax number also functions as a *resale certificate*, which you can present to any wholesalers you work with to save you from paying sales tax on the goods you purchase.

tip

You'll also need to create a merchant bank account for your business, separate from your personal bank accounts. Setting up a merchant bank account is different from setting up a personal account; ask your banker what's needed, and then shop around for the lowest fees.

Trick #4: Set Up a Professional Accounting System

Coincident with setting your eBay business up as a legal business entity, you'll need to set up some sort of professional accounting system. For any professional business, keeping accurate accounts is a necessity—both for managing your business on a day-to-day basis and for preparing your monthly or yearly taxes and government filings.

Why Accounting Is Important

Running a business is not something you can do on the back of an envelope—at least not anymore, and not with a business of any decent size. You need to set up a real, honest-to-goodness accounting system for your business, hopefully with the assistance of a real, honest-to-goodness accountant, to keep track of just how your business is doing.

To gauge the success of your business, you need to know how much profit you're making—not how much sales revenue you generate, but the actual end-of-day profit resulting from those sales. To do this, you need to know how much things cost and how much you sell them for, as well as how much you lay out for other expenses, and then do the appropriate financial calculations. A professional accounting system will do all this and then generate a series of regular financial reports, which you use to analyze the ongoing status of your business.

In addition, you need an accounting system to generate all the information necessary to report your business income and other information to the Internal Revenue Service and your state department of revenue. If you're incorporated, that also means reporting employment tax, sales tax, and the like. You just can't fulfill all these legal obligations without a decent accounting system.

Keeping Good Records

Any accounting system you create, however, is only as good as the information you feed into it. That means putting yourself into a mindset that collects and saves every little piece of information relating to your business so all that information can be input accordingly.

At the very least, you'll want to collect data on all the inventory you purchase and all the sales you make; this means tracking item cost, date sold, and sales price. You'll also need to track additional information relating to the costs of running your eBay business, such as the cost of office supplies, packing materials, shipping services, and the like. Whenever you spend money on your business, keep the receipt. Whenever you sell something, document it. That's the way to work.

You'll need to hold onto all these receipts and documentation for a minimum of three years, just in case the IRS decides to audit you. In fact, three years might not be long enough; the IRS, for example, requires that you keep documentation on all your assets for the life of the asset. And don't forget to hang on to all your bank statements, as well.

Setting Up an Accounting System

All accounting systems work to the same end, tracking two basic types of activities: *revenues* and *expenses*. Revenues are the sales you make to your eBay customers. Expenses are the costs you incur in the running of your business—the inventory you have to purchase, as well as all those other things you need to buy to make your business run.

When you subtract expenses from revenues, you get your business's *profit*. At the end of the day, you can't spend revenues (because they have to be used to pay your expenses); you can, however, spend your profits.

To make your accounting system work, you have to enter each and every financial activity of your business. Purchase some merchandise for sale, enter it in the books. (Or have your accountant enter it into the books.) Make a sale, enter it in the books. Buy some supplies, enter them in the books. You get the idea.

At regular intervals—typically at the end of each month—you add up all the revenues and expenses and take a snapshot as to how your business is doing. These snapshots are the financial statements you use to measure the financial condition of your business.

Choosing the Right Accounting Software

How do you put together all your business data and generate these financial statements? You have two practical options: hire an accountant or use an accounting software program. In fact, these are not mutually exclusive solutions; I recommend doing both.

There are many different programs you can use to keep your business's books. Some cost under $100, some cost over $1,000. The most popular include the following:

- Cashbook Complete ($120, www.acclaimsoftware.com)
- DacEasy ($449.99+, www.daceasy.com)
- Microsoft Money Home & Business ($59.99, www.microsoft.com/money/)
- MYOB BusinessEssentials ($99, www.myob.com)
- Peachtree Accounting ($69.99+, www.peachtree.com/peachtreeaccountingline/)
- QuickBooks ($99.95+, www.quickbooks.com)
- Quicken Home & Business ($79.99, www.quicken.com)
- Sage BusinessWorks ($599+, www.sagesoftware.com/businessworks/)

Of these programs, the one I recommend is QuickBooks. There are a number of versions of QuickBooks: Simple Start, Pro, Premier, Enterprise Solutions, and so on. For most eBay businesses, either the Pro or Premier version should do the job.

You can use QuickBooks not only to do your monthly accounting and generate regular financial statements, but also to manage your inventory, track your sales, and do your year-end taxes. QuickBooks even integrates with PayPal, so you can download all your PayPal-related transactions into the software program, and manage everything all in one place.

tip

If you use QuickBooks, download eBay's Accounting Assistant program, which lets you import eBay and PayPal data directly to QuickBooks. The Accounting Assistant program is free, but to generate the necessary data, you also need a subscription to either eBay Stores, Selling Manager (Basic or Pro), or Blackthorne Basic or Pro. Get more details—and download the program—at pages.ebay.com/help/sell/accounting-assistant-ov.html.

Working with an Accountant

In addition to QuickBooks or some similar accounting program, you'll still need the services of a professional accountant. Your accountant will handle all your tax-related issues, including preparing your quarterly tax estimates and year-end taxes, as well as all other government filing and reporting. And, let's face it, an accountant is well qualified to help you analyze the progress of your business and provide useful business advice.

Here's how I do it. I use QuickBooks to track all my business-related transactions (I enter all the information myself on a daily basis) and generate monthly financial statements. Then I call in my accountant to handle my payroll and prepare my quarterly estimated taxes and year-end tax statements. This is a pretty good combination; QuickBooks does the dirty work and feeds the necessary data to my accountant to do what he does.

Of course, you can also use an accountant to handle *all* your financial activities. This is a particularly good idea if your business gets really big, or if you're fairly useless when it comes to handling the books. Make sure that you find an accountant that you're comfortable with and you trust.

Trick #5: Track Your Performance

We touched on the issue of performance tracking when we talked about business plans earlier in this chapter. Obviously, you want to track your actual sales performance to plan, but there are a lot more metrics you can use to analyze your business's performance. How do you measure your business's success? Here are some of the more useful methods.

Dollar Sales

The easiest metric to measure is your gross revenue over a particular time period, typically monthly. This is simply the dollar value of your eBay sales. You should measure the dollar value of the item sales only, not including shipping, handling, or sales tax, and without subtracting any eBay or PayPal fees. So, if you sold $8,527 worth of merchandise in a given month, before S/H charges, your revenue would be that $8,527.

It might also be useful to create a second metric that measures the total dollar value of your sales, including the shipping/handling charges you tack on to each sale. This is useful if you view your S/H charges as a profit center—that is, if you intend to make a little money on your S/H charges, as opposed to just passing on the actual shipping charges.

caution

Gross revenues do not equal profit.

Unit Sales

Also useful is a measure of your unit sales—not dollar sales, but rather the number of units that you sold during a given time period. Unit sales are useful for tracking actual sales over time, ignoring any effect of price increases or decreases from period to period.

Gross Profit

Gross dollar revenue is an important metric, but it tells you only how much you've sold—not how much money you've actually made. To see how profitable your sales really are, you have to calculate your gross profit for each item you sell. There are several ways to define gross profit, but for eBay sales I like the following calculation:

	Final selling price
	Final selling price
MINUS	Unit cost
MINUS	eBay listing fee
MINUS	eBay final value fee
MINUS	PayPal fee

An alternative calculation figures in your shipping/handling charges, like this:

	Final selling price
	Final selling price
PLUS	Shipping/handling charge
MINUS	Unit cost
MINUS	Actual shipping cost
MINUS	eBay listing fee
MINUS	eBay final value fee
MINUS	PayPal fee

The second method of calculation is useful if you use S/H charges as a profit center.

In any case, what you're measuring is how much profit you've made on each item—that is, how much profit each item generates that can then be used to pay your business's other expenses (rent, salary, other overhead).

Let's calculate a quick single-item example, using the second calculation method. Assume that you have a gift basket that you paid $15 for, and it sold for $20 plus $5 shipping/handling; for this example, assume that the seller paid via PayPal, and that eBay's normal fees apply. Here's how the calculation works:

	$20.00 (selling price)
PLUS	$5.00 (shipping/handling charge)
MINUS	$15.00 (unit cost)
MINUS	$4.00 (actual shipping)
MINUS	$0.60 (listing fee)
MINUS	$1.05 (5.25% final value fee)
MINUS	$1.03 (2.9% PayPal fee—on the entire $25 charge—plus $0.30 transaction fee)
GROSS PROFIT:	$3.32

So, the $20 item you sold generated $3.32 in gross profit. You can't spend the $20; you can spend the $3.32.

You can then use the gross profit number to calculate your gross profit percentage, otherwise known as your *profit margin*. Simply divide the gross profit number by the revenue number (or, if you're using the second method, by the revenue plus S/H charge). In our example, we divide $3.32 by $25 and get a profit margin of 13.28%. Obviously, the higher the profit margin, the better.

You can calculate gross profit and profit margin for each individual item, and then for all the items you've sold in a given time period.

Net Profit

Gross profit describes the profit you make on each individual item. It doesn't take into account your business overhead and other expenses—packing materials, labels, Internet service, telephone calls, rent, salaries, you name it.

Your business's net profit is how much money you have left over after you pay all these expenses. The calculation is simple—you take your gross profit number and subtract all your other expenses. What's left over is your net profit—the measure of how profitable your total business really is.

Let's say you have $20,000 in sales in a given month. After you subtract item costs, eBay fees, and the like, you end up with $2,500 in gross profit on those sales. Now you subtract all your other expenses—$50 for Internet service, $150 for labels, $650 for boxes, $50 for your business phone line, $10 for bank charges on your business checking account, and $100 for other miscellaneous office supplies. (We'll assume that you're not paying yourself a salary at this point, and that you're not paying any rent.) Subtract this $1,010 from your $2,500 gross profit, and you end up with $1,490 in net profit for the month.

Net profit is, perhaps, the most important measurement of your business's success. And don't be surprised if your net profit is a negative number; that means you spent more than you made on your eBay business. It's not uncommon, but you need to know it—and deal with it.

Sell-Through Rate

The remaining metrics help you compare your sales in one period to those in another. We'll start by looking at your sell-through rate, which measures how successful your eBay auction activity is.

Sell-through rate is a percentage that measures how many of your auctions closed successfully, versus how many closed without a winning bidder. You calculate sell-through rate like this:

                    Number of successful auctions

DIVIDED BY   Total number of auctions

It's a simple percentage. Let's say, for example, that in a given month you listed 1,000 items for sale, and of those 650 closed successfully (had winning bids). Your sell-through rate is 650 divided by 1,000, or 65%.

> **note**
>
> The sell-through rate is sometimes called the *conversion rate*.

What is a good sell-through rate? It depends; some product categories have higher sell-through rates than others. In addition, you might settle for a lower sell-through rate if you list a higher number of auctions—that is, you may settle for a lower sell-through rate if you increase the actual number of closed auctions.

> **note**
>
> Some sources estimate that eBay's overall sell-through rate is less than 50%— meaning half of all auctions end with no winning bidder.

As I said, the real use of this metric is to measure your performance over time. If you start out with a 50% sell-through rate and six months later have a 60% sell-through rate, you've become more successful in your selling. If, on the other hand, you see your sell-through rate decrease from 50% to 45%, your selling has somehow become less effective. You should try to find out why.

Inventory Turns

Having a high sales or sell-through rate doesn't matter much if you have too much unsold inventory sitting in your garage or warehouse. This is why many businesses measure inventory turns, or how fast they move their inventory.

Inventory turns are typically measured on a yearly basis. That is, you measure how many times you sell through your complete inventory over the course of a year. To do this, you divide your annual dollar sales by the average value of the inventory.

As an example, let's say you sold $100,000 in merchandise last year and that, at any given point in time, you had $10,000 of merchandise sitting in your warehouse. Divide $100,000 by $10,000, and you find you turned your inventory 10 times last year. Compare that with a business that also sold $100,000 of merchandise, but had $50,000 of inventory in the warehouse. That business turned its inventory just 2 times, which isn't nearly as good as a 10X turn.

Successful and profitable businesses have a higher number of inventory turns. They move their inventory faster, generating more cash for their inventory investment; they don't have old, unsold inventory sitting around the warehouse. This results in better cash flow, and a higher return on investment.

tip

Some eBay businesses strive for 12X inventory turns, which means that at any given time they have only one month's worth of inventory in stock.

Market Share

This net measure is a bit harder to measure, and requires more research. When you measure market share, you measure how much sales your business generated versus those of all similar sellers on eBay.

The trick to this one is how you define your market. If you sell internal hard disks, does your market consist of all internal hard disk sales, all hard disk sales, or all computer accessory sales? In most cases, a tighter definition of your market is a more accurate measure of success.

In any case, you're going to have to do your research and measure all eBay sales within your category. You can do this by searching eBay's completed auctions for a given time period (typically a month), or by using one of the many third-party eBay research tools. After you've added up all your competitors' sales, you make sure that your sales are part of the total, and then divide your sales by the category total. The result is your market share—your share of the total category sales.

> **note**
>
> Learn more about the available eBay research tools in Chapter 2, "Tricks for Deciding What to Sell."

Let's say a given category, as you define it, has total one-month sales of $1.5 million. Let's say that your sales in that month amounted to $150,000. Divide $150,000 by $1,500,000, and you realize that your market share is 10%—that is, your business accounted for 10% of the sales in that category.

The bigger your market share, the more you can leverage your position. Bigger sellers can command slightly higher prices, and often gain even higher sales over time. (Size begets size.) And, again, market share is a great way to measure you company's growth over time; increasing your market share should be one of your long-term business goals.

Revenue/Profit Growth

Finally, measuring absolute numbers is fine, but you need to compare your numbers against prior numbers to measure how your business is growing. (Assuming that it is growing, of course.) It's well and good to sell $100,000 of merchandise in a given month, but is that more or less than you sold the month before? Has your profit margin increased or decreased? What about your market share?

I like to set up a month-to-month graph of each key metric to show how my business is trending over time. Obviously, you want to see the graph trend upward; a downward slope in any metric is a sign of potential problems.

That said, you need to take into account any seasonality of your particular business. Most businesses do more sales in the fourth quarter of the year than they do in other months, due to holiday sales. In addition, most businesses see somewhat of a slump during the summer months because people are out of school and on vacation. This might differ by product category, however; swimwear sales are stronger in the summer than they are in the winter. Don't rely solely on month-to-month comparisons; allow for seasonality and do year-over-year comparisons, in addition.

Tracking Performance via eBay Sales Reports

I would hope you would be able to track most of these performance metrics from the data you collect into your own accounting system. That said, you can supplement your own internal data with data supplied by eBay, via its Sales Reports feature.

eBay's Sales Reports (pages.ebay.com/salesreports/salesreports.html) let you view your following eBay sales data (from both traditional auctions and eBay Stores sales):

- Total sales
- Ended listings
- Successful listings (number)
- Successful listings (percent of total)
- Average sales price
- Net eBay and PayPal fees

In addition, the Sales Reports Plus tool offers the following advanced analysis:

- Number of total buyers
- Number of unique buyers
- Percent of repeat buyers
- Sales by category and format
- Key performance metrics by format
- Ending day and time
- Duration
- eBay and PayPal fee breakdown

Both the Sales Reports and Sales Reports Plus tools are free, although you do have to sign up for them. (Figure 1.1 shows the Sales Reports Plus summary page.)

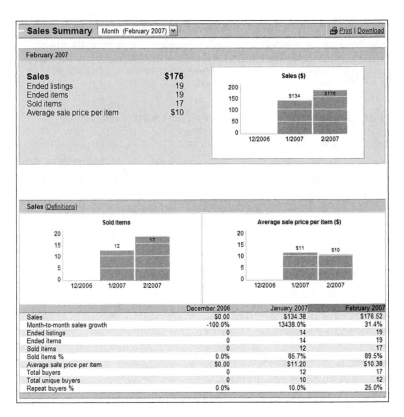

FIGURE 1.1
Viewing summary data from eBay's Sales Reports Plus.

tip

Also useful is Sellathon's ViewTracker (www.sellathon.com). This $4.95/month service provides very detailed analysis of your eBay auction activity, well beyond what eBay offers in its reports.

Trick #6: Don't Spend Money That Isn't Yours—Know How Much Money You're Really Making

One of the reasons we do the analysis discussed in the previous trick is so that we know how much money we're really making. One of the most common mistakes of eBay sellers is to look only at the gross revenue number, and think that all this money is theirs for the taking. As you now know, this isn't the case.

If you sell an item for $20, you can't (or shouldn't) go out and spend that $20. That's because, out of that $20 sale, you have to pay for the item itself, as well as the accompanying eBay and PayPal fees. And, sometime later in the month, you still have your phone, Internet, rent, and other similar bills to pay.

What you need to know is your estimated profit margin on each sale—the percent of the total sale left over after paying for the merchandise and all associated fees. If you know that your profit margin, on average, is 13%, you know (with a little math work) that when you sell a $20 item, you've actually made about $2.60 in profit. So, you can spend the $2.60, but not the $20.

Undisciplined eBay sellers tend to focus more on the cash flow (the $20 that showed up in their PayPal account) rather than the actual profit generated. They'll spend the $20, or some subset, without saving any money to pay the merchandise cost or their eBay/PayPal fees. This is a dangerous way to run a business. Because eBay fees aren't due until the following month, it's easy to spend the money that should be used to pay those fees. Just because the gross amount is in your bank account doesn't mean you can spend it all; you need to recognize and plan for all the fees that will eventually come due.

Some sellers enforce financial discipline by creating a second bank account used solely to pay their eBay fees. When a sale closes, they deposit the appropriate eBay fees for that sale into the second bank account. This way they won't be tempted to spend this money; they've set aside the necessary funds to pay all fees, when they come due.

Along the same lines, shipping and handling fees tend to create problems for undisciplined sellers. Some sellers want to count those S/H fees as their money, not funds to be used to pay the actual shipping charges. If you receive $5 in shipping and handling, you can't spend that $5 as if it's all yours; you have to set aside the appropriate amount to pay the actual shipping charges for that item. It's particularly tempting when you put shipping charges on your credit card, or charge shipping charges to a monthly account. Just because you don't fork over the cash at the time of shipment doesn't mean that you don't pay the fees. The shipping and handling charges you receive are really just a pass-through from you to the shipping service.

Trick #7: Prepare for the Taxman

As a small eBay seller, you probably didn't think a lot about stuff such as reporting your income for tax purposes, or collecting sales taxes, or the like. When your eBay sales grow into a real business, however, taxes become a real concern.

Sales Tax

As your business grows in size, it becomes more difficult to fly under the radar in terms of taxes—sales taxes, in particular. The bottom line is that you'll need to collect, report, and pay sales tax on all sales you make to residents of your state. (You don't have to collect sales taxes on out-of-state sales.) eBay makes the collecting somewhat easy when you click the appropriate sales tax option on the sell your item form.

Paying the collected taxes to your state department of revenue is a different story. You'll probably have to obtain a tax license and number from your state. You'll also have to file monthly or quarterly sales tax reports, and deposit your collected taxes on the appropriate schedule. This is definitely one area that demands the use of a professional; let your accountant handle it.

Income Tax

When you sell only a few old items from your garage or attic, nobody much cares about reporting these sales as income. But when you're running a real business—when you're purchasing items expressly for resale—you need to report the income that you generate.

If your business is set up as a sole proprietorship, your business income ultimately becomes your personal income. If you're set up as a corporation, your business income is separate from your personal income. In either case, however, it's your obligation to track the net income you generate from your eBay sales.

Note that I said you track your *net income*—not your gross revenues. Yes, you need to track your revenues, but it's not gross revenues that the IRS is interested in. Instead, it's interested in the profit (that is, your net income) you generate. So, you (or, more probably, your accountant) need to work with all your revenues, costs, and expenses to generate a final net profit or loss number.

When it comes to calculating the expenses for your eBay business, it pays to be inclusive. Every legitimate expense you register is a business deduction that lowers the net income you report; the lower your net income, the fewer taxes you pay. That said, many newbie businesspeople don't take full advantage of all the business deductions available to them. Here are just a few categories of deductions you should pay attention to:

- **Cost of goods sold**—Whatever you pay for your inventory (including the cost of shipping it to you and the cost of storing it) is a cost of goods sold (COGS) expense, as are all your eBay and PayPal fees. Make sure that you keep all invoices and receipts.

- **Selling expenses**—This is also a no-brainer. Keep track of all your selling-related expenses—postage, boxes, bubble wrap, shipping tape, labels, printer ink, paper, even pens and pencils. If you use it for your eBay sales, you can count it.

- **Office expenses**—Everything you use to run your business can be expensed. Printer ink, paper, pens, pencils, even your computer and printer (and Internet service) can be expensed. Document everything.

- **Home office expense**—If you run your eBay business out of a home office, you can deduct the cost of that office space. See your accountant for details (they're tricky), but in general you can deduct a fair percentage of your total home costs—utilities, rent, mortgage payments, and so on—based on the percentage of floor space your office represents.

- **Auto mileage**—You can deduct the cost of using your car for business purposes. Drive to the post office to ship your items? Deduct the mileage. Drive to Office Depot to buy bubble wrap? Deduct the mileage. Drive to the bank to deposit check payments? Deduct the mileage. Keep a mileage log in your vehicle and keep track of every business trip, no matter how short. Then multiply the miles you drive by an appropriate mileage rate, as determined by the IRS; it's this final number that you can deduct.

- **Meals**—If you meet any customers, suppliers, or advisors (including your accountant) for lunch or dinner, those meals can be expensed, at a 50% rate.

- **Education and research**—Subscribe to an eBay research service? Or an eBay-related magazine? Buy any eBay books (like this one)? Go to eBay Live, or attend any eBay seminars or classes? All these items count as education and research, and can be fully deducted.

The best advice I can give you in this regard is to hire an accountant and let him deal with all this. A good accountant will recognize deductions that you never thought of—and save you big money on your taxes.

Employment and Withholding Tax

If your business is incorporated, you have to pay yourself (and all other employees) a salary. Each paycheck you write has various taxes deducted—payroll taxes, Social Security taxes, Medicare taxes, and so forth. In addition, your business has to pay an employment tax on all salaries. These withheld taxes are typically paid to the state and federal governments on a monthly basis.

There's a lot of paperwork involved in these payroll taxes, which is why you really need to hire an accountant. Even if you're your business's only employee, the accounting and filing and such are extremely time-consuming. When your business is big enough to incorporate, it's big enough to hire the services of an accountant.

Trick #8: Use an Auction Management Tool

This is a big issue, and an important one to any growing eBay business. The process of listing, managing, and closing your eBay auctions is extremely time-consuming, especially so if you do it all manually via eBay's sell your item form and site-specific tools. You'll spend a good five minutes manually listing each individual auction; if you list 100 auctions a week, that's more than eight hours in front of your computer screen, doing nothing but auction listings.

After you reach a certain size, you have to automate this process. Fortunately, there are lots of auction management tools available. Unfortunately, not all of them are suitable for all sizes of businesses.

Understanding Auction Management Tools

Know that virtually every eBay business master says that using an auction management tool is essential for growing their businesses. Multiple sellers have told me that they couldn't have grown to their current size without the use of an auction management tool. (Some have also pointed out that choosing the wrong tool—one targeted at a smaller seller—can limit your growth.) To grow you business, you have to invest in this sort of tool; otherwise, you'll simply be overwhelmed by the volume of your operations.

What functions can you expect from an auction management service? While every site offers a different selection of tools, here are some of the tools you can expect to find at the major third-party auction sites:

- **Inventory management**—Enter and track all the items in your inventory, and automatically delete items from inventory as they're sold at auction.

- **Image hosting**—Host photos for your auctions on the service's website, and manage those photos in your item listings.

- **Bulk listing creation**—Create attractive item listings with pre-designed templates, and then list multiple items in bulk.

- **End-of-auction email**—Automatically send notifications to winning bidders, and notify customers when payment is received and items are shipped.

- **End-of-auction checkout**—Provide a dedicated page that customers can use to verify their purchases, and provide shipping and payment information.

- **Bulk feedback posting**—Automatically post customer feedback in bulk.

- **Sales analysis**—Generate reports and graphs to help you analyze your auction sales over time.

- **Storefront**—Provide other nonauction items for sale on the Web.

Not all sites offer all these services, nor at the same level. At the most basic, you can use eBay's free Turbo Lister (free; pages.ebay.com/turbo_lister/) to create bulk item listings, and eBay's Selling Manager (4.99/month; pages.ebay.com/selling_manager/) to track your in-process auctions and manage the end-of-auction process. However, these budget tools are effective only for relatively small sellers; get up to 50 or more auctions a week and you'll need something more powerful.

Move up in price and you get tools that better help you manage large sales volumes on eBay, as well as sales on other online marketplaces, as well as sales through your own e-commerce website. The more expensive services, such as ChannelAdvisor and Zoovy, also offer detailed inventory management and marketing functions; you can use these tools to manage virtually all facets of your burgeoning online business.

Choosing an Auction Management Tool

So what's the best auction management tool for your eBay business? Table 1.1 lays out some of the more popular tools, along with the features offered, with some attempt to judge the size of business for which each tool is best suited.

Table 1.1   Major Auction Management Tools

Service	URL	Target Business	Inventory Management	Image Hosting	Bulk Listing Creation	End-of-Auction Email	Checkout	Bulk Feedback Posting	Sales Analysis	Storefront	Pricing
Andale	www.andale.com	Small-to-large	X	X	X	X	X	X	X	X	"Quick Packs" for various-sized sellers; Small Office/Home Office (110 listings), $34.95/month; Small/Medium Business Seller (275 listings), $99.95/month; Merchant/Enterprise Seller (1,100 listings), $229.95/month; individual services also priced separately
Auction Hawk	www.auctionhawk.com	Small-to-medium	X	X	X	X	X	X	X		Various flat-fee plans available; Basic (220 listings), $12.99/month; Power (440 listings), $21.99/month; Professional (880 listings), $29.99/month; Unlimited, $44.99/month
Auctiva	www.auctiva.com	Small	X	X	X	X		X	X	X	Free
ChannelAdvisor	www.channeladvisor.com	Medium-to-large	X	X	X	X	X	X	X	X	Custom plans available; contact for more info
eBay Blackthorne Basic	pages.ebay.com/blackthorne/basic.html	Small			X	X	X (via eBay)	X			$9.99/month
eBay Blackthorne Pro	pages.ebay.com/blackthorne/pro.html	Medium	X		X	X	X (via eBay)	X	X		$24.99/month
eBay Selling Manager	pages.ebay.com/selling_manager/	Small				X	X (via eBay)	X			$4.99/month
eBay Selling Manager Pro	pages.ebay.com/selling_manager_pro/	Medium	X			X	X (via eBay)	X	X		$15.99/month
eBay Turbo Lister	pages.ebay.com/turbo_lister/	Small			X						Free

Service	URL	Target Business	Inventory Management	Image Hosting	Bulk Listing Creation	End-of-Auction Email	Checkout	Bulk Feedback Posting	Sales Analysis	Store-front	Pricing
Infopia	www.infopia.com	Medium-to-large	X	X	X	X	X	X	X	X	Custom plans available; contact for more info
inkFrog	www.inkfrog.com	Small	X	X	X	X	X	X	X	X	$9.95/month
Marketworks	www.marketworks.com	Medium-to-large		X	X	X	X	X	X	X	2% of final value; $29.95/month minimum
Truition CMS	www.truition.net	Medium-to-large	X	X	X	X	X	X	X	X	Custom plans available; contact for more info
Vendio	www.vendio.com	Small-to-medium	X	X	X	X	X	X	X	X	Various plans from $14.95/month plus combination of listing and final value fees
Zoovy	www.zoovy.com	Medium-to-large	X	X	X	X	X	X	X	X	Custom plans available; contact for more info

Which of these auction management tools is the best? Unfortunately, this is one area where the eBay business masters disagree. There simply is no single tool that gets consensus approval from eBay sellers. Some swear by Blackthorne Pro, others by ChannelAdvisor, still others by Vendio and Zoovy. Choosing the right tool for your business is really a matter of matching the tool's functionality and usability with the needs and style of your individual business.

That said, there are some tools that are better matches than others for particular types of businesses. For individuals selling on eBay, the eBay Turbo Lister/Selling Manager combination is functional and cost efficient, as are Auctiva's free tools. For small businesses just starting out, I recommend either Vendio or eBay's Blackthorne Pro, both of which provide good services and value for a business of this size. But as your business grows, check out the more advanced services offered by ChannelAdvisor, Marketworks, and Zoovy; these firms can help you grow your business beyond the eBay auction marketplace.

tip

Find even more auction management tools in eBay's Solutions Directory (solutions.ebay.com) and in the AuctionBytes Auction Management Services directory (www.auctionbytes.com/cab/pages/ams).

Of course, given the importance of these tools, you need to shop around before you make a decision. Look for those tools that offer some sort of free trial so that you can give the site a test run before you sign up. If something doesn't feel right, or isn't a good fit with your business, move on to the next tool.

Trick #9: Develop Your Own Business Management System

When I talk to the very biggest eBay sellers, they stress that the general auction management tools discussed in the previous trick don't do the job for them. Big businesses require custom management tools—processes and software designed specifically for their businesses.

The art of managing a large and growing business isn't a one size fits all affair. What works for managing a CD retailer doesn't include all the proper details for managing a clothing reseller. Different industries and types of products have their own unique features and needs; what works for one industry is likely to be a poor fit for another.

This is why many large eBay businesses invest in custom management systems. We're talking about inventory management software, database software, sales processing software, shipping and tracking software, and the like. The software is mapped to company-specific processes that just can't be duplicated by the generic auction management tools discussed previously.

Where can you find developers for this type of custom system solution? The best place to look is locally; there are no doubt many local software developers in your city who can take on this task. You might also be able to find prepackaged systems or available developers within your particular industry. Look in your relevant trade publications or consult with your industry trade associations for recommendations.

There are also several web-based development companies that offer custom eBay business development. The most popular of these companies include Dynamic Ventures, Inc. (www.dyve.com/dv/eBayDeveloper.htm) and JDT Technologies (www.jdttech.com/ebay.html). Do a Google search on "eBay customer software" to find similar firms.

As you might suspect, this sort of custom solution is not cheap. Expect to spend several thousand dollars, and perhaps pay a monthly licensing fee, to develop a system that best fits your business.

Trick #10: Treat Your eBay Business Like a Real Business—Because It Is

Do all the tricks in this chapter sound terribly business-like? Not much fun? Too much work? Tough. Building a successful business *is* work, and it requires business skills.

Sure, you can continue to sell odds and ends on eBay in your spare time, but that isn't a real business. A real business has quantifiable goals, and a plan on how to achieve those goals. A real business keeps good records and tracks its progress on a monthly basis. A real business is registered with state and federal authorities and pays taxes on the income it earns.

Equally important, a real business exists to make a profit, and to pay you a good income. Businesspeople don't sell stuff on eBay just for the fun of it (although it might be fun; that's a side benefit). Real businesspeople are in business to make money, and there's nothing wrong with that.

If you're serious about your eBay business, you can't treat it like a hobby; it's not a part-time thing. Your business should be the focus of your attention, and you should work full-time on making it successful and helping it grow. That means spending time not only on the day-to-day operational details (creating auction listings, managing in-process auctions, packing and shipping sold items), but also taking the time to analyze past performance and plan future operations. The more time you devote to your eBay business, the more successful it will be.

If you *don't* treat your eBay sales as a real business, you'll find that your sales (and profits) stall out after a time. You can only get so far on dumb luck and momentum. Growing a business takes time and a lot of hard work. Luck is only part of the equation.

Naturally, treating your eBay business like a real business requires the use of a whole range of business skills. You'll need the following skills to be successful:

- **Accounting** to put together and run your business's record-keeping system

- **Financial analysis** to analyze your financial reports and determine how well your business is doing

- **Purchasing** to identify items to purchase for resale, and to negotiate pricing on those items

- **Inventory management** to keep track of all your inventory and maximize inventory turns

- **Marketing** to create effective auction listings and promote your eBay auctions and business

- **Operations** to make sure that all your business's backend functions (packing, shipping, and so on) run smoothly

- **Management** to oversee not only the day-to-day management of the business, but also plan for future growth

If you weren't a business major in school, of if you don't have a real-world business background, you might not possess all of these skills. That's okay; you can learn. Many eBay sellers learn on the job; others take courses and read books to get smarter about everything they have to do. However you proceed, you need to possess and grow all of these business skills; without them, you'll soon be floundering.

So, this trick isn't really much of a trick at all; there's no magic to it. But it's still good advice—treat your eBay business like a real business, develop your own personal business skills, and devote all your energies to making your business successful.

Profile: Baseball Card Connection

Business Profile

Business name: Baseball Card Connection

eBay ID: bbcardconnection

eBay Store: stores.ebay.com/Baseball-Card-Connection

Website: bbcardconnection.beckett.com

Type of business: Sports cards and collectibles

Owners: Jon and Lisa Schafer

Location: Effingham, Illinois

Throughout this book we're going to profile several successful eBay businesses. I hope you can learn from these successful eBay business masters—both from their example and the advice they give.

Our first profiled business is Baseball Card Connection. This is a sports card and collectibles business run by the husband and wife team of Lisa and Jon Schafer—both online and off.

From Physical Sales to Online Sales

As the business name implies, Baseball Card Connection sells baseball cards, along with a variety of related merchandise—other sports cards, sports collectibles (team clocks, banners, lamps, and so forth), and Thomas the Tank Engine collectibles. The online business is an offshoot of the Schafer's existing bricks-and-mortar store, a 6,000–square foot superstore located in downtown Effingham, Illinois.

Inside the Baseball Card Connection bricks-and-mortar store.

Jon and Lisa had already established their retail business when they started selling on eBay almost 10 years ago, in 1998. They had heard that eBay was a great place to sell trading cards, so they started listing their current in-stock inventory on the eBay site. Their initial goal was simply to bring more exposure to their existing retail store; the sales they made on eBay were a welcome surprise.

Contrary to the advice in the preceeding chapter, not all sellers start out with a detailed business plan—especially those migrating an existing business to the eBay marketplace. That's certainly the case with Lisa and Jon; since they eased an existing business onto eBay, they didn't do a lot of planning for their online sales at the beginning. As the online business has grown, however, they're starting to do more long-term planning. Here's what Lisa says about business planning:

"We are currently trying to monitor all of our different products and sales figures to find out what products are bringing us the best returns. Our future growth consists of adding new innovative, fresh products. We try to add something new almost every week to keep our eBay Store fresh."

Managing the Business

The physical Baseball Card Connection is very much a family business, run by Jon and Lisa with one part-time employee. They utilize an outside accountant to handle the financial side of things.

For their eBay business, they use the Turbo Lister program to manage and list items in bulk. Lisa finds the program especially useful:

"I would recommend Turbo Lister even to users who are selling just a few items per week. It can really cut down on your listing times."

Selling Strategies

Jon and Lisa list all of their fast-selling items in the traditional auction format, with most items listed at a 1-cent starting price. This reduces their listing fees and gets multiple buyers interested in the item. Lisa explains the thinking behind this strategy:

"An example would be an Albert Pujols Baseball Card. If the particular card has recently sold for $40, $45, and $42, most likely our card will sell at those levels or higher, due to our good feedback. In this case, we would start the item at $.01 with no reserve."

On the other hand, the company sells less-popular and specialty items at a higher starting price with the Buy It Now option. As the Schafers see it, if you're selling an item that's of interest to only a small number of buyers, you must list it at the minimum price you are willing to accept, or it could sell for nothing. Lisa explains how they do it:

"An example of this would be a flag to fly outside your house. Most likely, buyers of this item are looking for a specific flag, like a St. Louis Cardinals house flag. This is an item that will sell if the buyer finds it, and it is what they are looking for. Price is really not that much of a concern. This item would be started near the full price of $19.00 with a $19.90 Buy It Now. There would be no benefit to reducing the price."

As to what makes for a successful listing, Lisa says that less is more:

"I view items every day that go on and on and on. Just keep it simple and let the product sell itself. Too many sellers try to hype up their listings, and in the eyes of smart buyers, it makes them seem desperate for bids. If I view an item that is hyped up, I just move on to the next one. That's the thing with eBay—there's always someone else with the same product."

* LARRY BIRD *

NICE LOT OF (7) DIFFERENT RARE CARDS

You are bidding on a nice lot of (7) different oddball Larry Bird basketball cards. The lot includes many tough to find magazine insert cards. What makes magazine insert cards so rare is the fact that they have to be cut from a full sheet inserted into the magazine. If you have ever tried you know how difficult it is to end up with a 2.5" x 3.5" card with clean, sharp edges. Since most collectors chose to leave the magazine intact, very few cleanly cut insert cards are in circulation today. A nice lot for a Larry Legend Fan. The lot includes:

1993 Ballstreet News Gold Card (No #) ~ 1991 Allan Kaye's Silver Card #9 ~ 1993 Investor's Journal Gold Foil Card #11 ~ 1993 Investor's Journal Blue Foil Card #11~ 1992 Investor's Journal Purple Foil Card #60 ~ 1992 Investor's Journal Gold Foil Card #60 ~ 1991 Legends Silver Card #52

The winning bidder will need to include $2.00 for shipping and insurance. Sorry, no orders outside the lower 48 states. We are a full time hobby store with a massive inventory. Be sure to view all of the other items we have up for bid under seller id "bbcardconnection". Thank You and Good Luck, Baseball Card Connection, Jon & Lisa Schafer, P.O. Box 1242, Effingham, IL 62401; Be sure to check our feedback to see comments from thousands of satisfied customers. Store Phone: (217) 342-2539; We accept Visa, Mastercard, and Discover through our store at no additional charge. We do not accept PayPal

Turbo Lister
Powered by eBay Turbo Lister

A typical listing from bbcardconnection—just enough information to sell the product.

The Schafers say that clear pictures are also important: "If your photo is bad, your results will most likely be bad."

Lisa also notes that they take full advantage of eBay's Second Chance Offer feature. "This is a great way to sell extra product and you have total control of the selling price," Lisa says—assuming that you have additional quantities in stock of the item you just sold, and that you had more than one bidder on the item. Just send Second Chance offers to everyone who bid a certain amount above your product cost. These are plus sales you make on the single original listing fee.

Other Online Sales

The Schafers sell on eBay via traditional auctions and through their Baseball Card Connection eBay Store. They currently list 3,000–4,000 items every month, with 50% of auction items selling through. Yearly eBay sales are in the $400,000–$500,000 range.

Lisa says that one of the things they like about their eBay Store is the cost—up to 90% cheaper than traditional auctions. As she says, "Having an eBay Store gives you the opportunity to put thousands of items up for sale at a drastically reduced cost."

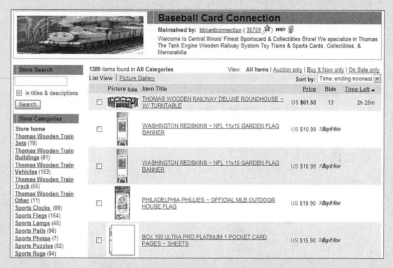

The bbcardconnection eBay store.

They supplement their eBay sales with another web-based store on Beckett.com, a major site for sports card buyers and sellers. This online store offers millions of trading cards for sale and is searchable by name, year, brand, and so forth.

Why two online stores? As Lisa notes, they cater to two completely different audiences:

"[The Beckett.com] website is geared towards the diehard trading card collector, whereas our eBay store is more geared towards customers that are looking for more general merchandise."

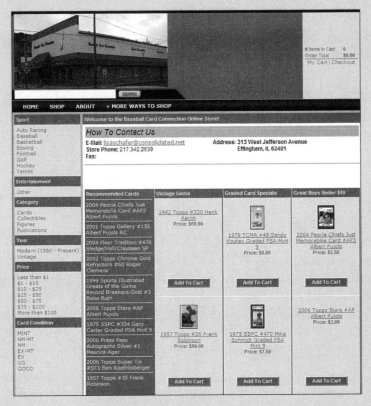

The Baseball Card Connection store on Beckett.com.

Finding and Managing Inventory

One of the challenges for any collectibles business, online or off, is finding new items to sell. Baseball Card Connection purchases most of its product directly from the manufacturers, using middlemen on just a few product lines.

To manage their large and diverse inventory, Jon and Lisa created their own inventory management system using Microsoft Works. Here's how Lisa says it works:

"When we receive deliveries during the day, we get the products put out in our physical store, and listed in our eBay store, as soon as possible, usually within a few hours. This keeps everything up to date and eliminates any backlog."

Jon Schafer managing his store's inventory.

The Schafers are continually trying to increase their inventory on the best-selling items. They try to have a month's worth of a particular product in stock at all times, and work hard at reordering products that are starting to get low. As Lisa notes, "This is one of the trickiest areas in the business world. You have to have product in stock to sell it, but every day the product sits on your shelf costs you money." It's a balancing act.

Managing Growth

Lisa notes that selling on eBay has become a bit more difficult in recent years, due to increased competition. But, as she notes, "If you have good products at good prices, and good customer service with fast delivery, you will come out on top."

They try to utilize all the free marketing tools that eBay offers—email newsletters, favorite store options, and the like. Using these free tools has helped the Schafers increase their eBay sales each year, by targeting repeat customers. They're also in the process of expanding their product lines and increasing the quantities available for most items they have in stock.

Keys to Success

I asked Jon and Lisa about some of the things they do to make their eBay business successful. Here's how they responded:

"We take pride in getting our shipments out fast. This shows up all of the time in our feedback, which gives us a great competitive advantage. We stress organization and efficiency when processing orders each day. If you get the order out fast, the customer will most likely receive it before they even have a chance to inquire about delivery times/and or delays. This, in turn, helps us alleviate having to respond to tracking requests and order status inquiries."

Lisa Schafer packing orders to ship.

And what advice would they give a new eBay seller looking to start up an eBay business?

"I won't say 'do your homework.' I will say that you must be selling something from an area of interest that you enjoy. You just can't start selling widgets because you heard selling widgets will make you money. You can start selling fishing lures if you are an avid fisherman and fishing is your passion. I have witnessed numerous people who think they are going to sell on eBay and make it big, until they find out how much work is involved. eBay is not a get-rich-quick website. It's like any other business; you are going to have to put in a full-blown effort to make it happen. Most likely you will struggle at first until you build a reputation and a client base. But once you get through the initial barrier to entry, and keep your nose to the grindstone, you can and will build a successful business."

In other words, eBay success requires a lot of work. Good advice for any eBay seller to know.

2

Tricks for Deciding What to Sell

The question I get asked most often from startup eBay sellers is "What can I sell that will make me lots of money?" As unanswerable as that question is (what's hot today is, more often than not, cold tomorrow), it does point to one of the key aspects of planning your eBay business.

Few sellers achieve long-term success by milking the latest fad or by selling the hodgepodge of products you find at a typical garage sale. True success comes from identifying opportunities in defined market segments and aggressively pursuing those opportunities.

How do the eBay business masters decide what product categories on which they want to focus? That's the gist of the ten tricks in this chapter; read on to learn how to focus your eBay selling.

Trick #11: Research the Market

This is the most important trick for deciding what type of products to sell on eBay. You can fly blind and trust your hunches, but that makes eBay selling a bit like gambling: You roll your dice and you take your chances. A much, much better approach is to research the market first, using facts and data to tell you what products are the hottest sellers in the eBay marketplace.

Researching eBay products sales is quite simple in concept. What you want to do is examine past auctions to determine what products are selling and for what prices. You want to gravitate towards those product categories with the highest or most rapidly growing sales and avoid those categories with slow or declining sales. It's common sense.

Of course, you also want to examine pricing trends in these categories. If a category is stagnant in terms of unit sales but seeing price increases over time, it might be worth investigating. Conversely, a stagnant category with decreasing prices is one to be avoided.

Market research can also help you determine how best to market your eBay auctions. Close examination of the data can tell you the best starting price for a given product, which day of the week is best to end your auctions, even what keywords you want to include in your auction listings. The key is to examine the most successful auctions and determine what made them successful; incorporate this information into your auctions to maximize your sales.

tip

The best categories for eBay success are those that are large and growing in both unit sales and average selling price.

caution

You should avoid those categories that, over the past several months, are shrinking in size or that have seen significant reductions in average selling price.

If analyzing past auction data is key, just where does all this data come from? It comes from eBay, of course. eBay keeps voluminous data on its past auctions, and makes most of it available to anyone with the time (and, in some instances, money) to analyze it.

The raw data is available free to any user willing to search eBay's completed auction listings. You can find up to 30 days of data readily available, which will tell you how things have been moving in the past month. Naturally, you can capture this data on an ongoing basis; create a big database or spreadsheet of results and you can see trends over time.

More detailed analysis is available from both eBay and a variety of third parties. This data is often accessible for a fee, although some sites offer their research services at no cost. What all these sites have in common is that they license eBay's data through the eBay Data Licensing Program. In this program, eBay provides the data to the third-party site, as well as applies some control over what the sites can do with the data. So, if you use one of these sites, be assured that you're getting genuine eBay data— but filtered through that site's own unique analysis.

However you obtain historical sales data, how best can you use it? The key is to look not only at what's currently hot, but also at trends. A category that's red hot this month might be ice cold the next. A snapshot of eBay sales really doesn't tell you much, but when you analyze sales and pricing trends over a period of several months, you get a much better sense of where that particular market is moving.

Because market research is so important, it's worth devoting a few pages to discussing the most popular eBay market research tools. Read on to learn about them.

tip

Use "what's hot" reports to identify those categories with the most potential. Use in-depth research to determine how best to sell specific products and in particular categories.

eBay Closed Auctions

If you have the time and inclination, all of eBay's sales data is available free of charge. All you have to do is search eBay's completed listings (not in-progress auctions) to extract sell-through and pricing data. The easiest way to search completed auctions is to click the Advanced Search link below the search box on eBay's home page; this opens the Find Items page shown in Figure 2.1. Enter the keywords necessary to locate a particular type of item, and then check the Completed Listings Only option. When you click the Search button, eBay will return a list of completed auctions that match your search criteria.

FIGURE 2.1

Searching closed auctions from eBay's advanced search page.

Note that these complete auctions aren't all successful auctions. eBay lists both auctions that closed successfully and those that ended without a winning bid. You can learn from both the successful auctions and the unsuccessful ones; in particular, examine *why* the unsuccessful auctions didn't receive any bids. Examine the starting price (often too high), the day of week the auction ended, whether photos were included, even the wording in the title and description. Then compare these unsuccessful auctions to the successful ones—why did the first auctions fail while the second ones succeeded?

After you generate a list of closed auctions, copy the relevant data into a database or Excel spreadsheet. I work with Excel, and like to create columns for starting price, ending price, success (yes or no), close date, and ending day (of the week). You might want to track more or less data. Create a row in the spreadsheet for each listing in your results; you can then work with the spreadsheet to analyze your data over time.

eBay Marketplace Research

If this auction-by-auction data collection seems a bit tedious (and it is), check out eBay's Marketplace Research service (pages.ebay.com/ marketplace_research/). Marketplace Research lets you search up to 90 days of historical listings and then analyze key metrics—average selling price, average start price, and so on. The data is presented in pretty-looking tables and charts, which makes it easier to view trends over time.

For example, Figure 2.2 shows a typical Marketplace Research report for a given product, complete with the following data:

- Average sold price
- Sold price range
- Average sold Buy It Now price
- Sold Buy It Now price range
- Average start price
- Start price range
- Average shipping cost
- Shipping cost range
- Last sold price
- Last sold date and time
- Number of completed items
- Number of sold items
- Average number of bids per item

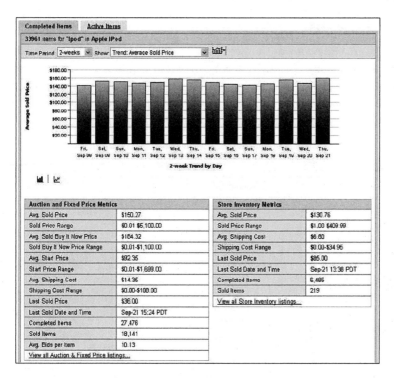

FIGURE 2.2

A typical research report from eBay's Marketplace Research.

There's also a chart of total dollar sales by day, for a two-week period. Most of this data is presented separately for traditional eBay versus eBay Stores sales.

Unfortunately, accessing the Marketplace Research data isn't free. eBay offers three subscription plans:

- **Fast Pass**—$2.99 one-time fee for 2 days access to 60 days worth of data
- **Basic**—$9.99/month for ongoing access to 60 days worth of data
- **Pro**—$24.99/month for ongoing access to 90 days worth of data

note

The Pro plan also offers several more advanced reports, including data for specific sellers, stores, and countries.

You might want to try Marketplace Research first with a two-day Fast Pass. If you like what you see, you can then subscribe to the Basic or Pro plan on an ongoing basis.

eBay Pulse

Not all eBay data has to be manually accessed. Particularly interesting is the eBay Pulse (pulse.ebay.com), shown in Figure 2.3. As you can see, eBay Pulse displays a lot of current information—top ten searches, five largest eBay Stores, and most watched items. You can display this information for eBay in general or for specific product categories.

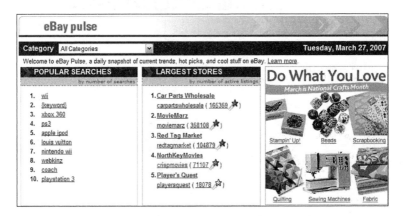

FIGURE 2.3
Viewing what's hot via eBay Pulse.

eBay Pulse is useful for determining what's hot at this point in time. It's not good for determining trends, but it will tell you what the current hot products are for any given category.

eBay Popular Searches

Also useful is eBay's list of its current most popular searches by category. The Popular Terms page (popular.ebay.com), shown in Figure 2.4, lets you select a category and then view the most popular searches within that category. For example, you might click the Baby Strollers category and see the most popular current items in that category, as determined by user searches.

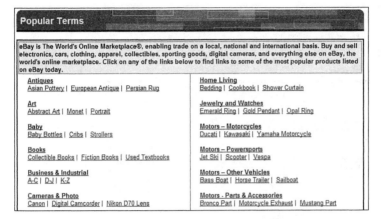

FIGURE 2.4

Viewing eBay's most popular current search terms.

Vendio

As noted previously, eBay doesn't have a monopoly on market research. A number of third-party websites have access to eBay's sales data and provide their own analysis and reports.

One of the oldest players in the eBay research market is Vendio (www.vendio.com). This site offers two key research tools: What's Hot and Research. You can use these tools to discover hot product categories and determine how to price and when to list your items.

note

Vendio's research tools were formerly offered by Ándale, which recently merged with Vendio.

The What's Hot tool provides detailed reports about the hottest selling eBay items, in any category. As you can see in Figure 2.5, the main What's Hot page lets you click through each category to find the hottest products in each category, or search for particular items to see their performance. Vendio also pulls out the hottest products in all categories (for the past four weeks) and lists them on this main page. When you click through to a specific product, you see the individual product report; Vendio uses a chili pepper icon to denote the relative hotness of any particular product. The cost to use this tool is $3.95/month.

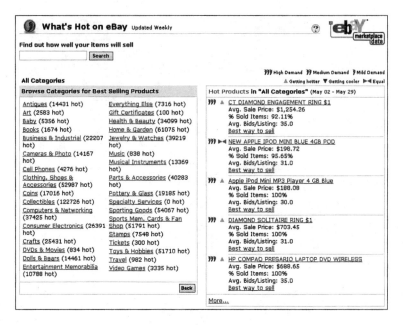

FIGURE 2.5

Discover hot products and categories with the Vendio What's Hot research tool.

Complementing the What's Hot report is the Vendio Research tool, which provides detailed pricing reports for any specific product or category on eBay. The main Research page, shown in Figure 2.6, lets you search for specific items. Enter the item or category in the Research Prices box, and then click the Research button. The search results page displays some key information (average selling price, number of total listings, number of items listed, total number of items sold, and success rate), along with three useful charts (average selling price, quantity listed and sold, and percentage of successful auctions, all over a four-week period). Even more detailed information is available when you click the How to Sell tab, which displays a very detailed report about the item or category you selected. This tool costs $14.95/month.

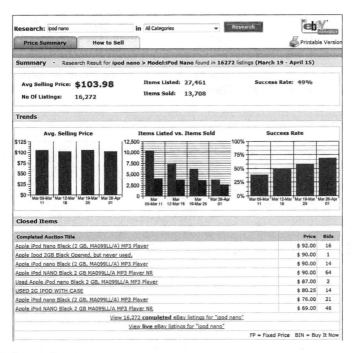

FIGURE 2.6
Research products or categories with Vendio Research.

Of these tools, What's Hot is good for identifying specific products to sell or general product categories to enter—and a lot more fully featured than eBay's superficially similar eBay Pulse page. The Research tool is essential for both determining what products to sell, and for fine tuning product listings.

AuctionIntelligence

AuctionIntelligence (www.certes.net/AuctionIntelligence/) is an auction analysis program available on a subscription basis. Downloading the software is free; you have to pay $14.99 per month to use it.

This program lets you search eBay by category or keyword. After it retrieves all matching auctions, you can generate a wide variety of sophisticated reports just by clicking the name of the report in the Reports list, and then you can customize the report based on your own user-defined parameters. You can generate reports that detail price over time; bidding and pricing trends; effects of auction duration, premium features, feedback, and PayPal; frequent bidders; common words in listing titles; and more.

For example, Figure 2.7 shows the AuctionIntelligence Search Summary report. This particular report displays the total number of auctions found; the sell-through rate for this item; the number of regular, reserve, fixed price, and Dutch auctions; the average number of bids for each auction; the average price for this item; and more.

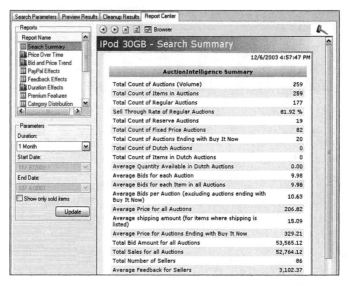

FIGURE 2.7

Basic auction sales analysis from the AuctionIntelligence Search Summary report.

AuctionIntelligence also offers Hot Items and Category Distribution reports. As such, you're looking at an extremely full-featured research program, although it's somewhat technically demanding (it requires the installation of a Microsoft SQL Server 2000 or MSDE 2000 database before it can run) and not the easiest program in the world to use. Given these caveats, AuctionIntelligence can generate some extremely valuable research reports for the serious eBay seller.

eSeller Street

A relative newcomer to the eBay research business, eSeller Street (www.esellerstreet.com) offers research reports on an a la carte basis. You can buy 20 reports for $8.95 or 60 reports for $21.00.

eSeller Street lets you research by product keyword or by seller. You can restrict results by category or by date range. A typical research report, like the one in Figure 2.8, details total revenue, total number of listings, number of successful listings, total number of bids, number of items sold, number of items offered, percentage success rate, and various pricing data. Scroll down the page to see results by listing type (auction, fixed price, and so on), hour of the day, auction duration, day of week (shown in Figure 2.9), and "listing promotion" (actually listing enhancement).

Keywords: Coach purse, **Seller ID:** , Category 0, Past 7 Days, US,

Categories	Totals and pricing			
Listing Types	Revenue:	$504,968	Average Sold Price:	$89.28
	Total Listings:	8,270	Lowest Sold Price:	$0.01
Durations	Successful Listings:	5,624	Highest Sold Price:	$1,025.00
	Bids:	64,605	Frequent Sold Price:	$51.00
Day of Week	Items Sold:	5,656	Average Start Price:	$35.11
	Items Offered:	8,420	Lowest Start Price:	$0.01
Promotions	Success Rate:	68%	Highest Start Price:	$550.00
			Frequent Start Price:	$0.99

Top Categories

Cat #	Category Name	Listings	Revenue	Sell-Through	Avg Sold Price
63852	Clothing, Shoes & Accessories > Women's Accessories, Handbags > Handbags, Bags:	7,642	$484,320	68%	$92.29
45237	Clothing, Shoes & Accessories > Women's Accessories, Handbags > Key Chains:	82	$1,247	80%	$18.07
3008	Clothing, Shoes & Accessories > Women's Accessories, Handbags > Wallets > Other:	68	$3,149	84%	$55.24
63889	Clothing, Shoes & Accessories > Women's Shoes:	64	$1,889	28%	$104.97
45260	Clothing, Shoes & Accessories > Women's Accessories, Handbags > Wallets > Coin Purses:	60	$992	65%	$25.44
1063	Clothing, Shoes & Accessories > Women's Accessories, Handbags > Other Items:	42	$986	55%	$42.85

FIGURE 2.8

A product research report from eSeller Street.

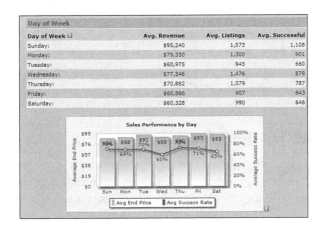

Day of Week

Day of Week	Avg. Revenue	Avg. Listings	Avg. Successful
Sunday:	$95,240	1,573	1,108
Monday:	$79,330	1,300	901
Tuesday:	$60,975	945	660
Wednesday:	$77,346	1,476	879
Thursday:	$70,882	1,079	787
Friday:	$60,866	907	643
Saturday:	$60,328	990	646

Sales Performance by Day

FIGURE 2.9

eSeller Street sales data by auction ending day.

If you need to do only a limited amount of research, eSeller Street is a cost-effective solution. All the data you need is presented on a single (long) page, which makes it easy to grasp.

Get4It

Get4It (www.get4it.com) is a free service that lets you do quick and easy searches for product pricing data. As you can see in Figure 2.10, when you enter a search term, the site generates a simple results page that includes the selling price range (on eBay and around the web), a pricing trends chart, and various selling data (average price per item, average number of bids per item, number of unsold items, and so on). The research isn't quite as robust as with other sites, but it is free—and will do the job for a lot of eBay sellers.

FIGURE 2.10

Free product pricing research from Get4It.

HammerTap Deep Analysis

HammerTap Deep Analysis (www.hammertap.com) is a software program that performs basic auction sales analysis. HammerTap provides fundamental information about any category or specific product, including the number of auctions in the past 30 days, the number of bids for each auction, percentage of items sold, average selling price, and so on.

HammerTap presents a variety of detailed analysis for both products and sellers. (Figure 2.11 shows a typical HammerTap category research report.) You can save individual searches within the program, as well as export your results to both spreadsheet and database formats. This versatile program works seamlessly with the data available on the eBay site, even if it is a tad pricey ($19.95/month subscription).

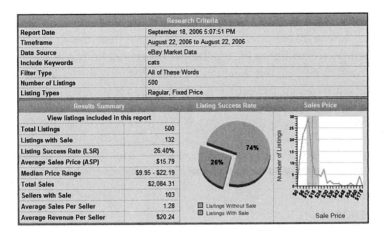

FIGURE 2.11
Category research with the HammerTap program.

Mpire Research

Mpire Research (www.mpire.com/products/researcher.html) is a very cool-looking and useful web-based eBay research tool. Enter a product or category and Mpire returns a report that tells you the average selling price of the top-selling listings and the most effective title keywords, listing enhancements, listing types, start price, listing duration, ending day and time, and product category. Figure 2.12 shows the top of a sample report.

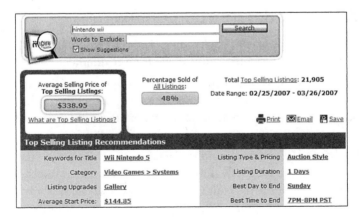

FIGURE 2.12
Easy-to-grasp listing analysis and recommendations from Mpire Research.

And here's the very best thing about Mpire Research—it's free. That's right, unlike all the paid research tools and services, there's absolutely no charge to search the Mpire database and generate research reports. You do have to register, but there are no fees associated with that. Just enter your search query and generate your free report.

tip

I'm a big fan of Mpire Research. The results are every bit as good as with the paid sites, but with a very easy-to-grasp presentation. (Particularly useful are the listing recommendations right at the top of each results page.) And it's free!

Terapeak

Another site offering free research is Terapeak (www.terapeak.com). Terapeak's free research includes much useful data about pricing, listing promotions, listing types, duration, day of week, keywords, time of day, and categories used. Formerly a pay service, Terapeak's switch to free research makes it worth considering for any serious eBay seller.

tip

Several other companies offer category-specific eBay research tools. These include MiBlueBook.com (www.mibluebook.com) for musical instruments; PriceMiner (www.priceminer.com) for antiques, art, and collectibles; and Vintage Card Prices (www.vintagecardprices.com) for baseball cards.

Trick #12: Test Before You Commit

Doing research on other people's auctions is one thing. Performing your own research to see what works for you is quite another.

Few businesses jump into new markets without doing some form of market testing. Before you commit huge resources (inventory, packaging, processes, and so on), it's smart to test the market by running a few auctions with the merchandise you're considering selling.

What do you learn by running test auctions? Lots of things. First, you learn whether there's really a demand for this particular merchandise. If no one bids, or if the bid count is disturbingly low, you just saved yourself a world of headache; there's still time to change your plans because you haven't made the final commitment yet. If your test auctions receive a large number of bids, you know you're into something good.

Second, you get a good idea of pricing trends. Run a few test auctions and see where the final prices end up; this will tell you what you can expect to average in terms of selling price if and when you go live with your real auctions.

Third, you can get smarter about *how* you list your items. For example, to determine the most effective starting price, run a half-dozen auctions of the same item, each starting at a different price. The auctions that garner the highest ending prices will tell you which starting price to use. Same with day of the week; start similar auctions on different days of the week and see which ones result in the highest selling prices. The more research you do, the more effective your auctions will be.

You can also use this type of market testing to determine the effectiveness of various listing enhancements. Should you purchase a subtitle for your listings? Run two listings, one with a subtitle and one without, and compare the results. The same with all other listing enhancements, auction length, even the Buy It Now option. Run tests with and without each enhancement and see which pulls best.

Let's work through an example. Let's say you're thinking about selling gift baskets, and you want to find out what to expect in terms of pricing. So, you put up three auctions, all starting on the same day and using the same title and description, and see what happens. When you calculate the results, you find that all three listings sell, at an average price of $25.

That's good news for finding out what you can expect to receive in terms of sales revenue. But now you want to fine-tune the model, and determine the best starting price for this item. This time around you start another three auctions, again starting on the same day with the same title and description, but starting at three different prices: $17.99, $19.99, and $21.99. See which of the three auctions results in highest final price, and that's the starting price you use going forward. (Of course, you'll want to repeat this test the following week to see whether the initial results hold or were just a one-time fluke.)

caution

Be wary of testing more than one factor at a time; you'll never know which factor produced the results. For example, don't change price and starting day in the same test. Test one factor first, and then run a second test for the second factor.

The bottom line is that the more you test, the more successful your auctions will be. And I'm not just talking about running one or two auctions and then making the commitment. Effective market research requires multiple test points in a variety of scenarios. Given the seven-day length of the average eBay auction, you might want to devote a month or more for your market tests. You'll want to test each individual combination of factors (price, starting day, and so on) more than once, as any given test can be skewed by any number of events. Run each test several times and take the average of your results; this will give you a better idea of what to expect when you go live with your real auctions.

What do you do if your tests produce disappointing results? Consider yourself lucky. If you hadn't run the tests, you might have already invested huge sums in inventory and such, sums that you might never recover. By testing a product before you sell it, you protect yourself from bad decisions. Purchase a few units for testing purposes (even if you have to pay a higher price for them), but buy larger quantities only if the tests are successful. If the tests show that the item doesn't sell or doesn't command a high-enough price, drop that item and move on to something else.

Trick #13: Sell What You Know

What should you sell in your eBay business? I'm always a little taken aback when I'm asked this question because it seems odd to me to enter into a random business. That is, most successful businesspeople I know are in their particular business for a reason. You don't find a lot of businesspeople jumping around from one type of business to another; most businesspeople tend to stick to a particular industry or discipline.

Granted, good business skills are transferrable across industries. But most people are more successful doing something they know something about—or, even more so, doing something they love. Someone who runs a successful music store will probably be less successful (and less happy) running a jewelry store. Yes, the skills required for each are similar, but it really helps when you know the product you're selling and the customers you're selling to.

For that reason, when people ask me what they should be selling on eBay, I ask them what it is they really like to do. What are their hobbies, their pastimes, the things that get them excited? What do they have experience with? Where have they worked before?

If you're a music lover, consider selling music-related items on eBay—CDs, musical instruments, that sort of thing. If you're a sports fan, consider selling sporting goods, sporting apparel, sports paraphernalia and collectibles, and so on. If you're a computer geek, consider selling computer hardware, software, peripherals, and the like. You get the idea.

Why should you stick to something you know? There are several good reasons for this.

First, you'll enjoy it more. If you're a collector of vintage toys, you'll enjoy selling vintage toys more than you would selling women's purses. eBay offers the unique opportunity to turn your avocation into your vocation—to make money doing the thing you love.

Second, you'll be better at it. When you know a category, you're better able to pick up on trends and know what's really going on. Sure, you can train yourself to learn a category, but you'll have a much faster start if you know the category going in. If you're a comic book collector in your spare time, you already know what the hot issues are, how to store and ship your inventory, even approximate pricing. Someone just starting out in comics won't know what you'll know; he'll make a lot of mistakes while trying to learn.

Third, you'll know the lingo. Whatever product category you pick, that category has its own private vocabulary—the slang that only those in that category or industry know. You've seen it before; everybody involved in a particular industry talks in their own peculiar language, with its own catchphrases, acronyms, and buzzwords. For example, record collectors speak of cut-outs, EPs, flexis, and radio copies; shoe sellers speak of ankle wraps, blucher toes, and jellies. If you're not connected to that category, you'll not only have no idea what those terms mean, you also won't know to use those terms when writing your auction listings. When you know the category, you know all the buzzwords—not only what they mean, but also when to use them. You'll be able to write item descriptions that both better describe what you're selling and better connect you to serious buyers. In this regard, insiders do better than outsiders.

Fourth, it's easier to find inventory. When you're familiar with an industry, you know who the players are—you know the top wholesalers and distributors, you know the manufacturers, you have established contacts. You don't have to make cold calls; you can work your contact list and start making purchases almost immediately.

In fact, you might even have your starting inventory in hand; if you're a collector, your starting inventory can be your private collection. You'll know other collectors and how to buy large collections. Someone just starting out won't have any of these advantages.

That's not to say that you can't sell merchandise in any category. You can, and if you're a good businessperson you'll probably do well—eventually. But you'll always be at a disadvantage to those sellers who come from that industry or hobby, an outsider selling against established insiders. Wouldn't you rather have that insider advantage? Well, you can—if you sell what you know.

Trick #14: Specialize

Inherent in the advice to sell what you know is that it pays to specialize. If you know one thing, sell that one thing. If you know a single product category, sell products in that category. Specialization is one of the keys to business success, on eBay or otherwise.

Don't believe me? Look at any list of top eBay sellers. What you'll find is that the vast majority of these sellers specialize in a single product category; few sell across categories.

For example, in September 2006 Sellathon (www.sellathon.com) produced a list of eBay's top 10,000 sellers, dubbed The Sellathon 10,000. I did a quick analysis of the top 50 sellers on the list and found just three sellers who sold in multiple unrelated categories. All the other sellers specialized in a single type of product: books, car stereos, cell phone accessories, computer peripherals, digital cameras, photo accessories, clothing, shoes, jewelry, CDs, DVDs, videogames, and so on. Think that's a coincidence?

In the real world there are certainly examples of successful multiple-product retailers. (Wal-Mart, anyone?) But online, the big successes come from specializing in a single product category, much like the single-category bricks-and-mortar big box retailers. So, if you want to be an eBay success, it pays to specialize.

Why is this the case? It has to do with product/category knowledge, purchasing power, and efficiency. Let's look at each separately.

Specialize for Knowledge

This ties back to Trick #13. The more time you spend in a specific category, or with a specific type of product, the more you'll learn about that category or product. And the more you know, the smarter you'll be about buying and selling in that category.

When all you sell is shoes, for example, you get smart real fast about everything shoe-related. You'll learn the major suppliers, the industry slang, the hot products, and so on. You'll learn what your customers like and expect, and how to make them happy. And you'll be better able to keep on top of the latest fads, and even anticipate market trends.

If you sold not just shoes but also jewelry, digital cameras, golf clubs, and snowmobiles, it would be a lot more difficult to stay equally informed about all those different categories. After all, can you really be an expert in more than one thing? It's possible, I suppose, but difficult—and highly unlikely.

The better approach is to specialize in a single category or type of product, then learn all there is to know about that category or product. Become an expert, and you'll become a more effective seller.

Specialize for Purchasing Power

Here's a very quantifiable reason for specializing in a single product category. When you stock multiple types of merchandise, you spread your buying across those multiple categories. But when you specialize in a specific type of product, you concentrate your buying within that single category—and often to a single supplier. The more you purchase from a given supplier, the lower prices you can negotiate. That's the way purchasing works; buy in larger volume, buy at lower cost.

Let's look at a numeric example. Let's say that you sell across four unrelated categories, and move $10,000 worth of merchandise a month in each category, for a total of $40,000 worth of sales. Purchasing at a 25% discount, you're buying $30,000 worth of inventory each month, spread across four suppliers.

Now let's say you do the same volume of sales, but concentrated in a single category. Instead of purchasing just $7,500/month from four different suppliers, you now purchase $30,000 every month from a single supplier. It's not hard to imagine that a supplier would allow greater discounts for a $30,000/month customer than it would for a $7,500/month customer. Let's say you were able to negotiate an extra 5% discount on the larger volume, so instead of paying $30,000 for your inventory, you now pay $28,500. That's an extra $1,500 in your pocket every month, just because you specialized in a single category and became more important to your supplier.

However the math works in your particular situation, you're better off consolidating your purchases than spreading them around. Consolidated purchases means higher volume through your remaining suppliers, and higher volume often means higher discounts and lower prices, which translate into increased profits for your business. Better to own a bigger fish in a single pond than smaller fishes in multiple ponds.

Specialize for Efficiency

Finally, we have the benefit of efficiency. When you sell multiple products, you also have to pack and ship multiple products. The more different things you sell, the more different packaging and shipping options you need—and the more different things you do, the more it costs you.

Conversely, if you specialize in a single type of product, you'll reduce the number of different operations you have in your business. And the fewer variables you have, the less it will cost you—both in time and materials.

Let's say you have a business that sells both golf clubs and digital cameras. When it comes time to pack and ship the items you sell, you're going to need two different sizes of boxes, two different types of packing materials, and probably two different shipping services. The two items have nothing in common, so you essentially double the size of your packing and shipping operation by selling both.

On the other hand, if you sold only digital cameras, you cut the size of your backend operation in half. You have to stock only a single size of box and a single type of packing material, and you have to use only a single shipping service. That means you can devote less space to storing your boxes and shipping materials, and you can probably save money on each by ordering more of the single type you stock. Because you'll now be sending more volume through a single shipper, you might be able to negotiate discounts there, as well.

Equally important, the fewer things you do, the more efficient your operation becomes. Packing and shipping both golf clubs and cameras requires that you develop two similar but slightly different sets of skills. Reduce that to a single product type and all of a sudden you get much more efficient in what you do. You have to learn how to pack only a single type of product, which means you can pack it faster. And, as we all know, time is money.

The same goes for preparing your auction listings. The fewer individual items you sell, the easier it is to write your titles and descriptions and to take your photos. The more different items you sell, the more onerous the upfront process becomes. Imagine selling 50 different types of products versus a single type of product 50 times over—you see how much more efficient specialized selling can make you.

The bottom line is that the biggest eBay sellers specialize, and there are many good reasons why. You should learn from these sellers, and strive to keep your eBay business as simple as possible.

Trick #15: Target Niche Markets—Avoid Commodity Products

As a new eBay business, you can learn only so much from existing businesses. It might be tempting to look at the list of top sellers and say that you want to duplicate everything they're doing. The problem with that strategy is that if you duplicate everything they do, you'll be in direct competition with them. And when it comes to competing with an established competitor, the established business almost always wins.

For example, a surprisingly high percentage of The Sellathon 10,000 sell CDs and DVDs. All fine and good, but CDs and DVDs are pretty much commodity products. That is, one Madonna CD is the same as the next Madonna CD; there's very little unique value that a retailer can add to the product. So, if you decide to sell that Madonna CD, you'll be competing with every other eBay retailer who's also selling that Madonna CD. Why should a customer buy from you instead from one of your competitors? What unique competitive advantage do you bring to the table?

The answer, of course, is that you don't bring anything unique to the table. One Madonna CD is the same as the next, so the customer is probably going to buy from the retailer that offers the lowest price. Unless you can offer the lowest price, you'll lose sales. (And you probably can't offer the lowest price because your larger competitors are no doubt buying at a lower cost; size has its purchasing advantages.)

Any new eBay business selling a commodity product has two strikes against it. First, it's offering a product sold strictly on price, and doing so at a purchasing disadvantage. Second, it's selling against established businesses that have built large customer bases and established efficient backend operations. Your ability to succeed in this situation is limited.

A better approach is to carve out a position in a less competitive category. Don't go head-to-head with the big boys; instead, offer a product that has fewer competitors and is thus relatively underserved to the consumer.

There are a number of ways to identify a niche category—you can go deep, you can go sideways, or you can go in a completely different direction.

Go Deep—Target a Narrow Niche

This strategy keeps you in the main category but focuses your business on a more specialized niche. It banks on the fact that most larger businesses tend to generalize within a category, aiming for the larger segments of a market, and thus leave smaller niches within that market underserved.

Let's take, as an example, the DVD market. If you were to enter the general DVD business, selling the latest hits and major studio releases, you'd be competing directly with some of eBay's largest and most established sellers. But these large sellers don't equally serve all subcategories within the DVD category. You might be able to carve out a profitable niche by specializing only in foreign films, going deep in a narrow category that is typically served only superficially by the larger DVD retailers.

You can envision a similar approach in the CD category. Instead of selling the latest hits by major artists, you could specialize in indie-label CDs by lesser-known artists, or in import CDs, or in rare and used CDs. You get the idea.

This approach might not be viable for all product categories, but when you can do it, you'll attract an audience. Just make sure that the niche is big enough for you to build your business on.

Go Sideways—Sell Ancillary Products

With this strategy, you don't enter the main category, but instead move sideways to sell products that service that category. Let the big boys sell the main stuff; you'll make your money selling items that supplement what they sell.

Taking the DVD category again, instead of selling DVDs you might focus your business on DVD cases, or DVD cleaners, or DVD cables, or something similar. Or, instead of diving head-first into the highly competitive computer category, you might instead sell computer cables, cases, stands, peripherals, and the like. With this approach, you make your money on the edges of the market—which can be quite profitable.

Go in a Different Direction—Change Your Plan

Finally, you might acknowledge that you can neither beat them nor join them, and instead choose to abandon that category and pursue something altogether different. Maybe there's no room for you at all in the DVD market, selling either niche DVDs or accessories. In this instance, you might opt to change your game plan and pursue a totally different category—tennis rackets, or leather gloves, or maybe pet supplies. It might simply not be worth your time to compete in your original category of choice. It happens.

Trick #16: Add Personal Value to Your Products

In the previous trick we talked about the dangers of selling commodity products. This trick is the mirror image of that one, demonstrating that you can stand out from the competition when you add unique value to the products you sell. Worked properly, this trick lets you turn even commodity products into unique items. And, as you might suspect, the more unique the item you have for sale, the higher the price it will command.

How do you add personal value to the items you sell? There are a number of ways, depending on the type of item.

One way to add personal value is to bundle a commodity item with another related item so that you're selling the custom bundle rather than the commodity. For example, you might bundle a commodity DVD player with a package of connecting cables, or a commodity MP3 player with a carrying case, or a commodity purse with an accompanying wallet. Because you're offering more value (or at least a different value) than your competitors, you can command a higher price than a seller offering the commodity product alone.

A second approach is to literally personalize the item. Instead of selling a generic carrying bag, stencil the buyer's initials on the side or include an engraved tag. Instead of selling a generic polo shirt, offer it monogrammed. You see how it works.

This personalization can even work with some consumer electronics equipment. Instead of selling a desktop PC in its stock configuration, upgrade the hard disk or memory, or throw in a USB hub or memory card reader. Instead of selling a stock videogame console, throw in an extra controller or a free game. This approach creates a unique SKU, something slightly different than all the other sellers are offering. And when you have something unique to sell, you're not tied to the normal commodity pricing.

The whole point is to sell something slightly different from what everyone else is selling. You want your products to be unique so that you're not competing head-to-head with larger commodity sellers.

Trick #17: Offer a Large Number of SKUs

Just because you specialize in a single product category doesn't mean that you offer only a single product for sale. No, the bigger eBay sellers tend to offer a large number of items for sale within their chosen category; the more products you have available, the more customers you'll attract and the more sales you'll generate.

note

SKU stands for *stock keeping unit,* which is a single item (model or item number) in your inventory.

The more SKUs you carry, the more choices your customers have. If you sell computer cables, for example, and only offer a single $10 six-foot USB cable, you're going to lose customers who want a different length or quality. To best serve your customers, you need to offer cables in three-, six-, and twelve-foot lengths, and at good-better-best pricing. Yes, you'll have to carry more (and more varied) inventory, but you'll have the higher sales to support it.

This makes particular sense in multiple-title categories such as books, CDs, DVDs, and videogames. You can't open a bookstore with just a single title in stock; you have to carry a width and breadth of titles to satisfy a diverse customer base. In many of these categories, the only way to succeed is to offer virtually every title available; every shopper who finds a title you don't carry is lost as a future customer.

The same goes with clothing. Not only do you have to offer a variety of styles and colors, you have to carry those items in a variety of sizes. Unless you specialize in big or petite clothing, or offer close-out merchandise only, you better have stock in all popular sizes. Again, this means increasing the number of SKUs you carry, and the corresponding total inventory.

And unless you're an authorized outlet for a given brand, it pays to offer merchandise from a variety of manufacturers. Few shoppers limit their interest to a specific brand of merchandise; most like to compare merchandise from multiple suppliers. So, if you carry Nikon digital cameras, you should also carry cameras by Canon, Olympus, Sony, and the like.

Look at it from your customers' perspective. Let's say you're shopping for a new memory card for your digital camera. You go to Store A and find a single 1GB SD card from SanDisk. Even though the price might be decent, that's not much of a selection; in fact, you might have been looking for a 2GB card instead. So, you next go to Store B and find 1GB, 2GB, and 4GB SD cards from SanDisk, Kingston, and PQI. You're more likely to buy from Store B simply because you have a better choice there.

It's a fact. The more SKUs you offer, the more customers you'll attract, and the more sales you'll close. Limit your product offerings and you artificially limit your customer base.

In addition, the more SKUs you offer, the higher the odds that your customers will buy more than one item. A person shopping for the latest Rilo

Kiley CD might also buy the latest CD from Arcade Fire, just because she saw it while browsing your store. How often do you see someone leaving Barnes & Noble with just a single book in his bag? The more SKUs you offer, the more add-on sales you'll make.

This also means offering products that are ancillary to your main product line. If you sell digital cameras, you should also sell camera cases, lenses, memory cards, and the like. If you sell men's shirts, you should also sell ties, cufflinks, maybe even belts. If you sell golf clubs, you should also sell carrying cases, golf balls, tees, maybe even golf shirts and shoes. Offer a complete solution and you'll keep more of your customers to yourself— and make more money in the process.

Trick #18: Sell Higher-Priced—And Higher-Profit— Items

This next trick isn't a universal one; there are plenty of examples to the contrary. But in general, you can make more money faster by selling higher-priced items than you can by selling lower-priced items.

Higher Prices Are Better—More Often Than Not

All other things being equal, you'll make more money (both revenues and profits) selling 10 $20 items than you will selling 10 $5 items. That's pretty easy to recognize. Not only is the higher-priced item priced higher (duh!), it also generates a higher return on your fixed costs. After all, it costs you about the same amount of time and money to photograph, list, pack, and ship that $20 item as it does the $5 item. The return on your effort is higher with a higher-priced item.

That's with all other things being equal, of course. It's easy to extrapolate out and come to the conclusion that all you need to do is sell items that go for $10,000 a pop. The problem with this logic (or lack of it) is that you'll probably sell fewer higher-priced items than you will lower-priced ones. It is, after all, easier to sell a $5 baseball card than it is to sell a $10,000 one. In reality, you'll sell multiple $5 cards for every $10,000 one you sell—if, in fact, you ever sell that high-priced card. In general, lower prices generate a higher sales volume.

That said, the strategy of focusing on higher-priced items is one way to success. You have to sell a lot of $20 memory cards to equal the revenues you generate from selling a single $500 digital camera. There's no denying that you can grow your revenues faster selling higher-priced items than you can with lower-priced ones.

An example. I typically sell CDs, DVDs, books, and similar items. But in the fall of 2006 I decided to sell off my collection of animation art. In contrast to the $10 items I normally sell, those animation cels sold for $300 or more apiece. In a single month of selling only about a dozen items, I generated enough revenue to qualify for eBay PowerSeller status, something I'd never achieved previously. I sold about $4,000 worth of cels in that one month; I'd have to sell at least 400 CDs or DVDs to generate the same amount of revenue. Obviously, a dozen sales are a lot less work than 400 of them.

Focus on Profit, Not Selling Price

There are complications to this strategy, however. For example, you don't always generate a proportionately larger profit on a higher-priced item. In fact, you might generate a higher dollar profit on a lower-priced item. This is particularly true in highly competitive categories, such as consumer electronics. For some consumer electronics products, it's not unusual to generate profit margins of 10% or less. So, selling a $200 DVD recorder might only generate $20 in profit. You might be able to make more money selling cables for that DVD recorder; a $40 component video cable might come with a 50% profit margin, thus generating the same $20 in profit than did the much higher-priced DVD recorder.

That means you need to focus on the profit generated by each item, not just the selling price. After all, it's possible to sell even a $1,000 item and lose money, in which case a 25-cent profit on a 99-cent item looks good. Look for those items that generate the most dollar profit while maintaining a level of unit sales, and that will be your best way to go.

Avoid Very Low Priced Items

Remember, I said to focus on profit dollars, not profit margin. That's because a high margin on a low-dollar item doesn't generate much absolute profit.

Another example. Let's say you have a $5 lens cleaning kit that generates a 50% profit. Do the math and you find that you make $2.50 profit on that kit. On the other hand, you have a $300 digital camera that generates only a 10% profit. Seems low, but in absolute terms that camera contributes $30 in profit. In this instance, do you want to sell the high margin (but low price) item, or the low margin (but high priced) item? The answer is in the dollars; $30 profit is better than $2.50 profit any old day.

Low-price items also come at a built-in disadvantage thanks to eBay's fee structure. Although eBay's final value fee is based on a percentage of the selling price, the listing or insertion fee is a fixed fee (within a given range). Listing a $5 item costs you $0.40 in insertion fees, which is 8% of the price; listing a $20 item costs you $0.60 in insertion fees, which is just 3% of the price. In general, lower-priced items end up costing you more, on a percentage basis.

In addition, PayPal charges a flat $0.30 fee per transaction (in addition to its standard 2.9% charge). That $0.30 fee is 6% of a $5 sale, but just 1.5% of a $20 sale.

As you can see, these flat fees add up to an exorbitant percentage of lower-priced sales. On a $5 item, you can easily rack up 14% or more in fixed fees; add that to the normal percentage fees, and you'll end up paying 22% or more of the selling price in eBay/PayPal fees alone. That's a lot of overhead.

note

On a $20 item, those same total fees add up to less than 13% of the final selling price. On a $100 item, the same fees are about 9%.

The bottom line is that it's difficult to make a profit on very low-price items. Think twice before you base your business model on products that sell for $5 or less, on average. To get past this so-called *flat-fee penalty*, you need to increase the average selling price of your items well above this level.

Don't Forget the Volume

So, higher prices are better—to a point. You don't want to sell items that are so high priced that volume suffers. Remember, in most instances it's easier to sell a $10 item than it is to sell a $1,000 one. High profit margins and high dollar profits-per-item matter only in relation to your overall volume of sales.

Remember, you have fixed costs that remain the same no matter what your sales level—rent, Internet service, salaries, and the like. You have to generate enough dollar profit to cover these costs, which means you need to work with a combination of profit margin percentage, dollar sales price, and unit sales volume. It's a tricky combination, and typically involves a variety of compromises. But in general, it's easier to achieve your dollar profit goals selling slightly higher-priced merchandise; it's tough to be a successful "dollar store" in the eBay marketplace.

What's the Right Price?

So, what average price do you need to create a profitable eBay business? Without going into all the math, you probably want to strive for an average selling price of at least $20. This gets you comfortably past the flat-fee penalty, and should provide a decent dollar profit per item to contribute to your business's fixed costs. For example, if you generate a 40% profit margin on a $20 sale, that produces $8 in profit dollars per item. If you can sell 100 items per week, that's $800 a week in profit generated—or enough profit to pay you close to a $40,000 salary (taking other fixed costs into consideration, of course).

Obviously, the profit gets greater if you can maintain that unit volume on a higher per-unit sales price. Average $30 per sale with the same unit volume and profit margin, and all of a sudden you're earning close to $60,000 a year. (And, in fact, your profit margin probably increases on that $30 item because eBay's fixed fees become a lower percentage of the costs.)

You see how it works. Look for products that sell for at least $20, and it will be easier to achieve eBay success.

Trick #19: Move Unwanted Merchandise in Large Lots

Not every product you buy for resale actually sells. If you carry 100 SKUs, you might find that 95 of them sell very well, but the remaining five are either slower movers or out-and-out dogs. What can do you to get rid of less popular merchandise?

Marking Down Merchandise

There are two popular strategies you can take. The first is to mark down the items and sell them at closeout prices. eBay makes this easy enough to do, especially with eBay Store items, with their Markdown Manager feature. Markdown Manager essentially lets you discount fixed-priced items by a specific percentage or dollar amount, and have those items appear in your listings with a special promotional look. Figure 2.13 shows a typical marked-down item listing—note the "25% off" icon.

FIGURE 2.13

An item reduced in price with eBay's Markdown Manager.

To use the Markdown Manager, go to your My eBay page and click the Marketing Tools link. When the next page appears, click the Markdown Manager link (in the Item Promotion section). When the Markdown Manager page appears, click the Create Sale button; this displays the Create Sale page, shown in Figure 2.14. You can give your sale a name (if you like), specify start and end dates for the promotion, determine the discount to apply (as either a percentage or a fixed dollar amount), and then choose which of your fixed-priced listings will have the markdown. You can select all the items in your eBay Store, all your fixed priced listings, all the listings in a specific store category, or individual listings. Click the Save & Submit button, and the sale begins.

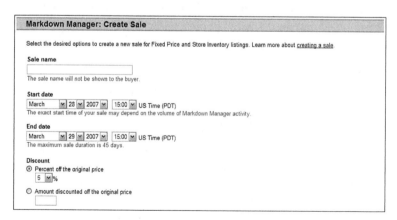

FIGURE 2.14

Applying an item discount with eBay's Markdown Manager.

Repackaging Product Lots

Discounting closeout items is a proven way to move otherwise unwanted merchandise—and the more you discount, the more likely the product is to sell. Unfortunately, if you discount an item too much, you lose money on it. Although this might be okay (you want to look at your average profit on all your sales, knowing that you make more on some than on others), there's another way to move old merchandise that might preserve your profit margins.

The trick here is to "hide" the less-popular merchandise in a package of more-popular items. I'm talking about creating a bundle or "lot" that includes a mix of products. The bundle has to have some sexy items, but it can be filled in with some of those less sexy items that you might not move otherwise.

Here's an example. Let's say you're a CD seller and you have a particular CD from some obscure 1960s band that's been gathering dust on your shelves. That CD won't move on its own, but it serves as decent filler in a "vintage 1960s" bundle you create with a half-dozen CDs from better-known 1960s bands. So, you have one CD each from The Mamas & the Papas, The Byrds, The Lovin' Spoonful, The Association, and The Grass Roots, and your "filler" CD from The Monks. The fact that nobody's ever heard of The Monks means less when they're getting value with CDs from the other more recognizable groups.

This strategy works even better when you're selling larger lots. Let's say that you regularly sell lots of 100 jeans. In that lot you have 90 pair in the most popular sizes, but then toss in 10 pair in those oddball sizes that haven't been moving. The buyer gets the overall value while you get to move those odd-sized jeans you were otherwise stuck with.

note

The reason this strategy works better for large lots is that you typically don't list the entire contents of the lot. The lot is sold as "100 Jeans, Mixed Sizes," and you don't list the sizes of all 100 individual pair.

If you do a good job averaging costs and price the bundle or lot competitively, you should end up making more money than if you tried to mark down the less-popular item to sell on its own.

Trick #20: Success Doesn't Come from One-Off Sales

For the final trick in this chapter, we examine the wisdom of selling multiple quantities of a given SKU—and not trying to sell a large number of unique SKUs.

You see, the real key to eBay success is to find a product that sells well, and then keep selling that same product over and over. Success is repeatable when you stick with a winning product.

Even if you offer a large number of SKUs, these should be consistent SKUs. Maybe you offer a thousand CDs for sale, but they're always the same thousand; you're not constantly changing the titles you have for sale. This provides a constancy in sales that makes your business very efficient—and improves your bottom line.

The point is that selling the same thing over and over ensures that your business is both predictable and efficient. Predictable because you know where your sales come from, and that they'll keep coming. Efficient because you develop processes to handle those predictable sales.

Let's say, for example, that you sell men's clothing. You want to develop your business so that a majority of sales come from a small number of consistent items—a particular brand and style of shirt, for example. As your business progresses, you know that you can depend on that particular style of shirt to contribute X amount of sales, week in and week out. And you develop an efficient process to handle those sales; you know exactly how to store your inventory, and to pack and ship that style of shirt.

It's certainly a lot easier than selling the same number of units but spread across a large number of different items. Say, for example, that instead of selling 100 of the same shirt every week you sold 10 units of one kind of shirt, 10 units of another shirt, 10 units of a particular pair of pants, 10 units of a specific type of jacket, and so on. First, you're less sure of where your future sales will come from. Second, you have to develop systems and processes to list, pack, and ship all those different items. Much less efficient than relying on a single SKU.

In addition, when you keep selling more and more of a single item, you can lower the price you pay to purchase that item. You'll get a lower price when you purchase 100 units of an item than you will when you purchase just 10 units of that item. As I've noted before, cost efficiency comes with increased unit volume.

Even though it's okay to refresh your product offerings from time to time, the thing you don't want to do is continually add single-unit items to your inventory. Every SKU you offer comes at a cost beyond its product cost; there are costs involved with entering the unit into inventory, taking product photos, writing the item description, even finding appropriate packaging and figuring out shipping costs. These one-time costs are better absorbed when you have more than one of an item to sell; the one-time setup costs become quite small when spread over 100 items than they are when applied to just a single item.

There are certainly successful eBay sellers who sell plenty of one-off items, and who move in and out of products and product categories with regularity. Good for them. It's easier to generate profits, however, by finding an item that sells and then repeating that success over and over. That one-off item you purchased might or might not sell; the item you sold 10 of last week, however, will sell 10 more next week.

Although there are no guarantees with one-off selling, repeated item selling is almost guaranteed success. Find an item that sells, and then keep selling it. It's the best way to build a successful business.

eBAY BUSINESS PROFILE

Profile: The Electric Quarter

Business Profile

Business name: The Electric Quarter

eBay ID: ElectricQuarter

eBay Store: stores.ebay.com/The-Electric-Quarter

Website: www.ElectricQuarter.com

Type of business: Videogames and accessories

Owner: Toby Paddock

Location: Franklin, New Hampshire

The best eBay businesses are built on the love of a particular subject. In the case of The Electric Quarter, the business grew from Toby Paddock's love of classic videogames. The result is an eBay business that's found success selling those classic games—and making lots of money doing so.

From Collector to Seller

Like many collectors, Toby started selling on eBay to add to his personal collection, and to get rid of extras he didn't need. That was back in February of 1999.

Like many eBay sellers, Toby didn't do a lot of planning up front; as he puts it, "not quite as much as I probably should have." He had a decent-sized vacation check coming from his previous employer, and enough inventory that he figured he could make at least as much as he was at his previous job. (That was $8 per hour as a supervisor at a local PETCO store.)

So, he jumped into eBay selling, and discovered that he was selling in a very profitable niche. The business grew over the years, and now Toby does do a fair amount of planning, due to the nature of his business:

"Especially in videogames it is *constantly* changing and evolving. Keeping up with current systems and what's popular for old consoles is quite a lot of work."

The Electric Quarter's Toby Paddock.

Just some of the classic videogames offered by The Electric Quarter.

Today Toby sells both classic and current videogames. His business is such that he manages it primarily himself, using a handful of family and friends to help out during the busy periods. Although Toby handles his own accounting, he does utilize eBay's Blackthorne Pro and Selling Manager Pro auction management program tools.

Selling Strategies

The Electric Quarter has between 1,400–1,500 items constantly listed on the eBay site, with 300–500 of these in the auction format. Of the auction listings, roughly 30% are successful.

Because Toby lists hundreds of similar auctions every week, he uses the same generic description text for most of his listings; the item itself is described via the listing title and picture. Given the huge number of classic videogame titles Toby has available, this is a more efficient option than creating new descriptions for every single cartridge.

A typical videogame listing from The Electric Quarter.

Toby always includes a Buy It Now (BIN) price in his auctions. He feels that BIN is important in the videogame category, as is accepting credit card payments via PayPal. He believes in listing all shipping charges upfront—and in not overcharging for shipping. He combines shipping charges on multiple-item purchases.

Other Online Sales

As noted, traditional online auctions account for just a quarter of The Electric Quarter's eBay listings. The remaining items are listed in Toby's eBay Store. As Toby notes, "the extremely low listing fees are a huge bonus for items that don't sell quite as fast. I can switch them over to auction format for a week, and then back to store inventory with very little work."

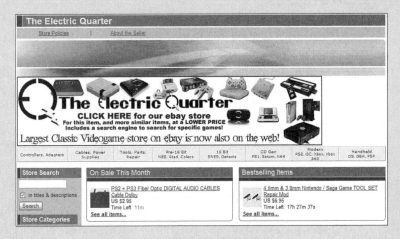

The Electric Quarter's eBay Store.

About five years ago, Toby started another online store, separate from his eBay Store. Both stores list similar inventory, but the non-eBay store has a higher profit margin per item—no eBay fees to pay.

The Electric Quarter's online web store.

Finding and Managing Inventory

Finding all the inventory that Toby offers for sale is a real challenge. He currently uses five different suppliers in four different regions: California, Japan, Hong Kong, and Europe. As Toby states, "getting new suppliers is the number-one challenge of being a successful business on eBay."

Toby manages his inventory visually. When he sees an item is getting low, he orders more. Fortunately, he's found suppliers that can deliver within 3–7 business days; he can also end a listing early if he runs out of product. On balance, however, he tries to keep a month or so of inventory on all his key items.

He also urged caution on edging into product categories with which you're not familiar. He related this story:

"If you think you found an excellent deal on wholesale for certain items that you really don't know much about, be cautious. We invested in a very large amount of body jewelry once that we purchased for roughly $1 apiece, and was selling in local shops for over $10–$15 per piece!!! So, of course, we bought it immediately. That was over a year ago. . . . We still have well over 75% of the stock still collecting dust, even with barely breaking a profit per item."

Yikes!

Managing Growth

Toby's business has grown as he's started carrying more new items and fewer used ones. This shift from used-to-new is also a big time-saver:

"The biggest challenge on used items is taking pictures. It became far too time consuming to clean everything, lay it out nice, take pictures, test the product for functionality, describe it, etc. . . ."

Keys to Success

When I asked Toby what was key to his business's success, here's what he told me:

"Believe in luck? You *have* to know what you're selling. If someone asks a question, you need to be able to answer it, without Googling your answer or guessing."

He also had this advice for would-be eBay businesspeople:

"Research, and as they say, 'keep your day job.'"

Toby also notes that selling on eBay is a lot of work—365 days of the year:

"I work 40 hours per week. There are no days off. People think it is *much* easier than it is. 'Why can't you go here? Just take some time off, you're your own boss.' That may be true, but for me to take off one week for vacation, I essentially have to suspend all sales for three weeks.

"For example, if I want April 14–21 off, I have to stop listing items on the 6th so they end before I leave and I can pack them all up and ship them out. I then have to wait until I return on the 21st to start listing items again that will end on the 28th. So, essentially, no new items are added from the 6th all the way to the 28th, just for seven days off. That is simply not at all feasible by any standpoint.

"I've learned that two–three day vacations with one day in the middle to get as much done as possible is okay, but that limits how far I can go away for vacation since I have to come home for one of those days. Now, I simply take smaller vacations, and keep the listings going, with a note at the top of the auction stating that there will be a shipping delay, and I bring my laptop for answering emails."

You've heard this before, and you'll hear it again: eBay selling is hard work. And, as Toby notes, it's constant work. When you go on vacation, your eBay business shuts down. (Unless you have employees you leave behind, of course.) Consider that before you start up your eBay business!

3

Tricks for Purchasing and Managing Your Inventory

As I noted in the previous chapter, the most common question I get asked by potential eBay sellers is "What's hot that I can sell?" That's quickly followed by question number two, "Where can I find stuff to sell?"

The second question is no easier to answer than the first. There's no single supplier that can provide a get-rich-quick solution, which is what I think a lot of folks are looking for. In fact, *where* you buy should be subsidiary to *what* you buy; a lot of potential sellers think all they have to do is find a cheap supplier and they're in business. Unfortunately, things don't work that way.

The way things *should* work is that you decide what kind of products you want to sell (as discussed last chapter), and then search out the best supplier(s) for those products. And, no surprise, there are some tricks for purchasing and managing that inventory that can save you both time and money. Read on to learn what the eBay business masters say.

Trick #21: Shop—And Negotiate—For the Best Price

Okay, this little bit of obviousness isn't a trick in and of itself. But there's good business sense behind it, and some tricks involved in pulling it off.

The business sense is simple. The less you pay for a given item, the more profit you can make on it when you sell it. Consider an item you sell for $20 on average. If you pay $15 for that item, you make $5 profit on each sale—a 25% profit margin. If you can find a different supplier that sells the same item for $14, you now make $6 profit per item, which increases your profit margin to 30%. An extra dollar might not sound like much, but if you're selling 100 of these items a month, that's an extra $1,200 in your pocket over the course of a year. That's real money.

How Much Profit Do You Need to Make?

That example of a 25% profit margin expanding to a 30% one might cause many successful eBay businesspeople to laugh. The reason is that you're not going to make a lot of money on eBay if your profit margins (before eBay fees) are in this range. If you want to be successful, you have to strive for much larger profit margins—which means taking a machete to your product costs.

How much profit margin do you need to make on your eBay sales? Every business is different, but you should probably look to at least double your money on every item you sell. (That's a 50% profit margin, if you're doing the math.) For example, if you buy an item for $10, you want to sell it for at least $20. Or, looking at it from the other direction, if you have an item that you know will sell for $20 on average, you want to purchase it for no more than $10.

Some sellers strive for much higher margins than this. For example, sellers specializing in liquidated merchandise might look for items that provide a 10:1, 20:1, or even a 30:1 return ratio—that is, selling for 10 times, 20 times, or 30 times the product's cost.

note

A 10:1 return ratio translates into a 90% profit margin. A 20:1 ratio translates into a 95% profit margin. And a 30:1 return ratio translates into a 97% profit margin.

Why focus on such high profit margins? For liquidators, it's because they buy bulk lots of merchandise, and not all the merchandise in a lot is sellable. They have to get a higher return on the sellable merchandise to warrant tossing the unsellable stuff.

That said, the higher your profit margin, the more dollars you'll make on each item to contribute towards your business's fixed costs, and to provide a nice net profit for you, personally. And, as you've learned, high profit margins are necessary to offset the various eBay and PayPal fees.

How to Shop for Lower Prices

Your goal, then, is to shop around and negotiate for the lowest possible prices on the merchandise you intend to sell. There are several tricks for doing so.

First, you should compare prices from more than one supplier. After you decide on a particular item you want to sell, try to source it from multiple vendors. Most items, commodity products especially, are available from more than one source; take advantage of this fact and play one source against another to get the lowest possible price.

tip

When comparing prices between two or more vendors, make sure that you're comparing apples to oranges. That means comparing your total price, including shipping charges; a vendor that has a lower unit price but then overcharges on shipping might not be the best deal.

Second, consider selling alternative items. Instead of sticking to a particular model from a specific manufacturer, consider selling an alternative model from that manufacturer, or a similar model from another manufacturer. You can often get a lower price by slightly changing the items you sell.

Third, it never hurts to ask whether lower prices are available. Most wholesalers will offer a standard price list, but not all price lists are the last word. Ask whether the price is negotiable, and then negotiate. That $20 unit price might come down to $18.50 if you do a little haggling. It never hurts to try.

Fourth, look for merchandise that's available for auction. When you're talking liquidation merchandise, large lots often go to the highest bidder. That doesn't mean you have to bid ultra-high; most of this merchandise goes for pennies on the dollar. You'll need to determine the original value of the merchandise, and then bid significantly lower than that. (One PowerSeller makes his bid one-sixth of a penny per dollar of the original cost.) The key here is to be unafraid to lose your bids. In fact, if too many of your bids are accepted, you're probably bidding too much. Figure that if 5% of your bids are accepted, you're doing good—and getting a good price.

Finally, here's the most important trick for negotiating a better discount: Buy in large quantities. Most vendors have quantity discounts, which means you can significantly reduce the unit price if you buy at the next-largest quantity break. For example, a vendor might offer an item at $20 for quantities of 1–100 units, $19 for 101–250 units, $18 for 251–500 units, $17 for 501–1000 units, and $16.50 for 1001 units and up. You should always buy at the highest quantities you can afford and have space for—and that you think will move in a reasonable period of time. If you move 100 units per month, buy at least 101 units to get the quantity discount. You might even want to consider buying a 2 1/2-month supply and purchase 251 units, to save another dollar per unit.

Remember, all per-unit savings go straight to your bottom line. So, it's in your best interest to negotiate the lowest unit cost possible.

Trick #22: Leverage Payment Terms to Improve Your Cash Flow

Unit cost isn't the only factor you want to take into consideration when purchasing merchandise for resale. You also need to consider your cash flow—how much money you have to spend *now* to pay for your inventory. Which means evaluating a vendor's payment terms.

If you're a small seller buying from a large supplier, the payment terms might be simple—pay up front or you can't have it. In most instances that means paying by credit card or PayPal, just as you would if you were buying via an eBay auction.

As your business grows, however, and gains a more legitimate appearance, you'll find that more payment options become available. What you want to look for are payment terms that give you "X" number of days to pay. These terms are typically listed as *net 10* or *net 20* or something similar. To decode, *net 10* means that the net amount is due in 10 days; *net 20* means the net amount is due in 20 days.

Obviously, the longer the payment terms, the better for you. A net 30 offering gives you a month to pay, and holding onto your money for a month is better than paying within 10 days on net 10 terms. In fact, if you can stretch the payment terms long enough, you essentially let your supplier finance your eBay purchases.

Let me explain. Assume that you purchase exactly 30 days of inventory. That is, the merchandise you purchase on January 1st is completely sold by January 30th. Now assume that you negotiated net 30 terms from your supplier. You receive the merchandise on January 1st, you're paid for the last item on January 30th, and then, also on January 30th, you send a check to pay for the merchandise to your supplier. In this scenario, you've sold all your merchandise before you've had to pay for it; you haven't had to risk a penny on inventory purchases.

Now, if you're savvy about numbers, you'll note a few small holes in this scenario. First of all, just because you purchase the merchandise on January 1st doesn't mean you receive it on January 1st; there's bound to be a few days' lag between when the clock starts ticking on your payment terms and when you can actually start selling the merchandise. Second, just because an auction ends on January 30th doesn't mean you'll get paid on January 30th, so there's another lag in terms of receiving your final customer payments. Still, the scenario works, if only because you receive more for each item than you paid for it (that's your profit margin, right?), so that you'll build up a balance of funds to pay for your purchase before the net payment period expires.

In any case, it's to your benefit to negotiate for longer payment terms—or simply to deal with suppliers that offer longer terms. Net 10 is good, but net 20 and net 30 are better. (In my experience, you'll be hard-pressed to find terms longer than net 30, unless you happen to be Best Buy or Wal-Mart.) The longer your terms, the more leverage you have with your funds. It's good to start generating revenues before you have to lay out funds for that inventory. Instead of investing upfront, it's more of a pay-as-you-go situation; you start making money before you start spending money.

But what if you can't find suppliers that offer these kinds of payment terms? That's not uncommon, especially if you're dealing with the whole-salers and liquidators used by the typical eBay seller. The key is to keep looking, and to position yourself as a legitimate business. Look beyond general wholesalers to those distributors that focus on a particular type of merchandise, or consider buying direct from the manufacturer. The bigger you are, the more options you'll have available.

In addition, be prepared to jump through all sorts of paperwork hoops to obtain this type of supplier financing. (It is financing, after all.) You'll need to prove your financial worthiness, which might mean providing income statements, banking information, and the like. It's a lot different from you personally purchasing merchandise with your credit card; this is big-boy business stuff here. And, as you can see, it pays to play with the big boys.

Trick #23: Find a Reliable Supplier

By now you're probably asking, just where do you find all these different wholesalers? It's not that hard, really; there are tons of suppliers that specialize in selling merchandise for resale on eBay. The key is to find those wholesalers that offer the perfect combination of appealing merchandise, low prices, and attractive payment terms.

What to Look for in a Supplier

Let's start by examining what you want to look for in a supplier. Not all wholesalers are created equal; some are more reliable than others, or offer lower prices, or are just plain easier to deal with. As you'll eventually discover, you want a supplier that you can trust—and that offers competitive prices. Here's a short list of desirable supplier attributes:

- A large selection of products
- Quality products that have obvious consumer appeal
- Adequate and consistent inventory levels
- Low unit pricing
- Timely shipment
- Reasonable minimum order quantities
- Extended payment terms
- Some sort of guarantee or refund policy for defective products, or if you're dissatisfied with your purchase
- 800-number customer service (so that you'll have a real human being to talk to if you have questions or problems)

Obviously, not all suppliers will possess all these attributes. In particular, not all suppliers offer extended payment terms; when you're first starting out, expect to pay for your inventory in advance, typically via credit card.

caution

Avoid suppliers that are exclusively web-based (no phone numbers posted on the site), or whose websites haven't been updated in some time.

In addition, not every supplier you contact will be willing to deal with you. Some suppliers don't like selling to online or home-based businesses; others don't like dealing with smaller businesses. It pays to check out the supplier's website to find out its minimum order quantity, or if it has a yearly minimum purchase requirement. If one supplier doesn't want to deal with you, just move on to the next. There are plenty of them out there.

Searching for Suppliers

So, how do you find a supplier for your eBay business? There are lots of places to look.

Start by using Google to search for suppliers of a certain type of merchandise. Enter a query that contains the product type and words like *supplier*, *wholesaler, distributor, wholesale merchandise,* and such. You can also check out Google's Wholesale Trade directory (directory.google.com/Top/ Business/Wholesale_Trade/) and Yahoo's Business to Business directory (dir.yahoo.com/Business_and_Economy/Business_to_Business/), both of which offer categorized listings of suppliers.

Next, check with the appropriate industry trade association. Trade associations are great sources for locating suppliers within a given industry. Ask whether the association publishes a supplier directory, which should include all the contacts you're looking for. (Use Google to find a given trade association, if you don't know it already.)

Most trade associations run one or more industry trade shows, which many eBay sellers swear by as the best way to find potential suppliers. Stroll the aisles of a typical trade show and you'll find dozens, if not hundreds, of manufacturers and wholesalers of a given type of product. There are many nice things about trade shows—you get a variety of suppliers under one roof, you get to physically assess product quality before you buy, and you get to meet personally with the manufacturer or wholesaler representatives. That face-to-face interaction might be the most valuable benefit of attending a trade show; the human element goes a long way when it comes to making a deal. You can check with a given trade association for that industry's trade shows, or with your local convention bureau for trade shows in your area.

tip

Don't limit your supplier search to U.S. companies only. There is a growing global market of manufacturers and wholesalers that might prove profitable for enterprising eBay sellers. There are several good directories of exporters and international suppliers available, including Alibaba.com (www.alibaba.com), EC21 (www.ec21.com), Export Bureau (www.exportbureau.com), Global Sources (www.globalsources.com), and Made-in-China.com (www.made-in-china.com).

In addition to trade associations and trade shows, you can often find suppliers just by asking for them. Find someone who's knowledgeable about a particular industry or product category and ask for the names of top suppliers. You might even receive a personal recommendation or inside contact in the process. You'd be surprised what people know, and what information they're willing to pass on.

Of course, you don't have to search just for wholesalers and distributors. For some products, the better approach is to go directly to the manufacturer. This might mean contacting the company's head office, or dealing with a manufacturer representative or sales rep.

You should be able to find manufacturer contact information on the company's website. You can also look up manufacturers via the National Association of Manufacturers (www.nambuyerseller.com), shown in Figure 3.1, or in the Thomas Register database (www.thomasnet.com).

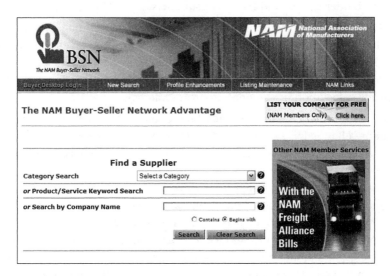

FIGURE 3.1

Use the National Association of Manufacturers website to search for manufacturers.

Know, however, that not all manufacturers sell directly to dealers. Others sell to an established dealer network, but not to everyone who calls them up or walks in the door. Still other companies don't allow their products to be sold over the Internet. And still others will sell to all comers, but have stiff minimum purchase requirements. So, don't be surprised if you get rejected going this route, or are redirected to a company's authorized distributor. In this type of scenario, going through the middleman might be your only option.

Using a Wholesaler Directory

There's not enough room in this book to list all the wholesalers in the world that can sell you merchandise to resell in your eBay business. (That would be an entirely separate book—and one that gets outdated as soon as it's printed!) Instead, I'll offer you a short list of sites that offer directories of wholesalers:

- 4WholesaleUSA (www.4wholesaleusa.com)
- Buylink (www.buylink.com)

- gowholesale (www.gowholesale.com)
- Top Wholesaler Suppliers.com (www.topwholesalesuppliers.com)
- Wholesale Central (www.wholesalecentral.com)
- Wholesale Distributors Network Directory (www.wholesaledistributorsnet.com)
- Wholesale Hub (www.wholesalehub.com)
- Wholesale Products Distributors Directory (www.wholesaleinone.com)

caution

Avoid those websites that purport to sell you listings of wholesalers and drop shippers. Most of this information is publicly available for free from other websites—so why pay for it?

These sites either organize suppliers by category, or let you search for particular categories or products. Most sites offer links to thousands of different suppliers in hundreds of different categories.

Of these sites, I'm partial to gowholesale, shown in Figure 3.2, which recently acquired another old favorite site, Wholesale411. You can either browse the site by category or specialty, or use the Find Products or Services search box to go directly to matching suppliers.

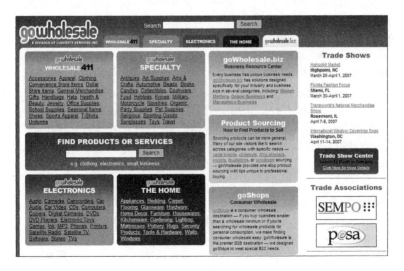

FIGURE 3.2

The gowholesale supplier directory.

Trick #24: Buy Liquidated Merchandise

Most wholesalers offer new, in-the-box merchandise for you to resell. Other wholesalers, however, specialize in liquidated merchandise—which provides a different way for you to increase your profit margins.

Liquidators are companies that purchase surplus items from other businesses, in bulk. These items might be closeouts, factory seconds, customer returns, or overstocked items—products the manufacturer made too many of and needs to get rid of. Liquidators help manufacturers and retailers dispose of this unwanted merchandise to the secondary market.

What kind of merchandise are we talking about? How about a lot of 80 320GB hard drives, 600 fashion necklaces, 13,000 assorted make-up items, or a pallet of assorted toys and games returned from Target? Pricing is typically pretty good, if you can take the quantities. For example, those hard drives went for just $4.81 apiece at a total lot price of $385. Assuming that you can resell them on eBay for $30 or more, that's a pretty good deal. The key is to pick an item that you know you can move in bulk over a period of weeks or months.

Pros and Cons of Selling Liquidated Merchandise

When you buy from a liquidator, you typically have to purchase large quantities of mixed items. In fact, you might not know exactly what it is you're purchasing; in the liquidation business, *mixed lots* truly means mixed. You might order a lot of 1,000 pairs of jeans, and have no idea what sizes or colors you're getting.

This known unknown is one of the challenges of buying and selling liquidated merchandise. The advantage, of course, is that you can buy this stuff really cheap—literally pennies on the dollar, in some instances. The low cost of liquidated merchandise can result in very high profit margins for you.

Know, however, that just because you can buy close-out merchandise cheap doesn't make it a good deal. Remember, there's probably a reason why items are being liquidated. They might be last year's models, they might be factory seconds, they might be used or returned, or they might just be items that no one wanted to buy. If an item didn't sell well originally, there's no guarantee that it will sell well (at a lower price, of course) in an eBay auction. And merchandise you can't sell doesn't help your overall profit margin one iota.

caution

When you buy surplus merchandise, check the warranty terms. Unlike the new merchandise you purchase from traditional wholesalers, most liquidators sell their goods "as is." That means if it's bad, you have to eat it—unless you also sell your goods with no warranty to your eBay customers.

Finding Liquidators Online

That said, where can you find liquidated and close-out merchandise? Here's a short list of some of the more popular online liquidation sites:

tip

Looking for a directory of liquidators? Check out Surplus.net (www.surplus.net) and The Closeout News (www.thecloseoutnews.com), which offer just that.

- America's Best Closeouts (www.abcloseouts.com)
- American Merchandise Liquidators (www.amlinc.com)
- AmeriSurplus (www.amerisurplus.com)
- Bid4Assets (www.bid4assets.com)
- Bookliquidator.com (www.bookliquidator.com)
- eBay Merchandise (www.ebaymerchandise.com)
- Fashions.net (www.fashions.net)
- Government Liquidation (www.govliquidation.com)
- Liquidation.com (www.liquidation.com)
- Luxury Magazzino (www.luxurymagazzino.com)
- Merchandise Liquidators (www.merchandiseliquidators.com)
- Salvage Closeouts (www.salvagecloseouts.com)
- TDW Closeouts (www.tdwcloseouts.com)
- Wholesale Apparel Source (www.appareloverstock.com)

note

Although you might think Overstock.com should be included in this list of liquidators, this site specializes in selling single units, not large lots, and thus isn't suitable for large-volume eBay sellers.

Even though all of these sites are legitimate and offer good values, my favorite is Liquidation.com, shown in Figure 3.3. It's a reputable site that operates on an auction basis; you place your bid on the lots for sale, and the high bidder wins. The goal, of course, is to win a saleable lot at the lowest possible cost. The less you pay, the more money you make.

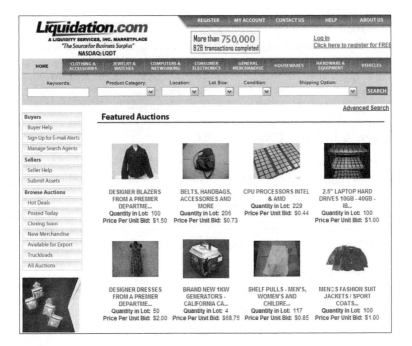

FIGURE 3.3

Bid on close-out merchandise at Liquidation.com.

caution

Never pay for any liquidated, wholesale, or drop ship merchandise by wire trans-fer. A supplier that asks for wire transfer payment is likely to be fraudulent because wire transfers are not traceable. Even with a legitimate supplier, you might not be able to get your money back in case of a problem or disagree-ment if you paid via wire transfer.

Trick #25: Buy on eBay to Resell on eBay

Here's another surprising source of wholesale merchandise: eBay. That's right, you can find a lot of merchandise for resale on the eBay site itself. Although you probably don't want to scour individual item auctions for that rare underpriced item, you can find a fair number of large lots avail-able at wholesale prices.

The first place to look is at the eBay Wholesale Lots directory (pages.ebay.com/catindex/catwholesale.html, or clickable from the Wholesale Lots link on eBay's home page), shown in Figure 3.4. Here you can find large lots organized by category, offered by a variety of whole-sale, manufacturer, and liquidation sellers.

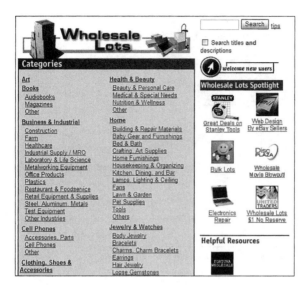

FIGURE 3.4

Find large lots for auction in eBay's Wholesale Lots directory.

If you're a big enough seller to achieve PowerSeller status, one of the best PowerSeller benefits is eBay's Reseller Marketplace, shown in Figure 3.5. Accessible only by registered PowerSellers, the Reseller Marketplace offers liquidation merchandise at competitive prices, via auction-format bidding. (Figure 3.6 shows a typical Reseller Marketplace auction listing.) It's a definite plus for eBay PowerSellers—and a resource the average eBayer is totally unaware of.

FIGURE 3.5

Liquidation merchandise for PowerSellers at eBay's Reseller Marketplace.

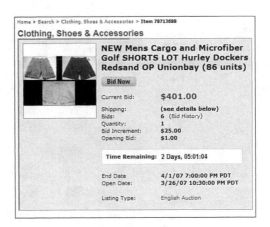

Home > Search > Clothing, Shoes & Accessories > **Item 78713688**

Clothing, Shoes & Accessories

**NEW Mens Cargo and Microfiber
Golf SHORTS LOT Hurley Dockers
Redsand OP Unionbay (86 units)**

Bid Now

Current Bid:	**$401.00**
Shipping:	(see details below)
Bids:	6 (Bid History)
Quantity:	1
Bid Increment:	$25.00
Opening Bid:	$1.00

Time Remaining: 2 Days, 05:01:04

End Date	4/1/07 7:00:00 PM PDT
Open Date:	3/26/07 10:30:00 PM PDT
Listing Type:	English Auction

FIGURE 3.6

Bidding on a merchandise lot in the Reseller Marketplace.

Trick #26: Consider Using a Drop Shipper

One of the drawbacks to buying merchandise in large quantities is finding a place to store all that merchandise. In addition, unless you can negotiate extended payment terms, you have to fork over the cash for that merchandise upfront—which can put a dent in the old pocketbook.

This is why many eBay sellers avail themselves of wholesalers that offer drop shipping services. At its most basic, a drop shipper functions as a combination wholesaler/warehouse/shipper; all you have to do is sell the merchandise, and the drop shipper does the rest. You don't have to buy the items up front, store them, pack them, or ship them. You just run your eBay auctions and collect the money.

How Drop Shipping Works

Working with a drop shipper can be quite simple. After you sign up with a drop shipper, you determine which available merchandise you want to offer in your eBay auctions or in your eBay Store. You use the information provided by the drop shipper (including a stock product photo) to create your item listing and description, and then post the listing to eBay.

When the auction ends, the buyer pays you and tells you where to ship the item. At this point, you notify the drop shipper of which item was purchased and where to ship it. The drop shipper ships the item to your customer, and you pay the drop shipper for the merchandise.

Naturally, you pay less to the drop shipper than you received from your customer; this is your profit margin. How much you mark up the item from the drop shipper's price is your business.

Drop Shipping Pros and Cons

It sounds simple enough, but drop shipping is a very controversial practice. Some eBay sellers swear by it; others swear at it.

What's good about drop shipping? Here are some of the pros:

- Access to a wide variety of products
- Professional packing and shipping to your customers
- No upfront costs—you don't have to pay for the product before you list it on eBay
- You don't have to pack and ship the product
- You don't have to warehouse the product

All of these benefits create one additional benefit for you—you have less time involved in the transaction. Because you don't have to manage inventory or pack and ship the items, that's a tremendous time savings. And, as you know, time is money.

That said, what appeals to most sellers is the ability to offer a wide variety of products without having to stock any of them. When you don't carry inventory, you can sell items that you couldn't sell otherwise—items too big for you to warehouse or ship personally, for example. And because you don't have to purchase your inventory in advance, you can start selling without a huge upfront dollar investment. You don't pay the drop shipper until you get paid by your customers. It seems like an ideal business model.

Except that it might not be.

Not all eBay sellers think that drop shipping is a good idea. In fact, many advise strongly against it. Here are some reasons why:

- You don't have control over the transaction; you can't affect any problems that the drop shipper might encounter
- If the drop shipper doesn't have the merchandise in stock, you're in trouble
- If the drop shipper is a slow shipper, you'll have unhappy customers
- Many competing sellers use the same drop shipper, so you won't be offering unique merchandise

In short, whatever the drop shipper does wrong, you take the blame for— in terms of customer complaints and negative feedback. If the drop shipper is slow, it's your fault. If the drop shipper doesn't have the item in stock or simply drops the ball, it's your fault. Your customers will hold you responsible.

In addition, that last point about competing against other customers of the same drop shipper can't be ignored. If too many eBay sellers are selling the same merchandise, the competition forces the selling prices down. This is a situation that really happens—uncomfortably often.

For example, one drop shipper offers a "deluxe civil war chess set" for $66.65 (with a "you sell for" price of $199.95), as shown in Figure 3.7. A recent search on eBay for this item found more than 100 different sellers (in both auctions and eBay Stores) offering the exact same item, priced from a high of $199.95 to a low of $61.20, as shown in Figure 3.8. With more than 100 sellers to choose from, why would any customer pay more than the lowest price? It's certainly unlikely that you could sell this item for the $199.95 recommended by the drop shipper, and you can't get rich buying an item for $66.65 and selling it for $61.20. (Sell at a loss, make it up in volume—not!) And here's the kicker—with all those chess sets on auction, there wasn't a single bid for any of them. Talk about unwanted product flooding the market!

Deluxe Civil War
Chess Set
Sell for: $199.95
Your Cost: $66.65
Your Profit: $133.30

FIGURE 3.7

A chess set offered by a given drop shipper—but don't believe that "sell for" price!

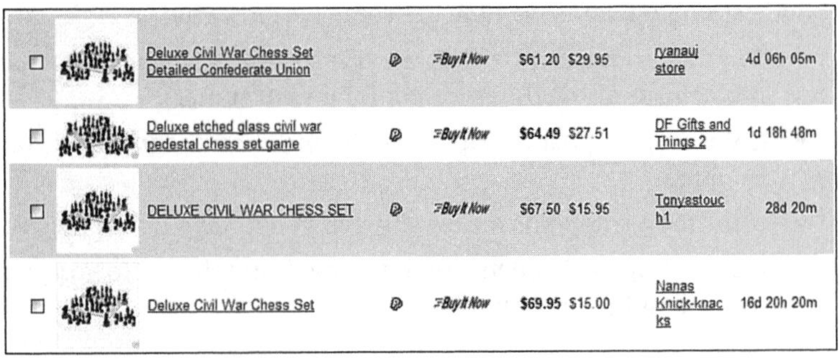

☐		Deluxe Civil War Chess Set Detailed Confederate Union	🔔	≡BuyItNow	$61.20 $29.95	ryanauj store	4d 06h 05m
☐		Deluxe etched glass civil war pedestal chess set game	🔔	≡BuyItNow	$64.49 $27.51	DF Gifts and Things 2	1d 18h 48m
☐		DELUXE CIVIL WAR CHESS SET	🔔	≡BuyItNow	$67.50 $15.95	Tonyastouc h1	28d 20m
☐		Deluxe Civil War Chess Set	🔔	≡BuyItNow	$69.95 $15.00	Nanas Knick-knac ks	16d 20h 20m

FIGURE 3.8

Just a handful of the 100 or so eBay stores selling the same "deluxe civil war chess set."

So, as you can see, although there might be compelling reasons to consider using a drop shipping service, there are also compelling reasons not to do so. The key is to find a drop shipper that offers unique merchandise, hasn't saturated the eBay market, and is reliable.

Finding a Reliable Drop Shipper

With that in mind, you need to consider several points when you're looking for a drop shipper.

First, check the eBay boards and do your research to determine whether a drop shipper is reliable. Some are, some aren't. An unreliable drop shipper will result in late or dropped shipments and very unhappy customers. You don't want that.

Next, make sure that you understand all the charges you'll have to pay over and above the cost of the item. Some drop shippers charge a larger shipping fee to cover the actual costs of drop shipping, whereas others charge a separate handling fee for the same reason. Some charge a flat, often excessive amount for shipping, and others calculate shipping based on the delivery ZIP code. (Although a variable shipping fee might sound best, you won't know how much you'll be charged for shipping until after the fact—which makes it difficult to pass on this charge to your buyers.) And many drop shippers require you to pay a monthly or annual "membership fee"; make sure that you factor this fee into your costs.

You'll also want to check out the merchandise offered by the drop shipper. Select a few items and then search for them on eBay. You don't want to be the hundredth seller offering the exact same item; you'll never sell any. Look for a drop shipper that offers a wide variety of merchandise within your chosen category of expertise, enough so that you can offer items unique from your competition.

And when you're looking at a drop shipper's merchandise, don't be fooled by the suggested retail price on the drop shipper's site. That price is seldom what the product actually sells for on eBay. Again, do some eBay research to find out what that product is really selling for, and then calculate your profit margin from the drop shipper's wholesale price.

It's also a good idea to understand how a particular drop shipper works. How do you notify them of a sale? What format do you use to submit customers' information? How will you be notified when an item ships? What is the best way to contact the drop shipper for expedited orders or to address issues? (Some work faster via email and other get things done by phone...) Are you assigned a contact at the company that you can work with directly?

Finally, make sure that you have access to accurate inventory levels (necessary before you decide to post an eBay listing) and that you're provided with tracking information for all items shipped. Given that you have no real control over the fulfillment of a drop-shipped sale, it's important to at least have as much information as possible about the shipment.

tip

Try to obtain a sample of the product you want to sell before you actually start selling it to your customers. You need to inspect the quality of the merchandise and make sure that your wholesale supplier is actually selling the item or brand name that it says it is. (It also helps you better answer any customer questions you might receive.) If a supplier won't provide a sample (either for free or for a one-off price), that supplier is probably to be avoided.

Searching for a Drop Shipper

When you want to find a drop shipper, where do you look?

First, know that many traditional wholesalers also offer drop shipping services. Find a wholesaler you like, and then ask whether it drop ships.

Second, goWholesale, eBay Merchandise, and most other wholesaler directories listed previously in this chapter also offer lists of wholesalers with drop shipping services. Search these sites for drop shippers.

Next, check out WebDropshipper.com (www.webdropshipper.com). This site offers a searchable directory of drop shippers in a variety of product categories.

Finally, here is a short list of drop shippers that some sellers have found legitimate:

- Doba (www.doba.com)
- DropshipDesign.com (www.dropshipdesign.com)
- E-drop-ship.com (www.e-drop-ship.com)
- National Dropshippers (www.nationaldropshippers.com)
- NetDropshipper.com (www.netdropshipper.com)

As with all things drop ship–related, however, look before you leap. Although these might be legitimate businesses, that doesn't mean you can actually sell the merchandise they offer, or generate enough profit to make it worth your time. Examine each company's merchandise and fees, do your research, and then decide whether drop shipping is for you.

---

tip

Even legitimate drop shippers sometimes have disgruntled customers. You can use the Rip-Off Report website (www.ripoffreport.com) to see what other sellers have to say about various online suppliers; too many bad reports are not a good thing.

Trick #27: Maximize Your Inventory Turns

Assuming that you use a normal wholesaler and not a drop shipper, one of the most important things you have to manage is the size of your inventory. You don't want too much inventory on your hands, for a number of reasons.

First, it costs money. The more unsold inventory you have, the more of your funds you have tied up in that inventory. Merchandise just sitting in your warehouse (or basement or garage) isn't earning you any money; it's just tying up your funds.

Second, it takes up space. The bigger your inventory, the more space you need to store it. Unless you happen to live inside a National Guard armory, your storage space is limited. When you exceed your available space, you have to pay money to get more. Space, in this context, costs money—and too much inventory takes up too much space.

For both of these reasons, you want to move your inventory as quickly and as often as possible. The quicker you turn your inventory, the sooner you have cash in hand to buy more inventory. The more inventory turns, the better.

Some eBay sellers strive for 12 turns a year—that is, to stock no more than 30 days worth of inventory. (In fact, some sellers do the math regarding shipment and payment lag and only want 21 days worth of inventory on hand.) Whatever number you arrive at, the point is to keep your inventory turning to free up your cash for future purposes.

Consider two scenarios. In scenario one, you purchase $10,000 worth of inventory and turn it in 30 days. In scenario two, you purchase the same $10,000 worth of inventory but only manage to turn it in 60 days.

In the first scenario, you've recovered your $10,000 investment well before the 30-day period is up. Assuming that you generate a 40% profit margin, you generate $16,666 in sales during the month, for $6,666 in profit. You can pocket the profit, use it to pay your expenses, or invest it in next month's inventory.

In the second scenario, you don't recover your $10,000 during the first month. Assuming that the merchandise sells at a steady clip, you generate only $8,333 in sales during the first 30 days, which is not enough to pay off the merchandise. Unless you invest more of your own money, you don't have any free cash to use for purchasing more merchandise until well into your second month of sales.

What we're dealing with here are the related concepts of cash flow, cost of money, and return on investment:

- You need to maintain a steady cash flow to pay your ongoing bills. If your inventory doesn't move fast enough, you don't generate enough free cash to keep your business solvent because too much of your money is tied up in slow-moving inventory.

- If you don't have enough cash to purchase more inventory, you'll have to borrow money for that task. Your banker doesn't give you money at no cost, which means you have to pay interest on any money you borrow. A 9% annual rate for a revolving small business line of credit means that you'll pay 0.75% per month on any funds you borrow. If you have to borrow $10,000 for 30 days, your cost of using that money is $75.

- The way to generate more long-term profit for your business is to maximize your return on investment. Any inventory sitting in your warehouse is not generating any return. The faster you move your inventory, the greater your return on investment.

There are other potential pitfalls to stocking too much inventory. For instance, seasonal merchandise "spoils" quickly if you hold it too long; those swimsuits you purchased in May lose most of their resale value by September. In addition, if trends change or fads go out of fashion, any older merchandise you might be holding could totally deflate in value.

So, you want to purchase wisely and efficiently to maximize your inventory turns. If you think you'll sell 1,000 units in a month, you should order only 1,000 units if you want to hold that inventory for only a 30-day period. Simple, right?

Not so simple, actually, when you also have to factor in the quantity discounts we discussed in Trick #21. Maybe the next price break is at 1,001 units, in which case you'll up your order by 1 to meet the minimum. But what if the next price break is 2,000 units? Do you order 2,000, knowing that you won't sell it for 60 days? How important is lower quantity pricing versus lower inventory turns? Do you risk carrying 60 days (or more) of inventory, just to get a lower unit price?

These are issues that face every business, small or large. It takes skill and experience to make the right decisions, and to strike the right compromise between inventory turns and unit pricing. There are no right answers, but there are plenty of wrong ones—in particular, when you order more inventory than you can afford, or tie up all your funds in unsold inventory, or end up with a large quantity of unsellable merchandise.

For novice sellers, the best approach is probably the conservative one; when in doubt, place a smaller order to keep your inventory low. Only more experienced businesspeople should gamble on being able to move larger quantities, or assume the financial risk of investing in and holding more inventory. For most smaller sellers, improving cash flow is more important than achieving a slight increase in profit margin.

Trick #28: Continuously Triage Your Inventory

One of the ways to improve inventory turns is to keep moving your inventory. That's glib advice, I know, but it's true; when a particular item starts to age, it's time to turn up the heat to move it faster.

The concept here is that of triage, the art of prioritizing items to identify and weed out the slow-movers. Not every item you stock has the same sales potential. Some items sell extremely well with little effort; other items have less appeal and thus don't sell nearly as well. Those slow sellers drag down your average inventory turns, and tie up your precious funds.

What you want to do, as early as possible in the process, is to identify those items in the lower 20% of your mix. Calculate sales rates and inventory turns for each item you carry, and then separate out the poor performers.

Your goal now is to somehow get rid of that slow-moving merchandise. This is where special attention is required. We discussed some tactics for this in Trick #19; to recap, you can deep discount these items, bundle them together into more attractive lots, or even use them as fillers or giveaways with your other merchandise. Worse comes to worst, you might just want to toss your doggiest items in the trash, or donate them to Goodwill or some similar charity. There is a point, after all, where you quit throwing good money after bad.

The point is to triage the nonsellers so that you can devote more of your attention (and inventory space) to your best sellers. You should do this on a regular basis, once a month perhaps, so that your inventory is continually fresh and free of dogs.

Trick #29: Find Low-Cost Inventory Space

The bigger your eBay business gets, the more inventory you'll be stocking. And, of course, the more inventory you stock, the more space you need to store it.

When you first start out, you can probably run your eBay business from your home. Your warehouse is your garage or your basement, outfitted with a few storage bins and metal shelving units. No problem at all.

Until your business grows, that is. The more merchandise you sell, the more merchandise you have to stock—and store. Soon enough, your garage or basement gets too small, and you have to start thinking about auxiliary warehouse space.

Perhaps your new warehouse space exists on your current property. I've heard of sellers storing inventory in backyard tool sheds, barns, unused garages, even oversized doghouses. For example, Home Depot sells a wide range of outdoor storage solutions, ranging in price from $300 for a small garden shed to more than $3,000 for a 14' x 31' model. Figure 3.9 shows a $600 walk-in model, perfect for storing small and mid-sized items.

FIGURE 3.9

An affordable backyard storage shed from Home Depot—perfect for warehousing eBay inventory.

For larger storage needs, consider renting a weather-proof storage container from PODS (www.pods.com), like the one in Figure 3.10. PODS units are available in 8' (h) × 8' (w) × 12' (d) and 8' × 8' × 16' configurations. You should be able to park either unit in your backyard or driveway. Pricing is variable, depending on unit size, how long you want to keep it, and where you live; you'll probably pay around $100 a month to rent the small-sized container, plus a delivery fee, but you should contact the company for an exact quote.

FIGURE 3.10

Another storage alternative—a PODS container.

note

PODS stands for *portable on demand storage.*

To store even more merchandise, consider renting an offsite self-storage unit. You should have at least one self-storage company in your area; prices vary wildly, depending on the size of the unit and your location.

tip

Search for self-storage companies at USStoragesearch.com (www.usstorage-search.com).

Beyond simple self-storage, you can also consider renting commercial warehousing space. If you go this route, it pays to compare costs, which are typically measured in price per square foot. You want to avoid renting space in retail centers, or in fancy office parks, both of which typically come with premium pricing. The best deals are found outside city limits in nearby suburbs, and outside major cities in smaller towns. Look for business parks with high vacancy rates; you can often pick up a bargain on a space that's gone unused for a period of time.

You can also consider sharing warehousing space with larger firms. Many large companies have bigger warehouses than they need, and you might be able to lease a corner of their space at a fraction of the going rate. There might be value in working with a commercial real estate broker to see what's available.

Remember, though, every dollar you spend on warehousing is a dollar that comes out of your pocket. You might be better off reducing your orders so that you don't need as much storage space for your inventory, or working on ways to improve your inventory turns, rather than spending the bucks for auxiliary warehousing.

Trick #30: Establish an Effective Inventory Management System

The bigger your business gets, the more inventory you have to carry—which, more often than not, means a larger number of SKUs. Managing all that inventory can very quickly become a major challenge.

Inventory management has both a physical and a virtual component. The physical component involves how you organize and store each item—in a bin, on a shelf, in a box, and that sort of thing. The virtual component is the data management, typically accomplished via a computer program, that lets you know what items you have in stock, how much they cost, and when you need to order more.

Why Inventory Management?

What do you want to achieve with an inventory management system? The Small Business Administration lists these goals:

- Maintain a wide assortment of stock—but not spread the rapidly moving ones too thin
- Increase inventory turnover—but not sacrifice your service level
- Keep your stock low—but not sacrifice service or performance
- Obtain lower prices by making volume purchases—but not end up with slow-moving inventory
- Have an adequate inventory on hand—but not get caught with obsolete items

As you can see, good inventory management is a constant balancing act. In essence, you want to achieve a balance between carrying too much and not enough inventory.

This is accomplished by creating a system that efficiently and effectively tracks every item you purchase and every item you sell, and where each item is in between the buyer and seller. As I said, the process is both physical and virtual.

Physical Inventory Management

Physical inventory management is all about organization. What you don't want to do is dump your inventory in a big pile. Inventory management by pile size just doesn't cut it, believe me. At the very least, you want to establish different piles for each of the items you carry—a blue shirt pile here, a red shorts pile there, and so on.

It's better, of course, if you can move beyond the pile stage. You want to store your inventory in a way that minimizes wear and tear and other damage to each item. That might mean storing clothing in individual plastic bags, or baseball cards in protective boxes, whatever is appropriate for the types of items you carry. It also means being neat about it; few items benefit from loose storage.

Your physical storage also has to be organized. Even if you could throw everything safely into a pile, that's not the best way to find things when you sell them. Order is important, which probably means using separate storage containers or shelves for each item you sell. Think of the way things are organized in a typical retail store—by item type, color, size, and the like—and then model your storage system on that. For smaller items, I like using small boxes or bins placed on larger shelves, with each box or container devoted to a specific model number, size, or color. For larger items, you might devote an entire shelf or shelving unit to a particular item.

In addition to organization, you need to consider access. This means knowing where every item is, and being able to physically get to it. You might want to create maps that you place at the end of each row or shelving unit that detail that area's contents. You could even get fancy, and note the location of each item in your inventory management program (which we'll discuss next). In any case, you need to know where each item is stored, and then be able to physically procure that item when it's sold.

How you organize your inventory should also take into account the relative popularity of each item. You don't want to bury your most popular items in the middle of a stack; you want your fastest-moving inventory out front and center, where it can be quickly grabbed. When you're moving a large number of items every day, physical efficiency is paramount.

You also need to consider the issue of inventory aging. In most instances, you'll take a first-in, first-out (FIFO) approach so that you're always selling your oldest merchandise of a given type. You don't want to organize your inventory so that newer stock is sitting in front of older stock; you want to put your oldest purchased items in front, where they'll be accessed first.

Finally, don't forget to label. I mentioned labeling the contents of each row or shelf, but you should also label the boxes or bins that hold individual items. Your warehousing system needs to be foolproof, and not rely solely on your own individual memory. Organize and label things so that any new employee you hire can easily find what needs to be shipped.

Virtual Inventory Management

Organizing your inventory physically is just one part of the process. You also need to establish a virtual inventory management system that keeps track of every piece of merchandise you own.

Setting up an inventory management system is actually quite simple, at least in theory. All you want to do is track when you got your stuff, how much it cost you, when you sold it, and how much you sold it for.

That's not rocket science. In fact, you can create a fairly effective inventory management system using 3" x 5" index cards, one card for each model number or item carried. You probably don't want to use index cards, however, especially when computerized solutions are readily available.

The simplest way to track your inventory on a PC is to use a database program, such as Microsoft Access. You can also use a spreadsheet program, such as Microsoft Excel, as a kind of simple database; Excel's database functions are good enough for most small business inventory management.

Just set up your database or spreadsheet with the following fields:

- Item name
- Item description
- Item model number (if appropriate)
- Item serial number (if appropriate)
- Manufacturer or vendor
- Cost of the item (sometimes called the *cost of goods sold*, or *COGS*)
- Date the item was purchased
- Date the item was sold
- Final sales price of the item

You should create a new record for each item in inventory. Whenever you purchase new inventory, create new records. When you sell an item, mark the record for that item sold, and fill in the date sold and sales price fields.

At the end of each month, have your program run reports that list the total cost of the inventory you currently have in stock, the total profit and average profit per item sold, and the inventory turns. These reports should provide the basic inventory and sales information you need for your accounting system.

tip

Another option for tracking your inventory is to use one of the advanced auction management tools discussed in Trick #8. The most sophisticated tools include inventory management modules that can track both your inventory and your customer activity. Most high-end accounting programs, such as QuickBooks, also offer inventory management functions.

After you get it set up, you can also use your inventory management system to help you decide when to order more inventory. Set a minimum quantity that you want to keep in stock for each item, and configure your program to alert you when the number of units on hand drops below this number. When used properly, your inventory management system will help you avoid out-of-stock situations as well as maximize your inventory turns.

What you want to avoid is having too many slow-moving items on hand and not enough of your fast-moving items. Just looking at a gross inventory number won't give you this item-by-item detail; you need your inventory management system to track your stock for each item you carry to maximize each item's performance—and your business's profit.

Profile: Yia Yia's Attic

Business Profile

Business name: Yia Yia's Attic

eBay ID: yiayiasattic

Type of business: Ephemera

Owner: Barbara Lemonakis

Location: Canonsburg, Pennsylvania

What is ephemera? The Merriam-Webster dictionary defines *ephemera* as "Something of no lasting significance," or alternatively as "Paper items (as posters, broadsides, and tickets) that were originally meant to be discarded after use but have since become collectibles."

To Barbara Lemonakis, ephemera is another word for "money." Her Yia Yia's Attic eBay business has achieved PowerSeller status by selling all sorts of ephemeral collectibles, focusing on paper items and postcards.

Taking Advantage of an Opportunity

For most people, getting fired from a job would be a major setback. Not so for Barbra Lemonakis. She had been an accountant for a construction firm for 16 years when a change in management resulted in her getting let go. Not a good day.

That was in 2001. When Barbara went to collect her unemployment compensation, she discovered that in the state of Pennsylvania, you can continue to collect unemployment while starting a business. She had already done a little casual eBay buying and selling of items around the house, but thought she could make more money on eBay than she could from another accounting job. It wasn't much of a plan, but it got her going.

"You'll run out of things to sell," her husband Steve told her. That turned out not to be true. Barbara and Steve began to attend local live auctions, at first just to watch, but eventually to buy things—mostly box lots that she could pick up cheaply. She started listing and selling the items she purchased, learning as she went.

In her second year of selling, Barbara realized that she really liked selling paper items. They were easy to pack and ship, and interesting to look at. "That was when I found my niche," she says. From that point, Barbara began to seek out auctions with paper, and soon narrowed her sales to 90% ephemera.

Seller Barbara Lemonakis with post office employee Bob Feathers—they meet every day!

Selling Strategies

Yia Yia's Attic made a small profit in year one, with some losses later on. The business turned around, however, and the past two years have been profitable. From the way 2007 is starting out, Barbara says it may be her best year yet.

She usually has between 100–200 auctions running at any given time. She lists almost every day, so auctions are beginning and ending all the time. About 50% of her items sell successfully.

Barbara doesn't sell too many high-end items, so her average sale is small—about $10 per item. She puts care into her item listings to best describe the collectible items she has for sale.

Romance Nite Club Drink Coupon Tijuana Mexico Vintage

A typical listing from Yia Yia's Attic—big picture, descriptive text.

By the way, Barbara has never opened an eBay Store or other online website. Why? "No specific reason," she says, "I just didn't ever feel the need to do so." She also doesn't like to use eBay's Buy It Now option, because "paper items can go for just about any price if two people both want the same item."

Finding and Managing Inventory

Barbara finds everything she sells at live auctions. She says she doesn't have time for estate sales, garage sales, or flea markets; "They are not good sources for paper anyway," she notes.

She claims not to have a method for managing her inventory:

"We just bring in the boxes, stack them up and I start listing. I try not to keep much inventory on hand. I move everything as quickly as I can. I don't keep buying and buying—although the buying is the fun part!"

Barbara tries to keep from 1–2 months of inventory on hand, on average. "For example," she says, "I attended a huge paper auction yesterday. I really stocked up. But before I went, I was down to one box of postcards!"

Managing the Business

Barbara runs the business by herself, with the unpaid help of her husband Steve, who is a teacher and musician. He attends live auctions with Barbara when he's not out of town for a band gig. Steve gets to carry everything to the car, "gets me food, and is generally just always there to help me." Barbara says that Steve wants to get more involved in the business after he retires, and will probably become her packer/shipper.

In terms of accounting, Barbara keeps simple records of gross receipts and expenses, making daily entries as she learned to do from her bookkeeping years. She uses the programs that came with her computer: Quicken and the Quattro Pro spreadsheet. Steve and Barbara do have an accountant who prepares their tax returns every year.

"Having been in accounting," Barbara says, "I knew that just about everything is legally deductible in a home-based business, and in self-employment. I was well disciplined in keeping records and receipts. I also knew from dealing with both federal and state tax entities in 30 years of working in the public sector, that it's always best to be honest in your declaration of gross earnings and deductions. I know I could probably deduct even more than I actually do, but I would rather sleep at night than deduct things that might be questionable."

For auction management, Barbara uses SpoonFeeder (www.spoonfeeder.com). "It's a simple and easy listing management [tool], which is very user-friendly and also has a great, responsive staff," Barbara says. "Reasonably priced, too."

Keys to Success

Barbara says that when she started selling on eBay, she knew nothing "and learned by trial and error (lots of error!)." She feels that the keys to successful eBay selling are the same as with any retail business:

"Be honest and fair to your buyers. I don't charge excessive shipping rates, and I really do take the time to describe my items accurately and honestly. If it's damaged I say so. As a buyer, I want to get what I paid for and I try to 'do unto others' as a seller, too. I also have to sometimes 'suck it up' when a buyer is totally unreasonable, complains about everything, leaves negative feedback for no real reason, etc. My only recourse is to block them from future bidding on my auctions."

Barbara goes on to say that she treats her sellers as she would like to be treated. "I answer all questions. I say please and thank you. I give them a little extra time to pay if they contact me and say they are having a problem or issue. I apologize if I made a mistake. I still agree with the old adage, 'The customer is always right,' even when you know they are not."

She also falls back on her accounting background to advise all sellers to "be legit. Get a tax number, keep records, tell Uncle Sam what you are earning. Pay your taxes if you show a profit."

All that said, Barbara wants it known that selling on eBay "is the best job I have ever had and I am the best boss I ever had. I worked in the public sector for 30+ years. Yes, a regular paycheck is nice, but being your own boss is wonderful."

"However," she continues, "I have never worked as hard or as long as I do now. I work seven days a week. I am online before 6:00 a.m. every morning as soon as my husband is off to school. I often work after dinner. I work on holidays and weekends when others are having fun. But I absolutely *love it*! And if I need to make a doctor appointment for myself or my in-laws, go shopping, or go to the gym, I can do it on my own schedule."

"I consider myself a 'real' business. I go to 'work,' even though it's in my home. I have a regular office. I never turn on TV during the day, or phone friends. I am *working*! I take a regular lunch break, and back to work. I think you have to be very disciplined to make this successful. If you don't take yourself seriously—who will?"

"And finally," Barbara says, "I no longer am ashamed to say 'I have an eBay business.' I am very proud of it. I wear my eBay shirt which I purchased at the convention with pride now. And I honestly think people are jealous of my home business. I just hope to run into the boss's son who fired me someday so I can thank him."

Getting fired was one of the best things to happen to Barbara. Now she runs a successful eBay business, and enjoys being her own boss. It's hard work, yes, but quite rewarding.

Barbara plans to keep her eBay business running until her husband retires. At that point she plans to scale down a bit so that they can enjoy their free time. Sounds like a good plan to me.

4

Tricks for Creating More Effective Listings

You've made your plans. You've decided what type of eBay business you want to run. You've identified the merchandise you want to sell, and found reliable sources from which to purchase that merchandise.

Your work has just begun.

Now it's time to start creating all your auction (and nonauction) listings. As the eBay business masters will tell you, it's your auction listing that makes the difference between a successful (that is, profitable) auction and an unsuccessful one. The more effective your listings, the more sales you'll close, and the more money you'll make.

So, how do you make your listings stand out from the millions of others on eBay at any given time? That's what this chapter is all about, so read on and learn what the eBay business masters recommend.

Trick #31: List at the Best Time(s) and Day(s)

If you think when you close your listings doesn't matter, let me give you an example of why your thinking is so, so wrong.

Let's say you opt to close your auction at 5:00 a.m. EST. Now, there are very few people awake and at their computers at 5:00 a.m. on the east coast, or 2:00 a.m. on the west coast. Anyone who's interested in your auction is probably asleep. So, you won't get any last-minute bids.

"So what," you say. "People can place their bids at any time; they don't need to be poised at their keyboards the exact second an auction ends. When the auction ends shouldn't matter."

Except that it does. In case you haven't noticed, for most listings most bids come in the final minutes of the auction. That's because smart eBay buyers have learned the technique of *sniping*, in which you wait until the last possible moment to place your bid; when you wait long enough, no other bidders will have a chance to respond and outbid you. This is why so many bids come at the end of an auction, whether it's a 3-, 5-, 7-, or 10-day auction. Smart bidders really do sit at their keyboards during the closing moments of an auction, waiting for it to end.

Picking the Right Time

This is why you don't want to close your auctions when people are asleep: You'll miss all those last-minute snipes, and in fact might receive zero bids on your listing. It's a simple fact—you want to close your auctions when people are awake and at their computers.

So, what's the best time of day to end your auctions? As I said, you want to pick a time where the most possible target customers are in front of their computers, ready and able to bid. When that time is depends on what type of item you're selling.

If you're selling to a general consumer audience, you want to end your auctions during prime time—those hours of the evening when most people are home from work or school and free to bid, and not yet in bed asleep. Knowing that you have to compromise somewhat between east coast and west coast bidders, I've found that ending between 9:00 p.m. and 11:00 p.m. EST (that's 6:00 p.m. and 8:00 p.m. PST) works best for this type of item.

If your auction ends on a weekend you have a little more leeway in terms of ending time. I'd avoid ending on Saturday evenings (it's a big date night; too many people away from home) and not start too early on Saturday (people like to sleep in), instead opting for an ending between 1:00 p.m. to 11:00 p.m. EST (10:00 a.m. to 8:00 p.m. PST). On Sunday, avoid the morning hours (customers at church and out to Sunday dinner) and end sometime between 4:00 p.m. to 11:00 p.m. EST (1:00 p.m. to 8:00 p.m. PST).

On the other hand, if you're selling to a younger audience—school kids of whatever age—then you want to end your auctions earlier. You need to catch kids after they come home from school but before they go to bed. A good window is 5:00 p.m. to 9:00 p.m. EST (2:00 p.m. and 6:00 p.m. PST).

But what if you're not selling to a home customer? If your merchandise is aimed at business customers, you need to end your auctions during the business day. Again allowing for coastal time differences, try ending between noon and 5:00 p.m. EST (9:00 a.m. and 2:00 p.m. PST) during the week. And, as you'll learn next, *don't* end anytime on a weekend.

Picking the Right Day

Which day of the week you end your auction is just as important as the time of day you pick. There are some days where you'll find more people at home and able to bid than on other days.

First, remember that you should be ending your auctions during the evening hours, at least for general consumer merchandise. So, what evenings are people likely *not* to be home?

The answer is simple. More people will be out and about (and not at home) on Friday and Saturday evenings. Weekend nights are date nights; people go to dinner, go to movies, visit friends, and just get out of the house on these two nights because they don't have to get up early for work or school the next morning. That's why television ratings are so much lower on Friday and Saturday nights; fewer people are at home to watch TV.

That leaves Sunday through Thursday nights as your better choices. Of those, Sunday is arguably the most effective ending night; for whatever reason, more people stay at home on Sunday nights than they do any other night of the week. (Again, look at the TV ratings, which are huge on Sunday nights.) So, for most merchandise, a Sunday evening ending should garner the most potential customers.

caution

Most savvy sellers know to end their auctions on Sunday evenings—which results in a glut of items ending on the same night. This can result in increased competition if you're selling commodity items, which isn't necessarily a good thing. It can also result in eBay's system slowing down under the weight of so many last-minute bids. For these reasons, some sellers *avoid* Sunday-night auctions, instead opting for a Monday-to-Thursday ending.

Obviously, this advice is totally wrong if you're selling to a business customer. You don't want to end any business auctions on the weekend, when most businesses are closed. End sometime during the working week, between Monday and Friday. Some sellers prefer Tuesday, Wednesday, or Thursday, banking that fewer employees call in sick or take early (or late) vacation on these days. Other sellers like Monday or Friday, when more traveling salesmen are in the office. It's a close call.

Days to Avoid

Given the general auction ending advice, there are also certain days of the year when you absolutely, positively don't want to end your auctions. You can probably name them; they're days when the majority of people are busy doing anything but computer work.

That's right, I'm talking holidays. Never, ever, ever end your auctions on a major holiday. That means no ending on Christmas day (or Christmas Eve, for that matter), New Year's Day, Easter, Thanksgiving, and the like. (Halloween and Arbor Day are probably okay, however.)

You should also avoid ending your auctions on other big event days. For example, you won't get too many bids if you end your auctions during the Super Bowl, or even during the NCAA basketball championship game. You should also avoid big TV events, such as the final episode of a popular TV show. You want your customers' full attention; you can't pull them away from the TV to make a bid.

Managing Seasonality

There are also certain times of the year that are better than others for eBay selling. In fact, you should plan for seasonality in your eBay business; in most instances, your sales will not be steady throughout the entire year.

The best time of year for most eBay sellers is the Christmas holiday season, followed closely by the post-holiday season. Holiday sales start to pick up in mid-October, and continue strong through mid-December. The best two weeks are those surrounding Thanksgiving; people start thinking about online ordering the Monday before "Black Friday" (the day after Thanksgiving), and stay in the buying mood for the next full week.

caution
Holiday sales die off in the last week or so before Christmas, when buyers realize they can't get items shipped to them before Christmas day.

Likewise, purchases really perk up right after Christmas, and continue strong through mid-February. I'm not sure what drives this post-holiday buying, but it's there. You'll see a gradual ramp-up starting just before New Year's, with sales peaking in mid-January and dropping off slowly for the next month or so.

Most sellers see another minor bump in sales starting in mid-August and continuing through mid-September. This is the "back to school" phenom-enon, and it affects most product categories—not just obvious school stuff. For this reason, many sellers start building their inventory and ramping up their auctions around August 1 so that they're ready when the increase comes.

The worst time of year for eBay sellers is during the summer. Sales start slowing down near May 1 and remain weak through the end of July. It's a simple thing: Kids leave school, people go on vacation, and your cus-tomers have better things to do than stay inside shopping. Summer is the weak season for retail sales of all kinds; it's especially cruel to eBay sellers.

In fact, you'll find some eBay sellers close up shop during the summer months. The reasoning is that there's no reason to list items when no one is buying. There's logic to it, but I don't necessarily recommend that course of action.

Most legitimate businesses don't close up shop during the summer. (Unless they're selling skiing supplies, that is.) Even if traffic is slow (and it will be), you still need to keep your virtual doors open. A good compro-mise is to decrease but not stop your eBay activity; cut back on but don't totally eliminate the number of listings you post. Maybe you reduce your listing activity by half or more, but you still keep your presence on the eBay site.

This strategy is good for a number of reasons. First, just because eBay traf-fic decreases doesn't mean it stops completely; there are still sales to be made during the summer months. Second, if you stop listing during the summer, you lose all visibility; you want customers to know you're there, even when they're not in the mood to buy.

So, slow down during the summer, ramp back up in the fall, go whole-hog over the holiday season, and ease off a little in the spring. For most businesses, that's a solid business plan.

tip

The exception to the summer slowdown rule is if you sell summer-specific mer-chandise. If, for example, you're in the swimsuit business, you should more or less reverse this selling schedule; you'll want to take your vacation in December, not in June.

Trick #32: Don't Overspend on Listing Enhancements

eBay is really good about providing you with different enhancements you can make to your auctions. You can change the auction length, add a subtitle, add a picture, you name it—all at an added cost, of course.

Unfortunately, most of these listing enhancements don't improve your auction sales one iota. They exist, not surprisingly, for eBay to make more money—for itself, not for you. So, with just a handful of exceptions, you should avoid these listing enhancements. Unless, that is, you like throwing money away and unnecessarily reducing your profit margins.

tip

Not sure which listing enhancements to use for a particular listing? Then check out the auction research services discussed in Trick #11; many of these tools (such as Vendio Research, eSeller Street, and Mpire Research) evaluate how the various enhancements affect sell-through and pricing for individual items, and recommend which enhancements are worth the added expense.

Gallery

The first listing enhancement we'll discuss is the Gallery option. This one started out as a way to display your items in a separate picture gallery. That gallery still exists, although few buyers use it. Instead, the Gallery option today displays a photo next to your item listing on all browsing category pages, as shown in Figure 4.1.

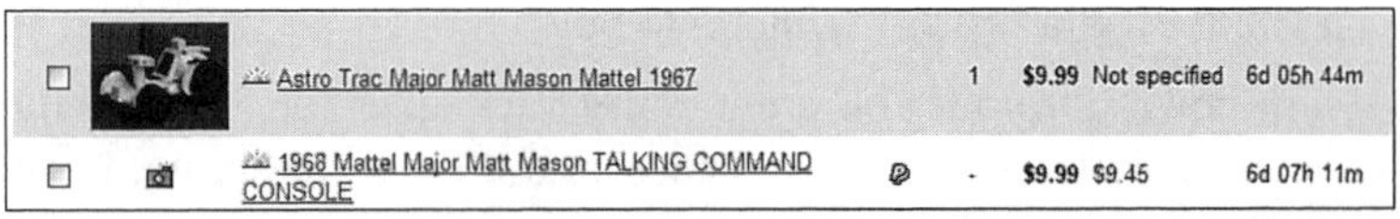

☐		Astro Trac Major Matt Mason Mattel 1967	1	$9.99	Not specified	6d 05h 44m
☐		1968 Mattel Major Matt Mason TALKING COMMAND CONSOLE		$9.99 $9.45		6d 07h 11m

FIGURE 4.1

Two search results listings—one with a Gallery picture, one without.

For most categories, the Gallery enhancement is an essential option, and well worth the $0.35 price. Unless you're selling a nonvisual item (and what would that be?), you should opt for the Gallery enhancement.

Gallery Featured

eBay also offers a second gallery option, called Gallery Featured. When you pay for this option, your item will periodically show up in the special Featured section above the general gallery. This option costs $19.95.

I do not recommend using this option. It's an expensive enhancement, and I'm not sure it gets you much; most buyers look beyond the first listings on a page.

Gallery Plus

Not to be confused with Gallery Featured, the Gallery Plus option puts an Enlarge icon below your gallery image on search results pages. Users who click the icon, or just hover over the icon with their mouse, display a larger (up to 400×400) version of your gallery picture.

note

To use Gallery Plus, you must have your pictures hosted by eBay Picture Services.

You pay an extra $0.75 for the Gallery Plus option—although this fee also gives you the standard $0.35 Gallery option, so it's really just 40 cents extra on top of the regular Gallery, if you think of it that way. That said, I don't recommend this option; if someone is interested in your listing, they'll click through to the listing itself and not bother with the little picture enlargement thing.

Subtitle

Can't get enough information in your listing's title? If you're that verbose (and you shouldn't be), eBay offers a Subtitle option, which appears below the title on your item listing page and on all search results pages, as shown in Figure 4.2. It's on the search results pages that a subtitle has the most value because it essentially provides another 55 characters for you to describe your item to potential bidders. Of course, you pay for this option, in the form of a $0.50 fee.

FIGURE 4.2
A listing with a subtitle.

In general, you should avoid adding a subtitle; it's an expense that isn't justified in terms of returns. That said, there are some categories where a majority of sellers have adopted the use of subtitles, so if you don't choose this option, your listings will look naked and somehow inferior. Do a search on your item or product category and see how the other listings appear; unless most of the results use subtitles, you can avoid this option.

In addition, some sellers of high-priced merchandise ($500+) use subtitles to provide additional information about their items. Instead of using valuable title space for words like "new," "sealed," or "MIB," you put these descriptive terms in a subtitle, instead. Again, it varies from category to category, so see what's common for the type of items you sell.

note

It's worth noting that adding a subtitle doesn't help potential buyers find your item. The text in a subtitle is not included in eBay's standard title search; it comes into play only if users expand their search criteria to include the item description.

Bold

How do you make your item stand out on a page full of search results? How about displaying the listing title in boldface? Well, if you don't mind spending an extra $1.00, you can display your item title in bold in the search results listings. A boldfaced item listing is shown in Figure 4.3.

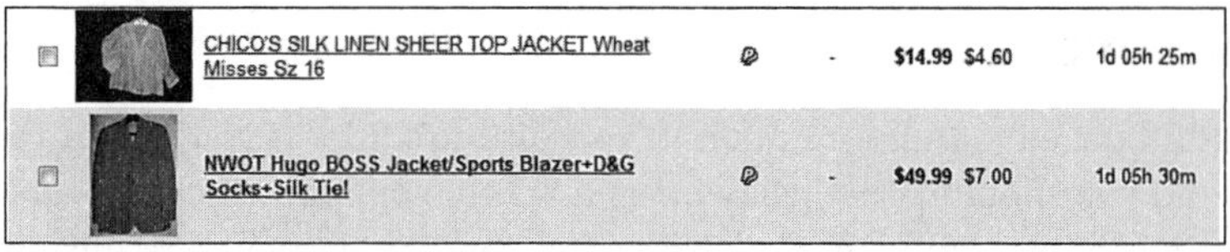

| | | CHICO'S SILK LINEN SHEER TOP JACKET Wheat Misses Sz 16 | | - | $14.99 $4.60 | 1d 05h 25m |
| | | **NWOT Hugo BOSS Jacket/Sports Blazer+D&G Socks+Silk Tie!** | | - | $49.99 $7.00 | 1d 05h 30m |

FIGURE 4.3

Two item listings—the second one in bold.

Because of the high price and minimal visual impact of this enhancement, I can't recommend you use it.

Border

If a bold title isn't attention-grabbing enough for you, how about putting a frame around your listing?

eBay's Border option puts a dark border around your listing on every search results page, as shown in Figure 4.4. This option is more expensive than the Bold option, costing you $3.00. It's not worth the money.

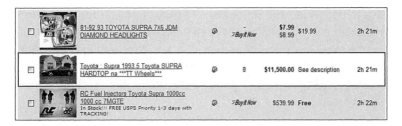

FIGURE 4.4
The item listing in the middle has the Border option.

Highlight

If you want to spend even more money, how about creating a *shaded* item listing?

When you select the Highlight option, your listing on any category or search results page displays with a colored shade, as shown in Figure 4.5. This little bit of color will cost you $5.00—and, as with the bold option, I find it too high-priced to recommend.

FIGURE 4.5
Two item listings—the second one enhanced with the Highlight option.

Featured Plus!

The Featured Plus! option displays your item in the Featured Items section on the appropriate major category page, as well as in the Featured Items section at the top of any search results page. This option will set you back a whopping $19.95, and I don't recommend it; it puts your "featured" listing at the bottom of the page, which is hardly a prominent position!

Home Page Featured

Ever wonder how much it costs to have your item featured on the eBay home page? Here's the answer: $39.95. (And this option doesn't even guarantee how often your item will pop up. What a deal—*not.*) All you have to do is select the Home Page Featured option, and your item will *periodically* be displayed on the home page, as shown in Figure 4.6. (For the same low price, your item also gets displayed in the Featured Items section of normal category and search results pages.) This is another option that I don't recommend, unless you're selling something really special.

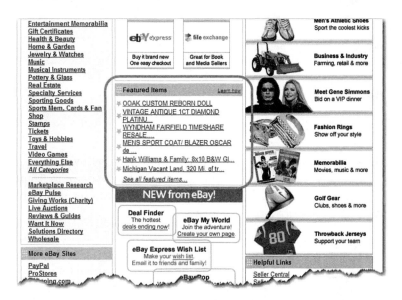

FIGURE 4.6
The Featured Items section in the middle of eBay's home page.

Gift Services

Think your item would make a great gift for a specific occasion? Then pony up $0.25 to add a Gift Services icon next to your item's listing, as shown in Figure 4.7.

FIGURE 4.7
An item enhanced with a Gift icon.

When you pay for the Gift option, you can also choose to promote any extra gift-related services you might offer—in particular, Gift Wrap/Gift

Card, Express Shipping, or Ship to Gift Recipient. It's an okay option for some sellers during the Christmas season, but otherwise fairly ineffective.

---

tip

eBay also offers two specially priced packages of listing enhancements that you might want to consider if you want all the individual enhancements. The Value Pack offers the Subtitle, Gallery, and Listing Designer options for $0.65. The Pro Pack offers the Bold, Border, Highlight, Gallery Featured, and Featured Plus! options for $29.95.

Skype Real-Time Communication

In 2005, eBay acquired Skype, a company that offers Internet phone service—that is, the ability to make phone calls from your PC over the Internet. eBay has since integrated Skype into its eBay auctions, so sellers now have the option (in many product categories) of including a Chat or Voice button in their listings. This lets potential buyers contact you in real-time, using the Skype service, to ask any questions they might have about your listing. This option is free, if you choose to use it.

Should you offer live chat or voice contact for your buyers? This is one feature that most sellers are not supportive of, for the simple reason that offering live customer service costs money—even if the technology itself is free. To offer this real-time support, you have to be available to answer the live questions. That means putting yourself (or an employee) in front of your computer for hours on end, just in case somebody asks a question. That's a huge time expenditure.

One of the appealing things about an online business, for many sellers, is that they don't have to have constant one-on-one interaction with customers. That's what makes online retailing more cost-effective than a bricks-and-mortar retail store. Do you really want to take live calls from customers? Most sellers I know don't.

Even if you're a large seller, eBay's customer support option might not make sense. If you're large enough to have your own customer support department, you don't need eBay to offer this service for you. You can simply put your own toll-free number or email address in your auction listings, and answer customer questions through the normal channels. Tying into eBay's Skype-based support simply isn't necessary.

Auction Length

This last option isn't really a listing enhancement, but rather a listing choice—which, in one configuration, comes at an added cost.

eBay lets you choose from five different lengths for your auctions: 1, 3, 5, 7, and 10 days. The first four options come at the standard listing price; 10-day auctions cost you an additional 40 cents.

The default—and most common—auction length is 7 days. Choose anything shorter, and you miss any potential buyers who check in only one day a week. Choose the longer option, and it's probably overkill. (Plus, you have to wait an extra 3 days to collect your money.)

Know, however, that some sellers like a 10-day auction that starts on a Friday or Saturday so that they get two weekends in their bidding schedule. Others prefer a shorter auction (as long as it runs over a weekend), recognizing that most bidding happens during the last few hours, anyway.

My recommendation is to go with the standard 7-day auction, with some exceptions. If you need your money quickly, go with a 3- or 5-day auction, but try to time the listing so that you get in a bidding weekend. Also know that some buyers expect and plan on 7-day auctions, so you might not get as much last-minute sniping if you opt for the shorter length.

note

A 3- or 5-day auction is also a good option if you have to start your auction mid-week but still want it to end on the weekend.

Trick #33: Invest in a Digital Photography Studio— And Take Professional Photos

The pictures you use in your eBay listings are equal to or more important than the words. The product photo first grabs most customers' attention; a product photo also helps customers get comfortable with merchandise that they can't personally see or touch.

The more and better photos you have in your listings, the more sales you'll get—at higher prices. Listings with no or poor photos don't draw well; all other things being equal, customers will choose the item with the better photos.

As you grow your eBay business, then, you need to develop a process that ensures a steady stream of professional product photos. For most types of merchandise, this means setting up your own semiprofessional digital photography studio.

Setting Up Your Studio

Don't freak; setting up a photo studio for eBay purposes isn't as big a deal as you might think. It does require a minor investment in equipment, and the dedication of a small amount of space. Beyond that, it's well within most sellers' expertise. To take professional-looking eBay photos, here's what you need:

- A quality digital camera—ideally one that offers a macro shooting mode, optional manual focus, and the capability to disable the internal flash. The higher-quality the lens, the better, although you don't need a lot of megapixels; you won't be shooting for large poster prints, just medium-resolution eBay photos.

tip

Look for a digital camera priced between $200 and $500. Models in this range should do everything you need them to do, in terms of taking good-looking product photos.

- A tripod to hold the camera. You don't need anything too fancy, just something solid and with a swivel head, like the Sunpak 6601UT ($34.99, www.tocad.com/sunpak.html) shown in Figure 4.8.

FIGURE 4.8

Use a tripod to steady your camera.

- A lighting kit with two or more floodlights. These lights will provide more even lighting than your camera's built-in flash, and without inducing glare on shiny objects or shrink-wrapped items. For budget-minded sellers, I like the Smith-Victor KT500U Thrifty Basic Kit, ($139.95, www.smithvictor.com), shown in Figure 4.9, which includes two 250-watt lamps with 10-inch reflectors and stands—more than enough lighting power for your needs.

FIGURE 4.9

The Smith-Victor KT500U lighting kit provides more even lighting than your camera's built-in flash.

- A table on which to set small items.
- A stand like the Interfit COR755 ($81.99, www.interfitphotographic.com) to hold seamless colored background paper, as shown in Figure 4.10.

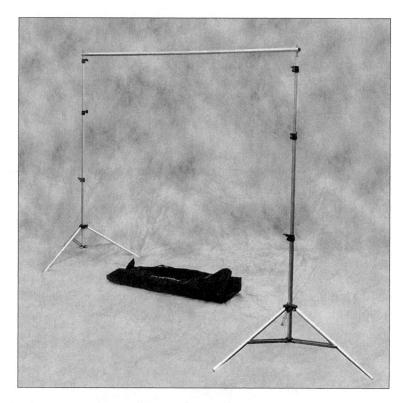

FIGURE 4.10

Put a roll of seamless colored paper on this support stand to provide a background for your product photos.

- One or more rolls of seamless colored background paper. For most items, you should stick with neutral colors, such as white or gray; used colored backgrounds only if you're shooting plain white or black objects, or clear crystal or glass items.

- A memory card reader for your computer to transfer the photos from your camera to your PC.

- A PC-based photo editing program for post-shoot editing. I like Adobe Photoshop Elements ($99.99, www.adobe.com) or Paint Shop Pro Photo ($79.99, www.corel.com), both of which let you crop, brighten, darken, and otherwise make your raw photos look more presentable for eBay use.

Shooting Small Objects

If you're shooting small items, you might want to ditch the lights and background paper and use a light box or light tent instead. A *light box* is a translucent cube or tent into which you place the items to photograph; light comes from outside the box to provide a soft glow around the object. They're ideal for shooting jewelry, crystal, small collectibles, and the like.

For example, American Recorder's Photo Studio in a Box ($120, www.americanrecorder.com), shown in Figure 4.11, is a translucent box with colored background. Similar kits are available from EZCube (www.ezcube.com), Interfit (www.interfitphotographic.com), Smith Victor (www.smithvictor.com), and XPro (www.xprogroup.com).

FIGURE 4.11

Shoot small objects with a light box, such as the Photo Studio in a Box.

The Photo Process

After you get your studio set up, it's time to start taking professional photos. The key, as you might have guessed from the equipment list, is in the lighting. Position your two floodlights in front of and to the side of the item you're shooting, to form a "V" (with the subject in the point of the

"V"). Experiment with how you aim the floods; you want to get good overall lighting with minimal shadows and no glare.

To this end, make sure that you turn off your camera's built-in flash. Flash lighting is harsh and directional, and often results in glare from shiny objects. (For example, shoot a shrink-wrapped CD with a flash and you'll get enough glare to obscure the face of the CD.)

---

tip

If you want to get fancy, you can add a "hair light" or backlight behind your item, positioned low and shooting up. This adds a glow around the item, for added contrast against the background.

Make sure that the camera is close to the subject and zoomed in to fill the entire camera frame. That's another symptom of amateur photography; the subject too small and far away from the camera. You want to get close enough so that potential customers can see all the detail in the product—which also means shooting from multiple angles. Shoot in three dimensions so that customers can see the item from all sides. And do close-ups of important product details or any blemishes you need to point out. (This might mean using your camera's macro mode for those ultra-close shots.)

Naturally, you want to mount the camera on a tripod, rather than holding it in your hands. A handheld camera is, more often than not, a shaky one that results in blurry pictures. Rely on the tripod to provide the stability necessary for razor-sharp pictures.

After you've taken your pictures, transfer them from your digital camera to your computer and load them into your digital photo editing program. Use this program to crop the pictures even tighter, correct the color (you want true whites and blacks), and adjust contrast and brightness, if necessary.

After you edit the photos, resize each one so that it's no more than 400×400 pixels in resolution. Anything larger is wasted on eBay, which displays that size as a default maximum. (Unless you pay for the Supersize option, which can display photos up to 800×800.)

Personally, I find 400×400 to be on the smallish size, especially if you need to show fine detail in your product. Fortunately, you can use larger photos if you insert the pictures manually into your listings via HTML (we'll discuss how later in this chapter), but you still don't want to get too large. I might go up to 600 pixels wide for detailed items, but typically max out at a width of 500 pixels.

---

tip

Photos are great for items that have a little depth, but if you're selling an essentially flat product (CDs, DVDs, books, and so on), you can scan the item instead of shooting it—and often get better results. If flat products are your bread and butter, invest in a decent scanner, and learn how to use it.

Trick #34: Use Third-Party Photo Hosting—And Post *Lots* of Pictures

eBay is happy to host the photos you use in your auction listings. It's even happier to charge you for extended photo hosting and display. The way it works is simple. eBay gives you first photo free, and then charges for anything else you want.

If you want to include more than one photo in your ad, you'll have to pay for it. Here's how eBay's fee structure works:

- Each additional picture (up to six, total): $0.15 each
- Picture Show (multiple pictures in a slideshow format): Free
- Supersize pictures (allow users to click a photo to display at a larger size): $0.75
- Picture pack (up to six pictures, supersized, with Gallery display): $1.00—or $1.50 for from seven to twelve photos

You can see how the costs can add up—and quickly, if you want or need to display a lot of photos for a product. That's why savvy sellers host their photos outside of eBay at a third-party photo hosting site.

Choosing a Photo Hosting Site

Several different websites offer to host picture files for your eBay auctions. Most of these sites charge some sort of fee, either on a monthly basis for a certain amount of storage space or on a per-picture basis. More often than not, the fees charged by these sites are significantly lower than what you pay to insert multiple photos via eBay's Picture Services. The most popular of these photo hosting sites include

- Image Hosting (www.vendio.com), with plans starting at $3 per month for 3MB of storage
- Auction Pix Image Hosting (www.auctionpix.com), offering 15 days of hosting for 20 cents per picture
- Photobucket (www.photobucket.com), which hosts photos at no cost

- PictureTrail (www.picturetrail.com), $19.95 per year to host 500 photos
- Vendio Image Hosting (www.vendio.com), with plans starting at $2.95 per month for 3MB of storage

Your Internet service provider might also provide image hosting services, often at no cost. Many ISPs give their users a few megabytes of file storage space as part of their monthly service; you might be able to upload your photos to your ISP's server and then link to that server in your eBay item listings.

In addition, if you subscribe to an auction management service, chances are it offers photo hosting as part of the package. Check to see what's available.

Finally, if you have your own online storefront outside of eBay, you can use your store website as a photo repository. Just use an FTP program to upload your photos to a separate folder, and then point to the photos in that folder from within your eBay auction listing. Any excess space on your website is yours to use as you like!

Inserting Photos into Your Item Listings

How do you insert photos hosted elsewhere into your eBay item listing? The answer depends on how you want to do it.

If you're adding a single photo, you can do so when you're creating your item listing. You do this from the Pictures section of the listing creation form. After you click the Add Pictures button to display the Add Pictures window, select the Self-hosting tab, shown in Figure 4.12. Now you should enter the full web address of your photo into the Picture URL box. If you have multiple photos, check the Picture Show option and follow the onscreen instructions to add additional URLs; you should also check the Gallery Picture URL option to use this photo as your gallery picture in search results. When you finish entering information, click the Upload Pictures button and continue with the rest of the listing creation process, as normal.

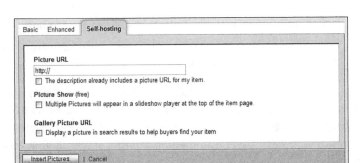

FIGURE 4.12
Add photos hosted elsewhere to your eBay listings via the Self-hosting tab.

If you're familiar with HTML code, you can insert one or more photos directly into the body of your item listing. This process isn't as hard as it sounds, assuming that you've already found a hosting service, uploaded your picture file, and obtained the full URL for the uploaded picture. All you have to do is insert the following HTML code into your item description where you want the picture to appear:

```
<img src="http://www.webserver.com/picture.jpg">
```

Just replace www.webserver.com/picture.jpg with the correct URL for your picture. Remember, when you use this method, you can include as many photos in your listing as you want.

How Many Photos Do You Need?

When you can include as many photos as you want in your listing at no cost, what's the right number of photos to include? It all depends on the type of item you're selling.

The simple answer is that you want to include as many photos as necessary to give potential customers a good feel for what you're selling. That might mean a single photo of a two-dimensional item, or six photos of a large, complex item. For example, if you're selling a collectible stamp, a single photo (or scan) is sufficient; there's no back or sides of the item to show. In contrast, if you're selling a used car, even a half-dozen photos might not be enough; you'll want to shoot the vehicle from the front, rear, and both sides, as well as include shots of the interior and under the hood.

Likewise, if the item you're selling has important areas of detail, you'll need to shoot those details. For example, I once sold a batch of animation cels, and I took close-up photos of the signatures included in the corners of each cel. The signatures might have been visible in a full-item shot, but it was important for potential buyers to see the signatures in close-up.

Can you include too many photos? Yes, you can—especially if they're large photos that take a long time to download. Not all potential customers have broadband Internet connections, you know; a third of all Internet users are still connecting via a slower dial-up connection. Use as many photos as you truly need to visually present your item, but no more than necessary.

Trick #35: Create a Unique Gallery Photo

By default, eBay uses the first photo you submit for the item's gallery photo—the picture that displays in all search results lists. That's fine and dandy, but maybe that photo isn't the best one to use.

For example, maybe the first photo in your listing is a group shot with a lot of small items in it. That photo might look good at normal size, but when displayed as a thumbnail. . .well, everything's just too small to have the desired impact.

That's why savvy sellers shoot a separate photo for the gallery thumbnail. You want this photo to show your item big and bold so that potential buyers can clearly see at a glance what you're selling. You might even want to crop the photo to show only the most important part of a larger item. The key is to recognize how the photo will look at thumbnail size, and optimize the photo for that thumbnail.

If you're using eBay Picture Services to host your photos, you can change the default gallery picture directly from the Sell Your Item form. After you select and upload your photos, click the Change Gallery Picture button in the Gallery Picture section of the form, shown in Figure 4.13. This expands the section to display all your uploaded photos; click the photo you want to use for your gallery picture.

FIGURE 4.13

Changing the gallery picture for a listing.

If you're using a separate photo hosting service, you can select your gallery photo from the Self-hosting tab of the photo upload window. Check the Gallery Picture URL option, and then enter the URL for the photo you want to use for your gallery thumbnail.

tip

Here's an added trick-within-a-trick: When you're creating a photo for gallery use, put a small colored border around that photo. A bright blue or red border will help your thumbnail picture stand out from all the others on the search results page—and draw more potential customers to your listing.

Trick #36: Organize Your Listings for Best Effect

It's always good to assume that potential bidders are in a hurry. For that reason, you need to make it easy for people to graze your listing without having to read every single word.

How do you make your listing easier to graze? Simple—put the most important information at the beginning and the least important at the end. Don't make the bidder read through to the end of the listing before placing a bid. Not everyone will read your entire listing; as they say in the newspaper business, you don't want to bury the lede. Make sure that even the most casual grazer sees the most important information about the item by putting it right at the top of the listing.

In addition, the most important information shouldn't be just the first thing on the page, it should also be the most *dominant* thing. You can use various page design techniques to separate different types of information and put them in different sections on the page. Make it easy for potential bidders to find the item overview, the detailed description, and your terms of service.

tip

Not every part of your item listing is of equal importance. Don't hide the most important stuff; put keywords and phrases in boldface or in a different color. You can also use bulleted lists to breakout discrete pieces of information. The key is to force the reader's eyes to focus on what's important.

So, what are the essential elements of an effective eBay listing? Let's take a quick look—going pretty much from top to bottom in your listings.

Title

Every auction listing starts with a title. Actually, two titles: the official 55-character title that eBay uses to index your auction (and is included at the top of the listing page), and the title that you place above the text description in the body of your auction listing. These two titles can be the same, although they don't have to be. That's because the title you include within the body of your listing doesn't have a character limit; it can be as long and descriptive as you want it to be.

And because you want the title to stand out from the body of your description, you probably want to format it somewhat differently. That means using a larger type size, a boldface type, a different type face, or a different color.

The key is to treat the title as you would the headline in a newspaper. It needs to attract the attention of potential buyers, and include all the keywords that touch the buyers' hot buttons.

tip

Including all essential keywords is even more important in eBay's official listing title. That's because most buyers use eBay's search function to find items to buy, so the title has to include the keywords that they're likely to search for. (Learn more about keywords in Trick #38, later in this chapter.)

That said, the title—although theoretically of unlimited length—shouldn't be *too* long. There's no need to limit yourself to just 55 characters, but you shouldn't let the title stretch more than two lines. Titles are for grazing, not for prolonged reading. If the reader can't absorb the title in a single glance, it's too long.

tip

If you need to go to a third (or fourth) line of type, consider breaking the title into a title and a subtitle, with the subtitle in slightly smaller, perhaps different-colored type.

Description

Below the title is the descriptive text of your listing. This text can be as short as a single paragraph or as long as you want. The key is to include as much information as necessary to describe what you're selling.

When you have a longer description, you should treat the initial paragraph separate from the balance of the text. In this situation, the first paragraph needs to serve as a short and pithy introduction to the more detailed description that follows. That's because many people read only so far before they lose interest. If the viewer reads nothing but that first paragraph, he gets a general overview of what the story is about. It's obviously not as detailed as the rest of the description, but it does the job of keeping the reader informed in a single glance.

note

Learn more about writing detailed descriptions in Trick #39, later in this chapter.

Photos

A text description is important, but a photograph is, in almost all cases, mandatory. Potential buyers need to know what an item looks like before they make a bid, and the only way to do that is to show them a picture. Or two. Or three. Or as many as it takes to accurately present the item.

Where should you place the photos(s) in your listings? That's a matter of taste and some debate. Some sellers like the pictures on top, either before or just after the title, as shown in Figure 4.14. Other sellers like the pictures after the description, as shown in Figure 4.15. Still other sellers are savvy enough to create a multiple-column layout that places the photos on either the left or right side of the description, as shown in Figure 4.16. There's no absolute right or wrong when it comes to picture placement; use the design that best showcases the product you're selling.

This auction is for one large green widget, perfect for any household. The widget is slightly used, and will ship in its original factory box. This widget was manufactured in 2003 by World Wide Widgets. It is model #572, part of the Incidental product line. The size of this widget is approximately 3" x 5" x 2.5".

FIGURE 4.14

A photo placed at the very top of a listing.

Large Green Widget

This auction is for one large green widget, perfect for any household. The widget is slightly used, and will ship in its original factory box. This widget was manufactured in 2003 by World Wide Widgets. It is model #572, part of the Incidental product line. The size of this widget is approximately 3" x 5" x 2.5".

FIGURE 4.15

The same photo, placed at the bottom of the listing.

Large Green Widget

This auction is for one large green widget, perfect for any household. The widget is slightly used, and will ship in its original factory box. This widget was manufactured in 2003 by World Wide Widgets. It is model #572, part of the Incidental product line.

The size of this widget is approximately 3" x 5" x 2.5". The official color is Forrest Green, and the actual paint job is a dark green metal flake.

Widgets from World Wide Widgets are made to be used by the average household. They are durable, long-lasting, and self-lubricating. When only the finest widgets will do, use World Wide Widgets!

FIGURE 4.16

An alternative approach, with the photo to the left of the item description.

Terms of Service

Now we come to the end of your item description, after which it's appropriate to talk a little bit about how you conduct your business. What I'm
talking about here is your *terms of service* (sometimes called the *terms of
sale* or just *TOS*), or what some folks refer to as the "fine print." It's important to include your TOS in your item listing, but not so important that it
draws attention to itself. Hence the position at the bottom of the listing
instead of the top; it's there for potential buyers to read, but not positioned as a key selling point for your auction.

tip

Format your TOS in a way that separates it from the item description, without making it appear too important. Different tricks include using a smaller or different-colored type face; placing a different-colored background behind the TOS; or putting the TOS in a text box or surrounding it with a border.

Just what should you include in your terms of service? Here's a short list:

- What payment methods you accept, and which you prefer
- Any restrictions for different payment methods (such as waiting 10 days for personal checks to clear)
- Which shipping services you use
- Your shipping and handling charge
- Whether or not you offer insurance or delivery confirmation, and if so, how much you charge
- Your return policy, if any
- Which countries you do or don't ship to
- Any other bidder restrictions
- After-the-auction checkout instructions

In short, your TOS should spell out any details that potential buyers need to know before they place a bid.

Trick #37: Create Your Own Auction Templates

A well designed, visually appealing auction listing not only attracts more buyers, it also makes them feel more confident about buying from you. A poorly designed listing will turn off some potential buyers. Because you never want to turn away any potential business, you want your listings to do as effective a sales job as possible.

All of which means that you need to design the look of your listings with every bit as much care as you choose the products that you sell. The better the job you do designing your listings, the more successful auctions you'll have.

Unfortunately, eBay's stock item listings are rather boring, visually. They're also the same; if all you do is enter text into eBay's Sell Your Item form, your listings will look identical to millions of other listings on the eBay site.

This is why many eBay business masters design their own listing templates. A *template* is simply a collection of design elements—colors, fonts, and graphics—that you apply to all your eBay listings. There are several ways to create great-looking eBay listing templates. We'll discuss several here.

note

Want to learn more about designing your own auction templates? Then check out my companion book, *eBay Auction Templates Starter Kit* (Michael Miller, Que, 2006). The book comes with a CD that contains dozens of templates you can use as is, or you can actually read the book to learn how to design your own templates with HTML.

Employing Good Design

However you choose to design your eBay listings, there are some common design elements you can employ to create more effective listings. In general, here's how you create a great looking and successful eBay listing:

- **Subtle design**—First, know that an effective auction listing uses subtle design elements. The design itself shouldn't knock you over the head; it should be noticeable without calling attention to itself. That means not using design elements for design's sake. The layout should be practical without being showy, and the font and color choices should be understated.

- **Logical page structure**—The structure of the page should work to draw the reader's eyes to the most important elements on the page. That might be the item's title or photo, or (ultimately) to the Bid Now button. There shouldn't be any speed bumps in the way from top to bottom. Subsidiary elements should be sectioned off; accessible, but not mandatory, in the reading scheme.

- **Columns and tables**—Multiple columns and tables should be used when necessary, but not overused. It's okay to place bulleted lists or photos in a separate column, but don't put the main description in a two- or three-column layout.

- **Flush left or justified text**—Text reads best when it's flush left or justified. Right-justified text is unreadable for many people, and you don't want to center large blocks of text. (Centering is okay for titles and subtitles, however.)

- **High contrast color scheme**—The whole design should work toward readability. That typically means dark text on a light background, like the black text against white pages of this book. Some reverse text can be used for effect, but know that it's difficult to read large blocks of light text against a dark background.

- **Understatement**—Nothing in the listing should scream at the potential bidder. That means no over-large fonts, no overly bright colors, no flashing graphics or animations. Pictures should be large enough but should not dominate the page. Fonts should be large enough to be readable, but not so large that body text looks like a headline.

In short, use design to help sell your item, not to draw attention to itself. Use discretion and subtlety to work towards readability and emphasis on the key features of what you're selling.

Using eBay's Listing Designer

Although you can do some simple formatting on the Sell Your Item page using eBay's normal text editor, a more effective method is to use eBay's Listing Designer. Listing Designer lets you apply predesigned templates, which it calls *themes*, to your item description.

note
Listing Designer isn't free; it costs 10 cents per listing.

A theme consists of some sort of background color or graphic, typically surrounded by a graphic border of some sort. A theme does *not* include any text formatting; you still have to format your item description text in the text editor. But by combining some simple text formatting with a colorful Listing Designer theme and custom photo layout, you can create listings that stand out from the standard eBay text-only listings.

Selecting a theme is as easy as scrolling to the Listing Designer section of the Sell Your Item page, shown in Figure 4.17. Check the Enhance Description with a Theme and Picture Layout option, pull down the Select Theme list to select a category, and then select a specific theme within that category. A thumbnail of the selected theme displays next to the pull-down list.

FIGURE 4.17
Selecting a theme for your listing with eBay's Listing Designer.

Listing Designer also lets you customize the placement of the photos in your item listing. eBay normally sticks your photos below the listing; you don't have a choice in the matter. But when you use Listing Designer, you can choose to put your photos at the top, bottom, left, or right of your item description. For many sellers, the customized photo placement alone is worth the ten-cent price of using Listing Designer.

note

Most auction management services also offer a variety of predesigned listing themes or, in some cases, a "design your own" listing designer tool. Check with the individual website to see what's available.

Using Third-Party Auction Templates

If you want more variety in listing design than Listing Designer provides, check out the many predesigned third-party auction templates available on the web. Some of these templates are free, others come with a fee; in either case, you should be able to find an attractive design that makes your listings stand out from the pack.

There are two types of auction template services available on the Web. The first type features a web-based form (sometimes called a *code generator* or *code generating website*) that you complete with the information for your particular auction. The second type features prewritten code that you download to your computer for editing. In both cases, you have to insert the final generated HTML code into the description of your eBay listing. Some of the more popular code-generating template sites include the following:

- Antique Central's eZ Auction (www.antique-central.com/eztemplate.html)
- Auction AD Creator (www.auctionlotwatch.co.uk/auctionadcreator.html)
- The Auction Insights code generator (www.auctioninsights.com/templates/)
- Auction Riches (www.auctionriches.com/freead/create.pl), shown in Figure 4.18

FREE AUCTION AD CREATOR

Title:	
Description:	
Photo URL:	(Must start with http://)
Shipping Terms:	
Your Email Address:	
Border Color:	navy
Background Color:	navy
Navigation Font Color:	white
Navigation Font Size:	+1

VIEW AD

FIGURE 4.18

Auction Riches, a typical code generator eBay template site; just fill in the form and click the button!

- Auction Writer (www.auctionwriter.com)
- AuctionSpice (www.auctionspice.com)
- BiggerBids (www.biggerbids.com)
- DeadZoom (www.deadzoom.com/auction-template/)
- K &D Web Page Design Custom Ad Creator (www.kdwebpagedesign.com/tut_tc2.asp)
- ListTailor (www.listtailor.com)
- Nucite (members.nucite.com)
- RobsHelp.com FreeForm Builder (www.robshelp.com)
- Wizard's Free Auction Template Creation Form (www.ambassadorboard.net/hosting/free-form.php)

If you prefer the ease of a predesigned template, here are some sites that offer free or paid templates for downloading:

- Alou Web Design (www.alouwebdesign.ca/free-ebay-templates.htm)
- AuctionSupplies.com (www.auctionsupplies.com/templates/)
- Auction Template Center (www.auctiontemplatecentral.com)
- DeSa C.S. (www.desacs.com); Figure 4.19 shows one of the many templates offered by this site

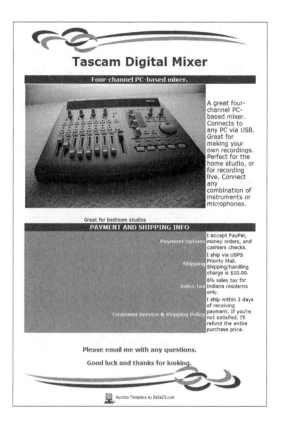

FIGURE 4.19
A customizable auction template from DeSa C.S.

- Free Auction Help (www.freeauctionhelp.com/free_auction_template.htm)
- K&D Web Page Design Premade Templates (www.kdwebpagedesign.com/pmt_1.asp)
- SaverSites (www.saversites.com/services_ebay_auction_templates.htm)
- The Ultimate eBay Resource (www.sellingonebay.info/templates.html)
- Xample.net (www.xample.net/templates.htm)

Whichever type of template site you use, the process ends when the site generates the HTML code for the template. You can then copy this code into the HTML tab in the Description section of eBay's Sell Your Item form. Edit the code as necessary and continue creating your eBay auction listing.

Designing with HTML

If you want even more-customized listings, you can design your own templates using HTML code. Although this isn't a task for the faint of heart, writing your own code lets you create highly individualized item listings—much fancier than you can do with a template-driven listing creator.

HTML is nothing more than a series of hidden codes that tell web browsers how to display different types of text and graphics. The codes are embedded in a document, so you can't see them; they're visible only to your web browser.

These codes are distinguished from normal text by the fact that they're enclosed within angle brackets. Each particular code turns on or off a particular attribute, such as boldface or italic text. Most codes are in sets of on/off pairs. You turn "on" the code before the text you want to affect and then turn "off" the code after the text.

You can create HTML code with any text editing program, such as Notepad or WordPad, or in a specific HTML editing program, such as Microsoft Expression (www.microsoft.com) or Adobe Dreamweaver (www.adobe.com). After you design your listing template, you cut and paste the resulting HTML code into eBay's Sell Your Item form; more specifically, into the HTML tab of the Description section.

Unfortunately, space does not allow a full discussion of HTML coding. If you want to learn more about HTML, I recommend that you pick up a copy of *Sams Teach Yourself HTML and CSS in 24 Hours, 7th Edition*, by Dick Oliver and Michael Morrison (Sams, 2005), available wherever good books are sold. It's a great primer for creating your own web pages with HTML. And my own *eBay Auction Templates Starter Kit* presents a variety of eBay-specific code you can use in all your auction listings.

Trick #38: Keywords, Keywords, Keywords

Most bidders find the items they want by using eBay's search feature, which searches item titles (*not* descriptions, by default) for specific keywords. What this means for you is that you need to inject as many keywords as possible into your listing titles so that your title is sure to include the words that interested customers will be searching for.

To do this, you have to think like the people who will be looking for your item. Imagine how you would search for this specific item, and then include the right keywords into your item title to make your item pop up on as many search results pages as possible.

What words should you include in your title? Well, if your item has a model number or series name, that's definitely something to use. As an example, you might be selling a **1956 Gibson ES-175 Red Jazz Guitar**. This title gets in the year (1956), the manufacturer (Gibson), the model number (ES-175), the color (red), and a brief description of what it is (jazz guitar)—which pretty much covers all the bases.

tip

You also need to make sure that your title "searches" well. That means adopting a few tricks that play to the way eBay's search engine works. For example, when describing an item in your title, you should use the full phrase or title for the item. Leave out a word—even if it's the word "and"—and your item won't come up as a hit on the search.

You can also use one of the third-party research tools we discussed in Trick #11 to find out which keywords customers are searching for. For example, Mpire Research (www.mpire.com/products/researcher.html) includes as part of its product research a list of the most keywords that buyers used to search for any selected item. The more you know about how your customers search, the more effectively you can construct your listing title.

Also useful, if somewhat less so, is eBay's very own Keywords page (buy.ebay.com). This page is a simple list of popular terms that people use to search the eBay site. The keywords are organized alphabetically, as shown in Figure 4.20; unfortunately, there is no indication as to the effectiveness of any of the keywords listed.

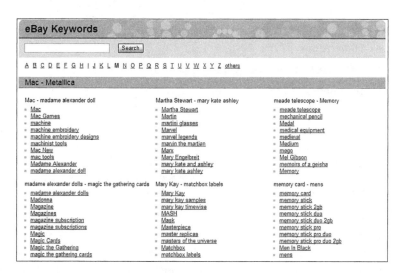

FIGURE 4.20

eBay's Keywords page.

Trick #39: Describe It Like There Are No Photos

Sure, a picture is worth a thousand words, but that doesn't mean that you can't also use a thousand words to describe what you're selling. An effective item description does everything a photo does; it describes in exquisite detail the item in question, in terms of what it is and what it does.

When you write your description, it helps to think like a copywriter for one of the big catalog or direct mail firms. Take a look at how L.L. Bean and Lands' End do it, and emulate that style and level of detail. The best advice I can give you is to describe the item as if there are no photos; imagine you're a radio announcer with the item in front of you, and use descriptive words to paint a word picture of the item.

What details should you provide in the item description? Here's a starter list:

- Manufacturer name
- Item name
- Model number
- Product line
- Year manufactured or sold
- Approximate age of the item
- Condition—new, used, like new, mint, fair, in original box, and so on
- Color
- Size
- Dimensions
- Short description of any known damage or defects
- Included accessories

---

tip

Notice how I presented the previous information? Instead of listing all those details about the details in a long, hard-to-read text paragraph, I broke them out into a bulleted list. This is a good technique to apply in your auction listings, too. Bulleted lists are much easier for readers to absorb than are long paragraphs— and they will improve the effectiveness of your listings.

You shouldn't stop at describing the item, of course. You also need to sell the item. That means listing not only the item's features, but also its benefits. It's not enough to say that this widget includes a 1/4" blowhole; you need to tell the buyer what that blowhole will do for him.

For example, if you're selling a DVD player with HDMI output, you should do more than mention the feature (HDMI output). You need to describe how the feature benefits the customer; in this instance, you could say "HDMI output upscales the picture to look sharper on a high definition TV."

See what I just did? I mentioned the feature, but then quickly turned it into a benefit. Customers buy benefits, not features.

Trick #40: Offer the Buy It Now Option

Here's one final trick for creating more effective auction listings. Although many eBay buyers are accustomed to the whole online auction process, many newer users don't want to wait seven days to purchase the item they want. (Plus, there's no guarantee that they'll win the auction when the seven days are up!) Impatient buyers see something they want, and they want it now. This is why savvy sellers, when they can, offer the Buy It Now (BIN) option in their auctions.

Selling with Buy It Now

eBay's Buy It Now option lets you add a fixed-price option to your auction listings. The way BIN works is that you name a fixed price for your item, as shown in Figure 4.21. If a user wants the item immediately, she clicks the Buy It Now button and pays the fixed BIN price; the auction is automatically closed and that user is the winning bidder.

FIGURE 4.21

An auction with the Buy It Now option.

note

Offering the BIN option does not preclude users from bidding below the BIN price via the regular auction process. When someone bids below the BIN price, the BIN option disappears and the auction continues as normal.

Using the Buy It Now option will cost you extra as a seller, however. Table 4.1 details the fees that eBay charges to add a BIN to your auction, over and above the standard listing fees.

Table 4.1   eBay Buy It Now Fees

Buy It Now Price	Fee
$0.01–$9.99	$0.05
$10.00–$24.99	$0.10
$25.00–$49.99	$0.20
$50.00+	$.025

Offering the BIN option is good if you think you can sell an item at a given price. It's especially popular for commodity products, where the price is pretty much dictated up front by the market. On the downside, the BIN option reduces the upside of unrestrained bidding; it's unlikely that bidding will progress above the item's BIN price.

All that said, the BIN option is popular among professional eBay sellers with a lot of similar inventory. If you place the same items up for auction week after week, the BIN price becomes the de facto retail price of the item and you can ship items as soon as you find a willing buyer. You don't have to wait the standard seven days for a normal auction to end.

You might also want to consider the BIN option around the Christmas holiday, when buyers don't always want to wait around seven whole days to see whether they win an item; desperate Christmas shoppers will sometimes pay a premium to get something now, which is where a BIN comes in.

Selling at a Fixed Price

Buy It Now isn't the only way to sell items for a fixed price on the eBay site. If you want to avoid the possibility for an item selling for less than the Buy It Now price (which is possible with a BIN-enabled auction), you can simply list an item with a fixed selling price. As you can see in Figure 4.22, eBay's fixed-price listings look just like regular auction listings and have the same duration (1 to 10 days, your choice); they just don't offer the option of placing a bid. When someone wants to buy your item, he clicks the Buy It Now button; there's no way to place a lower bid.

FIGURE 4.22

An item offered for sale at a fixed price in the eBay marketplace.

In years past, I would have never advised sellers to run anything but a traditional auction or an auction with the Buy It Now option. Today, however, an increasing number of transactions on the eBay site are of the fixed-price variety; more and more sellers are going the fixed-price route, and more and more buyers are buying fixed-price or Buy It Now items that they can receive faster than they can if they bid on an item listed for a seven-day auction.

Should you go the auction route or the fixed-price route? It all depends on the type of product you're selling, the type of competition you face (both on and off eBay), and your own business expectations. For many sellers, running a traditional auction with the Buy It Now option is a good compromise, the best of both worlds, as it were. But that's not the only way to go, or necessarily always the best. You have to make this choice for yourself—but know that the trends are moving away from traditional auctions and toward fixed-price sales.

eBAY BUSINESS PROFILE

Profile: Creative Sports and Home Decor

Business Profile

Business name: Creative Sports and Home Decor

eBay ID: Elrod7*

eBay Store: stores.ebay.com/CREATIVE-SPORTS-AND-HOME-DECOR

Type of business: Sports collectibles, crafts

Owner: Patty Manning

Location: Ozark, Missouri

Not all eBay businesses resell existing merchandise. Some businesses sell new items created by the owner. One such business is the subject of this profile; Creative Sports and Home Décor exists as an outlet for owner Patty Manning's creativity.

Creating New Product Categories

Eight years ago, Patty Manning's aging grandmother moved in with her and her family. It was a big lifestyle change (they even bought a bigger house, near Branson, Missouri), and Patty needed to find something she could do that would allow her to be home most of the time to take care of her grandmother.

Patty had always loved decorating, crafting, and football—kind of an odd mix of interests, but a mix that proved ultimately profitable. Looking around the house for raw materials, Patty found a Kansas City Chiefs Pocket Pro helmet and a Jack in the Box antenna ball. Here's what happened next:

"I cut the antenna ball down and hot-glued it into the helmet, and my husband listed it on eBay just to see what would happen. Amazingly enough, people thought they were the greatest things."

Almost by happenstance, Patty had created a new category of sports collectible—and built the foundation for a successful eBay business. She found a distributor where she could purchase the helmets and the yellow smiley-face antenna balls in bulk, and things started to take off.

Unfortunately, things didn't proceed as smoothly as they started. As many businesses discover, a profitable niche doesn't stay undiscovered for long. Several other companies jumped onto the helmet-ball band-wagon, utilized lower-cost Chinese suppliers, and even got their merchan-dise licensed by the NFL. Just like that, a profitable niche became oversaturated.

But that didn't deter Patty. She had a bunch of NFL helmets on hand, and needed to do something with them. Another light bulb went off, and Patty bought a scroll saw and starting cutting all those helmets in half. She used the now half-helmets to create 3D picture frames and license plate frames, thus creating yet another new category of collectible merchandise.

A 3D NFL picture frame, created and sold by Patty Manning (AKA Creative Sports and Home Décor).

Since then, Patty has expanded her business to include other craft items that she creates—in particular, decorative ceiling tiles. Here's how she describes this part of her business:

"I hadn't had much luck with the home decor part of eBay until I bought some reproduction metal ceiling tiles. I did a faux painting technique that gave them a distressed look and applied vintage looking centerpieces to them. I've done very well with those."

One of Patty Manning's decorative metal ceiling tiles.

Managing the Business

Patty's business strategy is to continue to pioneer unique crafts and collectibles categories. Her sales vary by year, but have approached the $100,000 level. One of the things Patty likes about eBay is that she can scale her business up or down to better manage her personal responsibilities. As she puts it, "eBay allows me to make the choice of how much or how little work I do."

Even though Patty is an established PowerSeller, she runs her business completely by herself. Patty hand-creates the items she sells, does all the listing and shipping, and keeps track of all her inventory. Patty can produce about 100 items per week (!), and typically ships within two days of receiving an order. She doesn't use any computer programs, and even does her own accounting—until tax time, that is, when she hands off everything to her accountant to figure out.

Patty Manning, tracking her eBay listings at her PC.

Selling Strategies

Patty sells via both traditional auctions and an eBay Store. She uses the Buy It Now option in the majority of her auctions. During the NFL season she has at least 100 auctions running each week; during the off-season, probably half that.

The Creative Sports and Home Décor eBay Store.

Her strategy is to list an item for auction twice, and if it doesn't sell by then, move it into her eBay Store inventory. In addition, when she has several duplicates of a particular item, she puts a few into the store in addition to the auction listings.

"We've had good luck with the store," Patty says, "as long as we have like items on auction, in order for people to find the store listings."

Keys to Success

The key to Patty's success is her creativity. As she puts it:

"I think for me, finding something that no one else has, or is original, has been the key to the success I've had on eBay. And these days that's not so easy to do. The fact that most of what I sell I have to make, and with the tiles being time-consuming, it can sometimes be a little overwhelming."

But there's an upside to selling on eBay, as Patty notes:

"eBay allows me a lot of freedom. Freedom to take care of my grand-mother when she lived with me, and when I had to put her in a nursing home a little over a year ago; it allowed me the freedom to be able to go see her everyday and spend quality time with her. It allows me the freedom to work in my yard and do things with my daughters that an 8–5 job wouldn't allow. And, depending on the time of the year, I can list more or less depending on how much work I want to do."

For Patty Manning, eBay provides a good income, the freedom to live life on her own terms, and a means to express her creativity. That's a nice kind of business to have.

5

Tricks for Setting Prices and Handling Payments

The price you set for a listing plays a big part in how many bids you get—and how high those bids go. Price too high and you scare away potential bidders; price too low and the bidding might not rise high enough to be profitable. In addition, if you aren't careful about how you price your items, you could end up paying more eBay fees than you have to. In other words, setting prices is a tricky business.

It's a good thing, then, that the eBay business masters have some tricks for optimizing your listing prices. They also weigh in on the best ways to handle your customer payments—which aren't limited to just accepting PayPal. Read on to learn more.

Trick #41: Price for the Type of Product You're Selling

Setting the price for an item is one of the trickiest parts of selling on eBay. This is true whether you're listing the item for an auction, for auction with the Buy It Now option, or for a fixed-price sale.

What's tricky about setting the item price is that every seller has a slightly different philosophy. Some sellers like to set the starting bid for their auction items as low as possible—99 cents, or even a penny—to attract attention and get the bids started. Other sellers like to set the starting bid as close as possible to what they think the item will actually sell for, thus turning the auction process into a simulation of a fixed-price sale. Still other sellers take the middle ground, setting the starting bid price at the price they paid for the item, knowing that any bids above that price are pure profit.

I'm going to recommend a few different pricing strategies, depending on the type of item you're selling.

Pricing High Demand Items

Let's start with items that are in high demand. You've done your research, and determined that the item you're posting will sell because there's currently a lot of demand for that item. You don't have a lot of competition, and you can be assured of the item selling at or near a particular price.

In this situation, you *could* price near the price you're likely to receive, but where's the fun in that? Bidders are going to stay away from your auction until the final moments; there's little incentive for them to bid at your higher price earlier in the auction. As a result, you'll receive fewer bids, and likely no bids higher than the going rate.

A better strategy is to set your opening bid relatively low. Doing so attracts a lot of buyer attention, and inspires some buyers to bid early, thinking that they're really getting a steal. However, as you already know, the item is worth a lot more than the opening bid, and serious buyers will bid the price up to the going rate—or even beyond, as the early bidders try to stay in the game. The price might end up exactly where you thought it would, or it could go higher; that's the beauty of this strategy.

As an example, let's say you're selling a collectible figurine that you know will sell around $50 because similar items have sold in that price range. Instead of starting the bidding close to that $50 price, you instead set the initial bid at $9.99. This attracts the attention of a few bargain hunters, and you see some quick bids at $10, $11, $12, and so on. By the time the end of the auction rolls around, bids are already in the $50 range, and a last-minute snipe or two could push the price up to $55 or $60.

The point here is that the more bidders you have, the higher the bidding is likely to go. And you attract a lot of bidders with a low starting price.

caution

You should use the low starting bid strategy only for those items that you're fairly certain will sell for a certain price. Do not use this strategy for commodity items, or for items where the market value is uncertain; you could end up selling the item for the price you initially set!

Pricing Commodity Products

Next up are those products that are commodities—inkjet cartridges, plain T-shirts, compact discs, just about anything that sells in mass retail. With these products, you're competing not just with fellow eBay sellers, but also with mass merchants such as Target and Wal-Mart. Your pricing on these products is dictated by the current market price, as defined by these merchants.

Let's say, for example, that you're selling electric toothbrushes. One particular model you offer sells, day in and day out, for $17.99 at the big mass merchant retailers. How should you price this item on eBay?

If you price this item too far below $17.99, that's what it will sell for. Price the electric toothbrush at $9.99, for example, and smart bargain hunters will snap it up for that price or something near it. Start the price too low, and you won't receive the full value for the product.

If you price the item *above* $17.99, it won't sell. Nobody is going to pay $19.99 for something they can buy for $17.99 at their neighborhood Target. Start the price too high, and no sales result.

If you price the item exactly at $17.99, it probably won't sell, either. That's because the price your buyers pay is actually higher than $17.99 after taking shipping and handling into account. Again, they're not going to pay more than what they pay locally.

This leaves a single strategy: Price the item slightly below the going rate. In our electric toothbrush example, you might set the price at $14.99 or so. The prospect of saving even a few dollars will attract savvy shoppers, and the bidding process will probably get the final price close to the $17.99 street price.

tip

One variation on this commodity pricing strategy is to set your starting bid price just below the street price, but then set a Buy It Now price equal to the street price. This lets eager buyers purchase the product right now, but at the going rate—and lets bargain shoppers still participate in the bidding process.

So, when you're selling commodity products, set your initial price just below—but not too far below—the average selling price.

Pricing Unknown Quantities

What if you're selling an item that isn't a surefire seller or a known commodity? There are lots of items you could sell that you won't know for sure what price you can command.

This situation is common when you're selling collectibles, antiques, and items you purchase from estate sales and the like. You know what you paid for the item, but you don't know how much it's worth to potential buyers.

In this situation, the recommended approach is to set the starting bid at or near the price you paid for the item. Then you let the eBay market-place do its thing and bid the price up to its true market value.

For example, let's say you purchased a rare comic book for $20 as part of an estate auction. You're pretty sure that you got a good deal on the thing, and that a serious collector would value it at $50 or more. Instead of pricing the item that high, you set the starting bid at $19.99. If the item happens to sell at this price, you haven't lost anything (save for your eBay fees, of course). More likely, interested collectors will bid the price closer to the $50 price—or even higher.

tip

An alternative strategy for collectibles is to set an even lower starting price, but set a reserve price equal to or slightly higher than your purchase price. The lower starting price attracts the interest of potential buyers, and the reserve price protects you from selling the item below a minimum desired level.

Pricing Based on Market Research

There's one final trick you can use to set your item's starting bid: Utilize a research service to find out how similar items have been priced. We dis-cussed a lot of different research services in Trick #11. For pricing pur-poses, I like the free Mpire Researcher (www.mpire.com/products/researcher.html). As you can see in Figure 5.1, all you have to do is enter a model number or product description, and Mpire Researcher returns key listing statistics, including advice as to the best starting price.

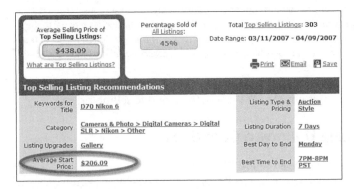

FIGURE 5.1

Find out the average starting price of an item from Mpire Researcher.

Even more useful is the How to Sell function of Vendio Research (www.vendio.com). Enter a product number or product description, and when the research results appear, select the How to Sell tab. As you can see in Figure 5.2, Vendio details the starting bid range that generates the best auction results, as well as other useful recommendations (such as whether to use a reserve). Follow the advice and you'll probably achieve the listed results.

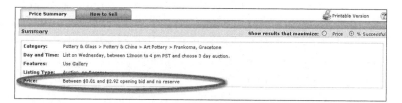

FIGURE 5.2
Get useful pricing advice from Vendio Research.

Trick #42: Price Below the Breaks

Whatever pricing strategy you embrace, you also need to keep in mind how much you're paying for each item you list. As you recall, eBay charges a listing or insertion fee based on the starting (or reserve) price of the item.

What you don't want to do is spend more than you have to in listing fees. The way you overspend on listing fees is to ignore eBay's fee structure, and price your items regardless of where the fee breaks occur.

To be smart about how you price your items, you have to know the breaks in eBay's fee structure—and then price your items just below the breaks. For your reference, Table 5.1 details eBay's listing fees, as of April 2007.

Table 5.1   eBay Insertion Fees

Starting or Reserve Price	Insertion Fee
$0.01–$0.99	$0.20
$1.00–$9.99	$0.40
$10.00–$24.99	$0.60
$25.00–$49.99	$1.20
$50.00–$199.99	$2.40
$200.00–$499.99	$3.60
$500.00+	$4.80

To see how this works, let's say you have an item that you want to price at around a dollar. If you set the starting bid at $1.00, eBay will charge an insertion fee of $0.40—which is a whopping 40% fee if your item actually sells for that price. On the other hand, if you price the item a penny lower, at $0.99, you only pay a $0.20 listing fee. Price for a penny less, save 20 cents—that's smart listing.

The same goes for items priced near any of eBay's insertion fee breaks. Instead of pricing an item at $10.00, price it at $9.99 and save 20 cents. Instead of pricing an item at $25.00, price it at $24.99 and save 60 cents. Instead of pricing an item at $50.00, price it at $49.99 and save $1.20.

These savings might not seem like much, but they add up fast. Besides, paying 20 or 60 cents more than you have to isn't very smart—and only smart sellers become successful eBay businesspeople.

Trick #43: Accept Multiple Payment Options

Let's now move beyond pricing to payment. It's a documented fact—the payment options you accept affect the success of your auctions.

Most successful eBay sellers recognize that the more forms of payment they accept, the more potential buyers they attract. Actually, this is more noticeable in the negative; the fewer payment options you offer, the more customers you'll drive away.

Let's say, for example, that you decide to accept only credit card payments. This is actually quite common because credit card payments (typically via PayPal) are both quick and easy for the seller, where other forms of payment (personal checks, especially) take longer before funds are bankable, and are a lot more hassle. So, what happens if a customer wants to pay by check? Your payment terms exclude that individual as a customer, that's what. You've just lost a potential customer; the more customers you exclude, the fewer bidders you'll have—and the less successful your business will be.

Smart sellers don't want to exclude any paying customers. Not everyone has a credit card, or wants to use it online. Not everyone wants to (or knows how to) go to the time and expense of purchasing a money order or cashier's check. Not every customer wants to write a personal check, and wait for that check to clear before receiving a purchase.

You see the theory. To maximize the number of potential buyers, you have to accept multiple forms of payment. In today's world, that means accepting payments via all the following methods:

- Personal check
- Money order
- Cashier's check
- Credit card

Exclude any one of these payment options, and you exclude a large number of potential buyers.

note

The one form of payment you don't have to accept—and, in fact, eBay won't let you accept—is cash. eBay now excludes cash as a payment option in most of its auctions, due to the high possibility of lost and stolen payments and fraud.

Trick #44: Limit Your Payment Options

Now for a piece of advice in direct opposition to the previous advice. Many successful eBay sellers *limit* the types of payment they accept. These sellers recognize that some forms of payment are either too risky (in terms of nonpaying bidders) or too much hassle to accept. They balance the costs of the payment method versus the number of customers who absolutely, positively have to pay by that method, and calculate that they save more than they lose by not accepting a particular method of payment.

The most common payment method excluded by eBay sellers is personal check. I have to admit, there have been days where I, too, wanted to drop payment by check from my accepted payment options. Personal checks represent the slowest, most risky, and most troublesome form of payment you can accept. What's bad about personal checks? Here's the short list:

- **Checks are slow**—It takes up to 10 business days for a check to clear after you deposit it. Add in the time it takes for the buyer to mail you the check and you're looking at two weeks before you can touch the payment funds.

- **Checks are a hassle**—Here's the routine. You have to wait for the payment to show up in your mailbox. Then you have to sign the back of the check, fill out a deposit slip, drive to your bank, and deposit the check. Then you have to wait those 10 business days before you ship the item—which means somehow tracking all the checks you receive and deposit. Lots of work, especially compared to other forms of payment.

- **Checks are risky**—The reason you wait 10 business days before shipping an item paid via check is because some people write checks for which they don't have the funds on hand. Bounced checks are a constant problem, and they're doubly unprofitable. Not only do you end up with an unconsummated sale (or, perish the thought, you shipped the item without waiting for the check to clear), you also get dinged $6 or more by your bank. That's right; your bank charges you for every NSF (nonsufficient funds) check you deposit. You can try to get the buyer to reimburse you for that expense, but if he wrote a bad check to begin with, chances are he's not going to have the funds to pay any extra fees. Bad deal.

For all these reasons, you might deem it inefficient to accept check payments. Yes, you might lose a few potential customers, but you reduce both your risk and your workload by not accepting those pesky personal checks.

Other sellers also ban payment by cashier's check and money order. Now, both of these forms of payment are a lot safer than personal checks, and you get your money faster (you don't have to wait 10 days for the check or money order to clear). But there's still the hassle factor, and the wait for the payment to arrive via mail. A lot of sellers want immediate payment, which is possible only when buyers pay by credit card.

note

In reality, you might receive your funds faster when someone pays by money order or cashier's check. When a buyer pays via PayPal, it takes 3–5 business days (after the payment is made) for those funds to be deposited into your own personal bank account. That is, you can't spend the money for five days or so after the payment is made. Contrast this with a buyer who promptly mails a cashier's check or money order after the close of an auction. A prompt buyer can get payment into your hands by the third day following the auction close—and you have immediate access to those funds after you deposit the payment.

What payment options you accept depend on your business philosophy. If you want to attract the widest possible number of customers, you'll accept everything—personal check, cashier's check, money order, and credit cards. If, on the other hand, you want to run a streamlined operation with as little effort as possible on your part, you'll limit your payment options, perhaps just to credit cards. The choice is up to you.

Trick #45: Accept Credit Card Payments—Via PayPal or Otherwise

Back in the old days (about half a decade ago), most buyers paid for their eBay purchases with personal checks. Today, 80% or more of all purchases are paid for via credit card. That's a major shift in payment patterns.

Today, you simply can't run a business of any sort without accepting credit card payments. That's especially true on eBay; if you don't accept credit cards, you could alienate half or more of your potential customers.

So, this trick is very simple. You have to accept credit card payments for all your eBay sales, auction, fixed-price, or otherwise.

Accepting Payments via PayPal

For most sellers, accepting credit card payments means signing up for PayPal. That's because it's a real hassle to set up your own merchant credit card account; setting up a PayPal account to handle your credit card payments is a lot easier.

PayPal (www.paypal.com) is an online payment service, owned by eBay, which lets any auction seller easily accept credit card payments with little or no setup hassle. PayPal works by accepting credit card payments from your customers and then sending you a check or depositing funds directly in your bank account for that amount—minus PayPal's fee, of course.

The PayPal service accepts payments by American Express, Discover, MasterCard, and Visa—and, although it's primarily a U.S.-based service, it also accepts payments to or from more than 103 countries and regions.

Of course, before you can use PayPal to accept payments, you must sign up for PayPal membership. You do this by going to the PayPal website, clicking the Sign Up link, and then following the onscreen instructions to complete your registration. You can choose from three different types of PayPal accounts:

- A **Personal** account is for eBay buyers only, not for sellers. Ignore this option.

- A **Premier** account is for small business owners and individual sellers. With a Premier account, you can accept both credit card and non–credit card payments for a fee. You sign up for Premier status by checking the appropriate option on the Personal Account Sign Up page.

- A **Business** account is necessary if you're receiving a high volume of payments. With this type of account, you can do business under a corporate or group name and use multiple logins. It's ideal for larger businesses that need a merchant credit card account—although the fee structure is identical to that of the Premier account.

For most eBay sellers, the Premier account is the way to go. If your sales volume rises high enough, PayPal automatically switches you to a Business membership.

Paying for PayPal

PayPal charges only the merchant for the transaction. The card user, of course, pays the credit card company a finance charge on the account balance at the end of the month. No charges result if the customer's account is paid in full each month. The merchant pays PayPal a percentage of the total transaction, plus a flat per-transaction fee. These fees are separate from your other eBay fees.

The fees you pay as a merchant are based on the *total amount of payment received* —that's the selling price plus any taxes and shipping and handling fees. So, for example, if a $10 item has a $5 shipping and handling fee, the buyer pays PayPal a total of $15—and PayPal bases its fee to you on that $15 payment.

PayPal's fees range from 1.9% to 2.9%, depending on your monthly sales volume. Table 5.2 presents PayPal's fee schedule as of April 2007.

Table 5.2   PayPal Transaction Fees (U.S.)

Monthly Sales	Transaction Fee
$0–$3,000.00	2.9%
$3,000.01–$10,000.00	2.5%
$10,000.01–$100,000.00	2.2%
>$100,000.00	1.9%

You're also charged a flat $0.30 per transaction, regardless of your sales volume. All fees are deducted from your account with every transaction.

Let's do a sample transaction. Imagine that you sell a DVD player for $55, with a $15 shipping and handling fee. The total that the buyer pays is $70; it's this amount on which your fees are based. Assuming that you're in PayPal's first payment tier (under $3,000 a month), you pay 2.9% of that $70, or $2.03, plus the $0.30 transaction fee. Your total fees for that transaction: $2.33.

If, on the other hand, you did more credit card volume and passed the $3,000 per month level, you'd only pay 2.5% of the $70, or $1.75. Add in the $0.30 transaction fee, and you pay a total of $2.05 to PayPal.

Activating PayPal in Your Auction Listings

To accept PayPal payments for your eBay sales, all you have to do is to choose the PayPal option when you're creating an item listing. When you choose this option, a PayPal Payments section is added to your item listing. PayPal will also appear as a payment option on your post-auction item listing page and in eBay's end-of-auction email to the winning bidder. Most third-party checkout tools will also recognize and accept PayPal payments.

Collecting PayPal Payments

When a buyer pays for an item via PayPal, those funds are transferred immediately to your PayPal account, and you receive an email notification of the payment. This email includes all the information you need to link it to a specific auction and ship the item to the buyer.

note

In most cases, the buyer's payments come into your account free and clear, ready to be withdrawn from your checking account. The primary exception to this is a payment made via eCheck, where a buyer pays PayPal from a personal checking account. Because PayPal has to wait until the "electronic check" clears to receive its funds, you can't be paid until then, either. PayPal will send you an email when an electronic payment clears.

You have to manually withdraw the funds due to you from PayPal; no automatic payment option is available. You can let your funds build up in your PayPal account, or you can choose (at any time) to withdraw all or part of your funds. I recommend clearing your PayPal account at the end of each business day; there's no reason to let PayPal hold onto your money any longer than necessary.

You have the option of okaying an electronic withdrawal directly to your checking account (no charge; takes three to four business days) or requesting a check for the requested amount ($1.50 charge; takes one to two weeks). Just click the Withdraw tab from the Overview tab and click the appropriate text link.

Trick #46: Establish an Alternative to PayPal

Of course, PayPal isn't the only credit card processor you can use—it's just the most convenient. If your eBay business is large enough, there are alternatives to PayPal. And many sellers are actively seeking such an alternative.

Why Some Sellers Dislike PayPal

Not all sellers like PayPal. Some dislike the (perceived) high transaction fees; some dislike the way PayPal operates; some have been dinged (or singed) by PayPal chargebacks to complaining customers; some simply don't like being locked into yet another service owned by eBay. Let's examine each of these complaints.

The sellers I meet who complain the most about PayPal tend to be the least experienced sellers. They look at the 2.9% (plus $0.30) they pay to PayPal on every transaction, and view that as more money going into eBay's pockets. (eBay owns PayPal, remember.) They view the fees as another example of eBay nickel-and-diming them to death, and resent paying them.

The thing is, it costs money to process credit card transactions. No matter who handles your credit card payments, they're going to bill you for those services. And PayPal's 2.9% fee (lower if you're a higher-volume seller) isn't out of line; you'll pay similar fees to a traditional credit card processing service. That doesn't mean you have to like paying those fees, but they're just a part of doing business. Factor the fees into your business's cost structure and get on with it.

PayPal, however, operates a bit differently from other credit card services. That's because PayPal isn't a traditional credit card processor; it's an online payment service. PayPal is set up for the convenience of the online buyer, not necessarily for the convenience of large merchants. Dealing with a traditional credit card processor is a little more automated than working through PayPal's one-thing-at-a-time screens; it's okay when you have a small number of transactions, but a bit cumbersome when your volume increases.

As to the chargeback issue, this is a legitimate complaint. If you have a complaining customer, it's possible that PayPal will automatically side with the customer and freeze the funds in your account. (This is another reason to clear your account every day—fewer funds to freeze.) I've heard of eBay sellers who had thousands of dollars in payments frozen for weeks on end as they tried to resolve a given situation. PayPal's attention to the customer is admirable, but retailers have some rights, too.

In addition, there might be some merit in the argument about putting too many eggs in eBay's basket. There's nothing wrong for paying eBay for services rendered, but you can also pay someone else to perform a similar payment service. There's no reason to tie 100% of your business services into the eBay behemoth; working with multiple vendors is good business practice.

Like PayPal but Different: BidPay

One alternative to PayPal is BidPay (www.bidpay.com), a similar online payment service that also lets buyers pay via credit card. BidPay operates a lot like PayPal, with a slightly lower 2.5% transaction rate—plus a slightly higher 50-cent per-transaction fee. That's probably a wash for most sellers, unless you sell higher-priced merchandise.

A Different Approach: Merchant Credit Card Accounts

If you're a high-volume seller, you might be able to get a lower per-transaction rate than that offered by PayPal by signing up for a merchant credit card account from a traditional credit card processing service. Most merchant credit card services have rates in the 2%–2.5% range, which beats PayPal's standard 2.9% rate. (Although it might be no better than PayPal's rates for high-volume sellers.)

However, there are a few issues around establishing this type of traditional merchant credit card account. First, it's more hassle than signing up for PayPal; you might have to submit various business documentation and possibly have your own credit checked. Second, getting everything up and running might also be more involved than simply plugging into the PayPal system. (For example, a credit card terminal might have to be installed and programmed.) Finally, upfront or monthly fees might be involved.

note

Setup fees for a merchant account can range from $25 to $400 or more, and there's probably some sort of minimum transaction amount that you must maintain each month. Some services also make you purchase expensive software or credit card terminals. Because these fees vary so much, make sure that you shop around before you commit.

If you're interested in establishing a merchant credit card account, Table 5.3 details the basic fees charged by some of the major online credit card processing services.

Table 5.3   Online Credit Card Processing Services

Company	URL	Discount Rate (Online Sales)	Transaction Fee
Cardservice International	www.expandyourbusiness.com	2.39%	$0.25
Chase Paymentech	www.paymentech.com	2.69%	$0.20
Charge.com	www.charge.com	2.25%	$0.25
Merchant Accounts Express	www.merchantexpress.com	2.33%	$0.24
Network Solutions Merchant Accounts	merchantaccounts.networksolutions.com	2.19%	$0.30
ProPay Platinum	www.propay.com	2.69%	$0.25
Total Merchant Services	www.merchant-account-4u.com	2.29%	$0.30

Note that these are just the base fees; you might also be charged a monthly service fee, as well as fees for software or terminal use. Some firms also charge additional fees for high-risk credit cards, or for different types of cards (American Express is typically higher than MasterCard and Visa). And remember, online rates are higher than rates for traditional retail transactions. Find out all the fees in advance.

tip

Both Costco and Sam's Club offer merchant credit card processing to their business members, at affordable rates. See each company's website for more information.

Tips for Choosing a Credit Card Processor

Before you sign up for credit card services, ask the credit card processor to do an analysis based on your previous month's credit card business. Get the results, and then compare the numbers.

When you inquire, ask about *all* applicable fees. In particular, check on software integration fees, monthly service fees, virtual terminal fees, and the like. You might also have to hit monthly minimums or pay an additional fee. And don't be surprised if your head starts swimming; most of these companies have extremely complex fee structures, based on the types of credit cards accepted (commercial cards, debit cards, private label cards, and so forth), the types of customers you have, the types of products you sell, and the types of transactions you make.

Bottom line: Check the fine print before you sign up; what sounds like a good deal might or might not be.

Trick #47: Protect Yourself Against PayPal Chargebacks and Disputes

If you're a big enough seller, it's bound to happen sooner or later. You sell an item, receive payment, and ship it out. But then, a few days or a few weeks later, the customer files a complaint with either PayPal or his credit card company, claiming he didn't receive the item or that it was defective. In response to the complaint, PayPal freezes the funds in your account for the amount in dispute, or simply deducts that amount from your account. The credit card company and PayPal take the customer's word, and you get screwed.

Or do you?

There are ways you can protect yourself against this type of unwarranted chargeback. Read on to learn more.

Understanding Chargebacks and Disputes

A *chargeback*, also known as a *reversal*, is when a buyer asks his credit card company to reverse a transaction that has already cleared. The customer can claim any number of reasons for the chargeback—he didn't receive the item purchased, the item received was substantially different from that described, the item was defective, or maybe he just didn't like it.

Many chargebacks are legitimate. The most common type of chargeback involves stolen credit cards; the credit card holder gets charged for merchandise he didn't order or receive. Chargebacks are also used to protect the customer when a seller tries to pull a fast one by not shipping an item or by selling defective merchandise.

note
According to a study by the Gartner Group, approximately 1.1% of online transactions result in fraudulent buyer chargebacks.

A customer can file a chargeback complaint with his credit card company, or can file a dispute with PayPal, via PayPal's buyer complaint process. When someone files a PayPal claim, you typically get notice of the complaint and have the opportunity to work things out with the buyer. If you can't reach agreement, PayPal might side with the buyer and charge your account for the amount in question.

Problems occur when unscrupulous buyers try to use the complaint process for their own personal gain. A buyer might claim he never received an item in order to get out of paying for something actually received. That leaves you, as the seller, hanging out to dry.

How to Avoid Unnecessary Chargebacks

You can't totally protect yourself against all chargebacks. In fact, some chargebacks are legitimate, especially if the buyer never receives an item you ship. That said, you can protect yourself against most chargebacks by embracing the following business practices:

- Describe the items you sell as accurately as possible, and include photos of all damage or blemishes. This should reduce the number of complaints about items not being as described in the listings.

- Clearly publish your returns policy in your auction listings. Make sure that your terms are simple and understandable; don't make the customer hunt for your returns policy.

- Sell the item "as-is," and clearly state this in your item listing and returns policy. You might also want to add a "no buyer's remorse" clause. This should protect you from buyers who want to return a product simply because they don't like it or no longer want it.

- Respond quickly and politely to any customer emails or complaints. You'd be surprised how many chargebacks can be avoided just by being responsive.

- Retain all records and emails for all your sales, including shipping receipts. You might need these records to dispute a chargeback.

- Ship only to the confirmed address listed on the PayPal transaction details page. Do not ship to an alternative address, even if the buyer emails with a different address. (Many scams come from someone other than the buyer diverting shipments to an alternative address.)

- Purchase delivery confirmation (or signature confirmation, for items over $250) so that you can track and confirm delivery of the item. Hang on to all proof of shipment and delivery.

- Purchase delivery insurance or require the buyer to purchase insurance for the item. This protects you and the buyer should the package be lost or damaged in transit.

Following these best practices won't completely protect you against all chargebacks, but it will reduce the number of potential chargebacks you receive.

Fighting Chargebacks and Disputes

What happens when a buyer files a chargeback or dispute? It's a straight-forward process.

First, the buyer notifies his credit card company of the problem. The credit card company then notifies PayPal's merchant bank, and pulls the disputed funds from the bank. The merchant bank then notifies PayPal, and pulls the disputed funds from PayPal. PayPal then notifies you, via email, and pulls the disputed funds from your account. If there aren't enough funds in your account to cover the dispute, PayPal freezes your account.

You can dispute a chargeback, but ultimately it's the credit card company that decides the validity of the buyer's claim. PayPal will, however, help you fight any such claim.

First, PayPal offers a Seller Protection Policy that covers you for up to $5,000 against fraudulent transactions. To qualify for this protection, you must have a verified Business or Premier account, sell a tangible good (no virtual products, such as e-books), ship the item to a confirmed U.S., UK, or Canadian address (no other foreign addresses), ship within seven days of receiving payment, retain proof of delivery (such as USPS delivery confirmation), and, for items over $250, obtain a signature receipt.

Next, you should respond to the dispute via the PayPal Resolution Center (www.paypal.com/us/cgi-bin/webscr?cmd=_complaint-view). You can also respond via email (chargeback-response@paypal.com) or fax (402-537-5755). You'll need to provide PayPal with all the evidence you have supporting your side of the claim—original item listing, sales receipt, delivery confirmation, and so on—and you'll need to respond quickly, usually within 10 calendar days.

PayPal then takes your data, along with any other information it has, and disputes the chargeback with the credit card company. Unfortunately, the resolution process can take 75–100 days, during which time your funds are frozen. If PayPal wins the dispute, the charged back funds are redeposited into your PayPal account. If PayPal loses the dispute, you lose your funds.

caution

If you lose a dispute, PayPal not only withdraws the funds for the transaction, but also charges you a $10 payment for the investigation.

Trick #48: Protect Yourself Against Deadbeat Bidders and Fraudsters

A credit card chargeback is just one way a fraudulent buyer can scam you out of your hard-earned cash. Let's look at a few of the ways unscrupulous customers might try to cheat you—and how you can avoid being cheated.

Dealing with Deadbeat Bidders

One of the most frustrating things about selling on eBay is when you have a high bidder who never pays. This type of deadbeat bidder leaves you holding now-unsold merchandise, which you then have to relist to sell it again. (Fortunately, you haven't shipped the item yet; you might not have been paid, but at least you still have the item in your possession.)

If you find yourself a victim of a deadbeat bidder, you can report your case to eBay, ask for a refund of your final value fee, and maybe offer the item in question to other (unsuccessful) bidders. But you have to initiate all of these activities yourself; eBay doesn't know that you've been shafted until you say so. Here's what you want to do:

1. **Contact the unresponsive buyer**—It's on your shoulders to go to whatever lengths possible to contact the high bidder in your eBay auctions. This contact should start with the standard post-auction email, of course. If the buyer hasn't responded within three days, resend your original email with *URGENT* added to the subject line. You should also amend the message to give the buyer a specific deadline for responding. If another two days go by without a response, send a new message informing the buyer that if you don't receive a response within two days, you'll be forced to cancel his or her high bid and report the buyer to eBay as a deadbeat bidder.

2. **Initiate eBay's Unpaid Item Dispute process**—If you haven't heard from the buyer in 7 to 10 days, or haven't received payment in two weeks or so, it's fair to write off the buyer and move on. You do this by filing an Unpaid Item Dispute. Go to eBay's Security & Resolution Center (pages.ebay.com/securitycenter/), check the Unpaid Item option, and then click the Report Problem button. When the Report an Unpaid Item Dispute page appears, enter the auction's item number, click the Continue button, and follow the onscreen instructions.

3. **Ask eBay to refund your fees**—After an Unpaid Item Dispute has been filed, eBay sends a message to the bidder requesting that the two of you work things out. You then have to wait seven days before

you can request a refund of your final value fee. To request a refund, go to your My eBay page and click the Dispute Console link. When the Dispute Console page appears, click through to the item in dispute and select the I No Longer Wish to Communicate With or Wait For the Buyer option. eBay then issues a final value fee credit, and your item is eligible for relisting.

4. **Leave negative feedback**—Naturally, you want to alert other eBay members to the weasel among them. You do this by leaving negative feedback, along with a description of just what went wrong (no contact, no payment, whatever). Limit your comments to the facts—avoid the temptation to leave personally disparaging remarks—but make sure that other sellers know that this buyer was a deadbeat.

5. **Block the bidder from future sales**—Next, you want to make sure that this deadbeat doesn't bid in any of your future auctions. You do this by adding him or her to your blocked bidders list. You do so by going to eBay's Site Map page and clicking the Blocked Bidder/Buyer List link. Follow the onscreen instructions to add this buyer's ID to your blocked list.

6. **Offer the item to the next-highest bidder**—If you had other bidders in the auction, you can offer the now-available item to the next-highest bidder(s) via eBay's Second Chance Offer feature. To make a Second Chance Offer, return to your original item listing page and click the Second Chance Offer link. When the Second Chance Offer page appears, as shown in Figure 5.3, select which buyer(s) you want to make the offer to, select a duration for the offer, and then click the Continue button to make the offer.

FIGURE 5.3

Making a second chance offer to nonwinning bidders.

tip

Second Chance Offers can also be used, in a successful auction, to offer duplicate items to nonwinning bidders.

7. **Relist your item**—If you don't have any takers on your Second
   Chance Offer, you can always try to sell the item again by relisting
   it. The nice thing about relisting an unsold item is that eBay refunds
   the second listing fee—essentially giving you the relist free.
   (Obviously, you still pay a final value fee if the item sells.)

Dealing with Product Switchers

Here's a common scam: You ship an item and the customer claims that
the merchandise was damaged, or that she never received it, in the hope
of you sending their money back—no questions asked. If you send a
refund, the customer essentially gets free merchandise.

There's nothing in the customer-is-always-right manual that says you
have to offer no-questions-asked refunds. Instead, ask buyers to return the
item if they're unhappy, and then issue a refund when you receive the
merchandise. (In this situation, the buyer is typically responsible for paying the return postage.) Someone trying to scam you won't send the stuff
back, and that's the end of it.

Even then, you could still be scammed. Some fraudsters like to return merchandise different from what they received. That is, they order a new item
from you, receive it, ask to return it, but then return to you a different
item from the one you shipped. Maybe it's the same model, but damaged;
maybe it's something completely different. In any case, you get scammed
if you refund their money without realizing they've pulled a switch.

The best way to protect against this type of scam is to not refund any
money until you've received the returned item. Carefully inspect the
returned item, and compare it to photos you took of the original item. If
you've been switched, don't refund the money.

Dealing with Address Switchers

You're selling an item, the auction ends, and you get an immediate notice
of payment (typically via PayPal). Then the buyer emails you and asks
you to ship the item to a different address as a gift to someone else or
because he recently moved. Although this could be a legitimate request, it
could also be a scam.

Unless you can verify the legitimacy of this request, you should *not* ship the item. That's because it's likely that someone has hijacked the buyer's account and is trying to get the item shipped to their own address. (And the payment is likely fraudulent, as well.) If you ship the item to the second address, you'll probably lose both the item and the payment. When in doubt, double-check with PayPal or hold onto the item long enough for the payment to be verified or cleared.

Dealing with Escrow Scams

Our final form of scam is the escrow scam. In this situation, the buyer, after winning the auction, decides he'd rather pay via an escrow service. There are many legitimate escrow services out there, but that's not how this scam works. The buyer recommends a particular escrow site, and shortly thereafter you receive an email from the site confirming that the buyer has paid and that you should ship the item. The problem, of course, is that the site is fraudulent; the buyer hasn't paid anything, and you just shipped an item that you'll never receive payment for.

How do you avoid escrow service scams? First, deal only with Escrow.com, eBay's officially authorized escrow service. Second, don't respond to any escrow messages sent via email. No legitimate escrow site sends "confirmed to ship" messages via unsecured email; instead, you'll be directed to a secure website for all communication. And check out the discussions on eBay's Escrow & Insurance discussion board; it's a great place to learn about all the latest escrow-related scams!

Trick #49: Sell Internationally—And Prepare for Foreign Payments

Even though most U.S. sellers sell to U.S. buyers (and most Canadian sellers sell to Canadian buyers, and most Japanese sellers sell to Japanese buyers, and so on), eBay is a global marketplace. There's nothing stopping you from offering your goods to bidders in other countries—nor is there anything stopping you from restricting your auctions to your fellow countrymen.

In fact, many successful eBay sellers recognize the increased profit potential of opening up their auctions to buyers outside the U.S. The more potential bidders you have, the more likely you are to sell your item—and command a higher price.

If you choose to sell internationally, include in your auction listings a sentence welcoming international bidders. ("International bidders welcome" should do the trick.) You'll also want to specify international shipping charges for your item in the shipping section of the listing.

You'll also have to determine how you want to handle non-U.S. payments, which can be a bit of a hassle, especially if you're dealing in foreign currency. First, you have to convert it to U.S. dollars. (How many lira to the dollar today?) Then you have to receive it in a form that is both secure and trusted. (Do you trust a personal check drawn on a small Spanish bank?) Then you have to find a way to deposit those funds and convert them to U.S. dollars. (Does your bank accept foreign deposits?)

tip

If you need to convert foreign funds, try the Universal Currency Converter (www.xe.net/ucc/).

The easiest way to simplify the whole international currency issue is by specifying bidding and payment in U.S. funds only. This puts the onus of currency conversion on the buyer, which is a plus for you.

The payment process can be further simplified when the buyer pays by credit card, using PayPal. PayPal is active in more than 100 foreign countries and can handle all the payment, conversion, and deposit functions for you. Just specify foreign payments via PayPal only, configure PayPal to block payments sent in a currency you don't hold, and let PayPal handle all the details for you.

Trick #50: Offer a Money-Back Guarantee

You attract more customers when you can provide peace of mind about what you're selling. And the best way to provide peace of mind is to offer a money-back guarantee.

eBay lets you include a Return Policy section in your auction listings. You can also detail your return policy in the Terms of Service section in your item description. In fact, if you offer a money-back guarantee, you might want to state it upfront, near the top of your listing. For many sellers, it's a unique competitive advantage.

Most money-back guarantees are simple. You offer to refund the customer's purchase price if he's dissatisfied with the purchase. The item doesn't have to be defective; all the customer has to say is that he isn't happy, and you refund his money, no questions asked.

---

note

You can choose to refund (1) just the purchase price; (2) both the purchase price and the original shipping and handling charge; or (3) the purchase price, the shipping and handling charge, and the customer's costs to ship the item back to you. Make it clear which it is before you ask the customer to return the item.

And here's the trick about a money-back guarantee. You'll probably never have to pay out. The number of customers who will actually take you up on a money-back guarantee is, for most sellers, extremely small. You might sell several hundred items before you have to issue your first refund. That's a small outlay for all the good will you built simply by offering the guarantee.

You do, however, need to determine how long your guarantee lasts. Certainly, most retailers guarantee their merchandise to arrive intact and in good working condition—or at least as described in the auction listing. Should you respond to customer complaints if the item stops working after 30 days, or 90 days, or even a year after the auction? Although a manufacturer might offer an unconditional one-year guarantee, you probably don't have the same obligation. I'd say that any problems that crop up after the first 30 days shouldn't be your obligation. Most customers will understand and agree.

Profile: Boston Drum Center

Business Profile

Business name: Boston Drum Center

eBay ID: fromthecurve

eBay Store: stores.ebay.com/Boston-Drum-Center

Website: www.bostondrum.com

Type of business: Drums and percussion

Owner: Sean Kennedy

Location: Acton, Massachusetts

Sean Kennedy is a drummer and a businessman, which is a fairly unique combination. He sells drums and percussion instruments online, via both eBay and his own web-based store.

From Drummer to eBay Seller

Sean Kennedy does a lot of planning. That's important because he runs both an eBay business and a physical drum shop. He's a real businessman running real businesses.

Sean has been playing drums since he was a child. Like most musicians, he upgraded his equipment over the years, but rarely traded or sold any of his old instruments. In his mind, "dealers never offered a fair price for used gear, and selling through the classifieds required time and patience that I didn't have. I thought that eBay would be a quick and effective way to reach buyers around the world."

When he first joined eBay, in 2003, Sean had the simple goal of selling off some of his own instruments. He started as an amateur eBayer, "buying and selling occasionally, dealing only in my own possessions, mostly musical instruments. But I saw the potential for a business, even early on. I had some basic photography skills, knew something about the items I sold, and enjoyed researching what I did not know. With good pictures and detailed descriptions, my auctions usually fared well, often better than those of other sellers with similar items."

In 2005, Sean began to purchase used and vintage instruments locally, restoring and repairing them as necessary, and then reselling them on eBay. At this point, Sean considered his eBay sales a sideline to his musical career, not a real business. However, this experience prepared him for the next step:

"In March 2006, I acquired a 'bricks-and-mortar' drum shop in Boston, Massachusetts. The retail storefront would enable me to buy and resell new merchandise from percussion manufacturers and distributors, and thus take my eBay selling to the next level."

At the same time he took over the retail store, he moved his online business to a warehouse in Acton, Massachusetts. He knew that online sales would ultimately be more important than in-store sales. As Sean states:

"The modern business model requires a significant Internet presence. Profit margins are slim on musical instruments, volume is crucial, and more and more 'mom and pop' retail stores are finding it impossible to compete with the online giants. My Acton location houses the shipping and receiving, eBay, and other mail-order aspects of the business, serving both the retail and online operations. As a bonus, the warehouse is zoned for retail, so I established a showroom there as well."

Other Ways to Sell

Sean opened his eBay Store in May 2006—shortly after he acquired his retail business. Here's why he did it:

"I believe that having a Store sets professional eBay sellers apart from non-professionals, and provides buyers a traditional online shopping experience. In addition, a Store allows sellers access to important tools such as store inventory listings and auction management programs."

Not surprisingly, Sean put a lot of thought and planning into his eBay Store. He spent two months developing the look and feel of the Store, designing the logos and graphics, photographing merchandise, writing copy, and creating an HTML template for use in all his item listings.

In addition, Sean also sells through his own www.bostondrum.com website, through various online drum forums, and directly to customers who come to him, sometimes after first dealing with him on eBay. Sean views these supplemental sales channels as "an important growth area, especially if eBay fees continue to rise."

Sean Kennedy's eBay Store.

The Boston Drum Center website.

Sean recognizes the synergy that exists between all these sales channels. Here's how he puts it:

"I knew that eBay would play an important part in establishing my online drum shop. Customers may navigate directly to the websites of the well-known online retailers, while eBay provides visibility for the rest of us. It is an open, democratic playing field where my fledgling operation could be listed right alongside much more established businesses."

Selling Strategies

Sean tries to keep between 100–200 eBay listings active at all times. Of these, approximately half are eBay Store inventory format and half are fixed-price format. He lists between 1–5 traditional auctions of used and vintage items each week, and also holds a used cymbal sale every few months, pricing cymbals to sell at a Buy It Now price, determined on a cost-plus basis.

As to what makes a successful item listing, Sean thinks "A professional appearance is critical. Too many eBay sellers, even Stores, use unattractive auction layouts, replete with poor grammar, spelling errors, and bad photographs!"

A typical template-based listing from the Boston Drum Center.

To help create a professional appearance, Sean has designed an HTML template to build listings for every item he sells on a recurring basis. He believes that the consistent format simulates a traditional retail shopping experience; he hopes that buyers are as comfortable paging through his listings as they would be browsing in their favorite drum shop.

As to what makes for a great listing, Sean believes that "Any surprises experienced by buyers should be pleasant ones. So while this may be cliché and obvious, good photos and detailed descriptions are the most important elements of a successful eBay listing." As Sean says, "Honesty and diligence generate high bids on eBay."

And here's what Sean says about those product photos:

"By good photos, I mean flattering but not deceptive. The item should look its best, but any issues should be clearly depicted as well. I use eBay Picture Manager, so for no extra charge, I can add as many pictures as I can take to my listings. When I sell something like a vintage drum kit, I will include as many as 40 photos.

"Similarly, descriptions should include both the good and the bad, and should describe any faults of the item, even if they are also pictured. Along with an objective and subjective description of the item, I try to include any history or background information that might be relevant, whether I know it or have to research it."

Dealing with Industry-Specific Issues

The reason that Sean lists so many fixed-price or Buy It Now items is because of the unique nature of the musical instrument business. Most major manufacturers enforce "minimum advertised price" policies on their products, which means that no dealer, online or off, can advertise an item below a specific price. If Sean were to list an item for less than the minimum price, the manufacturer could cut him off as a dealer.

"The price regulation is a challenge," Sean says. "Musical instrument manufacturers enforce minimum advertised price policies, and dealers must abide by them in order to get products. With all authorized dealers selling at the same price, each must differentiate its listings somehow; this is why many sellers offer free shipping, free items, package deals, and the like. Furthermore, authorized dealers must compete with non-authorized dealers, who may undersell without recourse since they do not get the merchandise directly from the manufacturer."

This pricing issue isn't unique to the musical instrument category, but it does pose a unique challenge. It's to Sean's credit that he's able to come up with product bundles, freebies, and such to present a distinctive value to his customers.

Another issue in this product category is that of hearing how an instrument sounds; musicians want to see and hear instruments before they buy. That's easy enough in a traditional music store, but it's a challenge for online buyers. To this end, Sean is investigating the use of sound files and video clips, so customers can "hear" the instrument online. Although he's yet to incorporate such items into his eBay listings, he does use sound files to demonstrate several of the cymbals he offers via his other online store.

Finally, Sean faces the logistical challenge of shipping delicate and sometimes large and heavy items. (Ever try to lift a 24" bass drum—or a 22" cymbal?) Here's how Sean handles this challenge:

"I use different couriers for different items, since each has its own rules and rates for packages of certain sizes. I have also observed how the manufacturers pack and ship their merchandise, techniques which they have developed over the years for economy and efficiency."

Managing the Business

Sean's business is a relatively big one, at least compared to other eBay businesses. That's due in part to his multiple websites and to his bricks-and-mortar location. He currently has four employees who work in the retail store, one of whom also helps him with his online business. (Sean notes, "I could use more help!")

Sean does all of his own accounting, although he's considering implementing QuickBooks as an electronic solution. He uses eBay Selling Manager Pro to manage his eBay activity.

Purchasing and Managing Inventory

As an official dealer for many drum and cymbal brands, he purchases most of his new inventory direct from the manufacturers. His primary vendors read like a who's who of the percussion industry: Bosphorus, Canopus, DDrum, Drum Workshop, Dunnett, Meinl, Pacific, Sabian, Sonor, Stagg, Taye, Tempus, UFIP, Wuhan, Zildjian, and more.

Sean notes that only by having an official physical presence can he order from many of these supplies. Many musical instrument companies don't sell to online-only dealers; they require their dealers to have a storefront. In this regard, Sean's retail store provides him with a unique advantage over online-only competitors.

Of course, Sean also deals in used and vintage instruments. How does he find used drums to sell? He explains:

"Some items are traded in by customers at my retail store. Others I find locally through Craigslist or other classified ads. Very occasionally, I find items on eBay which sell for less than they should, or can be repaired or restored. Usually I sell these at the retail store, but sometimes they end up back on eBay!"

As to managing all that inventory, the only software he uses is eBay Selling Manager Pro. However, because it's tied to eBay sales, the web-based tool doesn't manage his non-eBay sales. That's why he relies on physical inspection, usually taking a complete inventory once a week. As a general rule, he tries to keep about three months' worth of inventory on hand. That said, his inventory varies wildly by item and supplier. And, Sean notes, "Thanks to my warehouse facility, I can take advantage of closeouts and the like and stock up big."

Managing Growth

The Boston Drum Center sells about $1,000 a day on eBay. That number continues to grow, of course, the longer that Sean sells online.

"I would say that it is getting easier for me," Sean confessed, "because it was such a challenge to start from scratch and build the business to its current state. But now all of the pieces are in place, and I can quickly add new items as they hit the marketplace. Plus, I am gaining a reputation, and many of my early customers are now returning for more gear."

Keys to Success

I asked Sean what made his particular eBay business so successful. Here's what he said:

"I think that to many buyers, the experience of acquiring gear is just as important as the gear itself. So my number-one priority is to make that experience an enjoyable one. The components of this approach are elementary: friendly emails, fast shipping, tracking numbers where applicable, professional packaging, and service and expertise both before and after the sale.

"Our tagline is 'Talk to a drummer, not a customer service rep,' and I think that's one of the most important aspects of the business. We compete with the low prices and vast selection by the online giants, but we can also offer advice about which ride cymbal to use in a piano trio, or walk a customer through the spring tension adjustment of a bass drum pedal."

What advice would Sean give to a prospective eBay seller? "Do it!" he says. Or, more specifically:

"Know what you sell. Buyers take a risk when buying items without seeing them in person, but an informative listing created by a reputable seller puts them at ease. Buy a good digital camera and learn how to use it effectively. If you don't know something about your item, research it. All of the above leads to higher bids; the more time you put into your listing, the more money you will make."

Sean has become an eBay success by carefully thinking through and planning every aspect of his business. He's also leveraged the benefits of both online and physical sales, using one to complement the other. In addition, he offers some very neat equipment for sale, at competitive prices. (As a drummer myself, I can vouch for that!)

It's all working for him—because he planned it that way.

6

Tricks for Packing and Shipping

The more items you sell on eBay, the more items you have to pack and ship. Packing and shipping is the unglamorous part of running an eBay business, but it has to be done. If you do it wrong, you can cost your business time and money. If you do it right, however, you can create a very efficient packing and shipping operation, minimize your costs, and maybe even turn a little profit.

Make a profit on packing and shipping? It's possible, and that's just one of the tricks presented in this chapter. Read on to learn more about shipping and handling from the eBay business masters.

Trick #51: Find Low-Cost Packing Supplies

Many eBay sellers don't realize how much they're spending on packing supplies until they run their profit and loss statement at the end of the month. Unless you keep tabs on your shipping and packing purchases, you could end up spending more on packing supplies than you charge for shipping and handling.

Many small sellers like to save money on packing supplies by recycling existing boxes. That's well and good, but if you're running a real eBay business you want to present a more professional image than you can by shipping your products in used boxes. Besides, as your volume increases, it gets harder and harder to scrounge up enough recycled boxes to meet your needs.

To establish a professional image and ensure a steady supply of boxes and envelopes, a growing eBay business needs to arrange wholesale purchases of packing supplies. Buying in bulk has the added benefit of costing you less per box; purchase in volume to reduce your packaging costs.

Evaluating Your Packing Needs

Before you write a check for a box of boxes, evaluate your packing needs. There are lots of options available to you, depending on the types and quantity of items you ship.

That said, here's a quick checklist to work through before you start shopping for packing supplies:

Packing Supplies Checklist

❑ What types of products do you typically ship?

❑ What is your shipping volume—how many items do you typically ship each week?

❑ How much packing material is used for each shipment?

❑ Do your shipping needs warrant purchasing packing materials in bulk?

❑ Can you use standard packing boxes and supplies, or do you need custom packaging materials?

❑ Do your shipping services have special requirements for packing materials?

❑ Do your shipping services supply their own free packing boxes and envelopes?

Choosing a Supplier

You can find boxes, envelopes, Styrofoam peanuts, and the like at a variety of different retailers and wholesalers. For example, your local Office Depot or OfficeMax probably has an entire aisle of packing supplies. But just because you find packing supplies there doesn't mean that you're getting the best deal. In fact, these office supply stores typically offer a slim selection at high prices. They're okay in a pinch, but not a good source for buying in bulk.

When it comes to both selection and pricing, there are better choices available. Here are some of the best sources for low-cost boxes, envelopes, and other packing supplies, as recommended by the eBay business masters:

- Bags & Bows (www.bagsandbowsonline.com)
- eSupplyStore (www.esupplystore.com), shown in Figure 6.1

- Onepak (www.onepak.com)
- PackagingSupplies.com (www.packagingsupplies.com)
- Pac-n-Seal (www.packnseal.com)
- Paper Mart (www.papermart.com)
- U.S. Box Corp. (www.usbox.com)
- Uline (www.uline.com)
- Wholesale Packaging (www.wholesale-boxes.net)

FIGURE 6.1

eSupplyStore—a favorite supplier of many eBay sellers.

tip

If you ship items that require temperature-controlled packaging, check out TCP/Reliable Inc. (www.tcpreliable.com).

When you're ordering large quantities of packing materials, it pays to shop for the best price. Pick one or two items that you use regularly and check the prices from several suppliers. It's also a good idea to check the quality from a new supplier before ordering large quantities; order a small quantity to test before you commit to buying in bulk.

Finding Free Packing Supplies

Some shipping services offer free packing supplies to their customers. Depending on what and where you ship, this might be a great way to cut your packaging costs.

For example, the U.S. Postal Service offers a variety of free boxes and envelopes for its Priority Mail service. You can find some of these supplies at your local post office; a greater variety is available online, which is also where you can place bulk orders. Just go to The Postal Store (shop.usps.com) and click the For Mailing/Shipping link. When the next page appears, click the Priority Mail link to see all the supplies available, as shown in Figure 6.2. You can order directly from this page and have your postal carrier deliver them to your door.

FIGURE 6.2

Free Priority Mail boxes and envelopes from the USPS Postal Store.

Another good option, depending on what type of products you sell, is the Postal Service's flat-rate Priority Mail boxes and envelopes. There are several different-sized flat-rate boxes and envelopes available, with equally low flat shipping rates. You pay the same flat shipping rate no matter the weight of what you ship or its destination. Table 6.1 details the flat rate boxes and envelopes available, as of May 14, 2007.

Table 6.1   Flat-Rate Priority Mail Packaging

Order Number	Type	Size	Postage
EP 14-F	Envelope	12 1/2"×9 1/2"	$4.60
0-FRB1	Box	11"×8.5"×5.5"	$8.95
0-FRB2	Box	11 7/8"×3 3/8"×13 5/8"	$8.95

These flat-rate boxes are great when you're shipping small, heavy objects, where the weight would normally kill you in shipping fees. An added benefit is that you can quote a single flat shipping and handling charge in your auction listings.

tip

Another source for free packing supplies is Freecycle (www.freecycle.org), an organization that offers recycled shipping supplies at no charge. The organization is composed of numerous local groups; just locate a group near you and put in your request. (Freecycle is a particularly good place to get Styrofoam peanuts!)

Trick #52: Pack Professionally

The sign of a professional eBay business is the quality of its packaging. Individual sellers might be able to stuff old newspapers in used Amazon.com boxes, but a real eBay business needs to project a more professional image. That not only means using new, quality boxes and envelopes, but also requires sturdy and efficient packing.

Picking the Right Shipping Container

We'll start with the shipping container itself. Your first decision is whether to use a box or an envelope. If you have a very large item to ship, the choice is easy. But what if you have something smaller and flatter, such as a baseball card or a coin? Your choice should be determined by the fragility of your item. If the item can bend or break, choose a box; if not, an envelope is probably a safe choice.

Box or envelope, you need a container that's large enough to hold your item without the need to force it in or bend it in an inappropriate fashion. In addition, make sure that the box has enough extra room to insert cushioning material—but not so big as to leave room for the item to bounce around.

If you're shipping a breakable or bendable item in an envelope, consider using a bubble-pack envelope or reinforcing the envelope with pieces of cardboard. This is especially vital if your item shouldn't be bent or folded.

If you're shipping in a box, make sure that the box is made of heavy, corrugated cardboard. Thinner boxes, such as shoe boxes or gift boxes, simply aren't strong enough for shipping. When packing a box, never exceed the maximum gross weight for the box, which is usually printed on the bottom flap.

Packing the Box

Packing is a skill you can and must develop. Fortunately, there's a bit of logic behind it.

The first step is to cushion the bottom of the box. That means putting a layer of cushioning materials—Styrofoam peanuts are always good, as is shredded paper—in the box, a few inches deep. Now place your item on top of this cushioning layer, and fill up the rest of the box with more peanuts. You want the item itself surrounded by 2"–3" of cushioning on every side.

The item itself might also need to be cushioned against shock, in addition to the box's cushioning. That might mean wrapping it in tissue paper or bubble wrap, depending on its fragility.

tip

When you're shipping books, postcards, and other items that need to stay dry, you should wrap the items in some sort of waterproof packaging. One very effective approach is to seal your item in a plastic gallon freezer bag, and then place it in the envelope or box you normally use.

If your item has any protruding parts, cover them with extra padding or cardboard. And be careful with the bubble wrap: Although it's great to wrap around objects with flat sides, this kind of wrap can actually damage more fragile figurines or items with lots of little pieces and parts sticking out. If the bubble wrap is too tight, it can snap off any appendages during rough handling.

---

tip

If you're shipping several items in the same box, be sure to wrap each one separately (in separate smaller boxes, if you can) and provide enough cushioning to prevent movement and to keep the items from rubbing against each other. Items in the box should be separated from not only each other, they should also be separated from the corners and sides of the box to prevent damage if the box is bumped or dropped.

After you think you're done packing, gently shake the box. If nothing moves, it's ready to be sealed. If you can hear or feel things rattling around inside, however, it's time to add more cushioning material. (If you can shake it, they can break it!)

Different Packaging for Different Items

Packaging differs, of course, depending on the types of items you ship. Here are some specific tricks for packing different types of items:

- **Books**—For normal books, pack in a bubble wrap envelope. For vintage books, wrap in bubble wrap and then pack in a box surrounded by peanuts or other cushioning material.

- **CDs and DVDs**—Pack in appropriately sized bubble wrap envelopes. Don't use unpadded envelopes; you need the bubble wrap padding to protect the item during shipment.

- **Clothing**—Fold the item neatly and place it in a thick poly bag, or even a Ziploc bag. Fold over the open end of the bag and seal it with a piece of tape. Then place the bagged clothing into a Tyvek envelope, a flat-rate Priority Mail envelope, or a box.

- **Coins**—Place in an airtight plastic container. Ship in a padded envelope or small box.

- **Electronics**—Whenever possible, ship the item in its original box. Depending on the item, you might have to put the original box inside a larger, sturdier shipping box; be sure to pad the outer box with plenty of peanuts.

- **Glassware and pottery**—Wrap the item in several layers of tissue paper or foam padding. Stuff all hollow areas with tissue paper. Wrap a layer of bubble wrap around the item and then place it in a box, surrounded by at least 2" of Styrofoam peanuts.

- **Jewelry**—Place each piece of jewelry in tissue paper, and then place it in a Ziploc bag. Wrap the bag with bubble wrap, and then pack it in a small box.

- **Plates and china**—Similar to packing glassware. Wrap each plate individually in tissue paper, and then surround it in bubble wrap. Place it in a box surrounded by peanuts or other cushioning material.

- **Postcards and magazines**—Do not bend or fold. Put the item in a page protector or Ziploc bag, and then sandwich it between two layers of cardboard. Tape the cardboard pieces together at the edges, and then place them in a padded envelope.

- **Stamps**—Encase the stamp in a thin transparent envelope, against a sheet of black construction paper (for show). Then place this envelope inside a larger padded envelope for mailing.

Sealing the Package

After your box is packed, it's time to seal it. A strong seal is essential, so always use tape designed for shipping. Make sure that you securely seal the center seams at both the top and the bottom of the box. Cover all other seams with tape, and be sure not to leave any loose tape or open areas that could snag on machinery.

You should use sealing tape designed for shipping, such as pressure-sensitive tape, nylon-reinforced Kraft paper tape, glass-reinforced pressure-sensitive tape, or water-activated paper tape. Whichever tape you use, the wider and heavier it is, the better. Reinforced is always better than nonreinforced.

note

Don't use wrapping paper, string, masking tape, or cellophane tape to seal your package.

One last thing: If you plan to insure your package, leave an untaped area on the cardboard where your postal clerk can stamp "Insured." (Ink doesn't adhere well to tape.)

Trick #53: Compare Shipping Costs—Then Choose a Single Shipper

Ideally, you pass on your shipping costs—the fee charged by your shipping service—to your customers. There's still value, however, in shopping around for the lowest-cost service; lower shipping charges can win you more customers.

In addition, you want to find the shipping carrier that best fits your business needs. You want a carrier that does a good job with the types of items you sell, offers convenient drop-off or pick-up services, has relatively rapid shipping schedules, and doesn't have a big problem with damaged or lost shipments.

Available Shipping Carriers

You have a number of choices when it comes to shipping your package. I've detailed the services of the major carriers in Table 6.2, along with two shipping examples—a one-pound envelope and a five-pound box, both shipped from New York to Los Angeles.(Note: These rates area a snapshot in time; since rates change often and vary by specific Zip code, don't expect to duplicate the exact rates listed in this table.)

Table 6.2 Major U.S. Shipping Services

Carrier	Website	Service	Delivery Time	Cost of 1-Pound Envelope	Cost of 5-Pound Box
DHL	www.dhl.com	Next Day	1 day	$34.27	$49.39
		2nd Day	2 days	$14.56	$25.65
		Ground	4 days	$4.98	$7.26
FedEx	www.fedex.com	Standard Overnight	1 day	$36.80	$51.98
		2 Day	2 days	$17.05	$28.11
		Express Saver	3 days	$14.69	$23.10
		Home Delivery (Ground)	4 days	$6.89	$9.17
UPS	www.ups.com	Next Day Air Saver	1 day	$36.52	$53.02
		2nd Day Air	2 days	$17.71	$30.14
		3 Day Select	3 days	$13.53	$22.22
		Ground	4 days	$7.27	$10.59
U.S. Postal Service	www.usps.com	Express Mail	1 day	$16.25	$30.70
		Priority Mail	2 days	$4.60	$11.90
		First Class Mail	3 days	N/A	N/A
		Parcel Post	7 days	$3.96	$6.76
		Media Mail (books, CDs, DVDs, and so on)	7 days	$2.13	$3.49

note

USPS First Class Mail is available only for envelopes weighing 13 ounces or less.

Of all these shippers, the one most-used by eBay sellers, large and small, is the U.S. Postal Service. Dealing with the Postal Service is relatively convenient because most sellers have a post office within a short driving distance, and it is set up to easily handle the shipping of small items from individuals. In addition, with so many shipping options available, you're sure to find an option that best fits the type of merchandise you sell.

The one exception to this recommendation is if you're shipping larger, heavier items. The post office doesn't do as good a job with big items as it does with smaller ones, so using an alternative courier is often necessary. For larger items (electronics, artwork, and so on), I like FedEx Ground (AKA Home Delivery). It's relatively affordable and surprisingly fast—plus, you can ship from any FedEx Kinko's location.

Comparing Shipping Services

To compare costs among all these carriers, you can go directly to each site and use its online shipping calculators. Make sure to use the same data for all your price comparisons—size and weight of package, to and from ZIP codes, and type of shipping service or option.

There are also several websites that let you do your price comparisons all in one place. These sites let you input your data and then get rates from all the major carriers. These shipping comparison sites include

- iShip (www.iship.com), shown in Figure 6.3
- RedRoller (www.redroller.com)
- Shipping Sidekick (www.shippingsidekick.com)

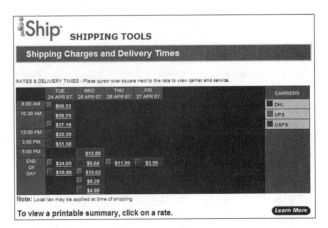

FIGURE 6.3

A comparison of shipping costs from iShip.

Choosing a Single Shipper

The main thing to keep in mind is that you want to, as much as possible, settle on a single shipper and method of shipping for all your eBay sales. The last thing you want to do is to make trips to multiple shipping stations each day, and deal with a myriad number of packing boxes and shipping instructions. It's much more efficient to stock a limited number of box types, travel to a single drop-off location (or schedule a single daily pickup), and learn the shipping rates for a single carrier. You want to minimize the options to maximize your efficiency.

Standardize on a single shipper and you'll make your business's shipping operation much more efficient. Don't standardize, and you'll waste a lot of time unnecessarily.

Trick #54: Establish a Shipping Routine

As your eBay business grows, packing and shipping becomes much more burdensome. This is especially true if the things you ship are different sizes and weights. It's much better if you can standardize what you ship in order to establish a more efficient packing and shipping operation.

It's important that you get your packing and shipping down to a manageable routine. If you find yourself hip-deep in different-sized boxes, and then schlepping those boxes down to the post office every day, you're not doing it right. Read on to learn how to be a more efficient shipper.

Setting a Packing and Shipping Schedule

When you're running a high-volume eBay business, you have to distance yourself from the "ship it immediately" syndrome common to smaller sellers. Novice eBay sellers hover over their computer screens or mailboxes, waiting for payments to come in. As soon as that payment arrives, they rush to send out a confirmation email, print an invoice, and pack the merchandise. Then they hop in the car and drive as fast as possible to the post office, stand in line, and ship the thing out.

This might work when you're selling one item a day (or a week), but not when you have to ship dozens of packages daily. As your shipping volume increases, you have to establish a routine—a schedule that you follow for all your packing and shipping. You have to control your packing and shipping, and not let it control you.

If your sales volume is moderate and your time free, it's okay to pack and ship once a day. But do it at the same time each day, on an appropriate schedule. For example, you might want to pack and ship all items the first thing every morning. This lets you process all payments received the previous day, and then get your orders packed and shipped by noon.

You don't have to ship every day, however. Many high-volume eBay sellers ship only a few days out of the week so that they're not wasting time traveling to the post office every day. You might choose to ship all your packages on Monday, Wednesday, and Friday, for example—or maybe just Tuesday and Friday. Whatever days you choose, you let your paid orders build up until your scheduled shipping day and then get your shipping done all at once.

Creating a Packing Assembly Line

When it comes to packing your items, it pays to have the process down to a science. Have all your boxes and packing material lined up and ready to go so that you can run each item through the "assembly line." Wrap, pack, cushion, seal, and label—that's the routine. And the more uniform the items you sell, the more automated this procedure can become.

What you don't want is to have your routine interrupted. That means not running out of tape or peanuts or having to rush out and purchase a special box just for that one special item. (Which is yet another reason, of course, to standardize the items you sell.) The smoother the process and the fewer interruptions, the faster you can get everything packed and ready to ship.

Getting It There

When it comes to shipping your items, be prepared. If you use the U.S. Postal Service for shipping, try to time your visits so that you don't have to stand in long lines. That means avoiding lunch hour and the last half hour or so before closing; avoiding Mondays and Saturdays; and avoiding peak shipping periods around major holidays, such as Christmas and Valentine's Day. Early morning and mid-afternoon are typically low-volume times at the post office window.

tip

If you have a lot of packages to ship, don't go to the post office by yourself—take a helper. If large shipments are common, invest in a small hand truck to help you cart all those boxes to the counter.

You should also investigate printing your own prepaid shipping labels, which we'll discuss in Trick #55. When you do this, you don't have to stand in line at all; instead, you can either drop off your packages at the front of the line, or arrange to have your packages picked up by your postal carrier.

Trick #55: Print Prepaid Postage Labels

One of the biggest time-savers offered by eBay is the capability to print prepaid shipping labels—that is, labels with prepaid postage. You can do this directly from eBay, via PayPal, for both U.S. Postal Service and UPS shipping. When you print prepaid labels on your own printer, you can arrange for your postal carrier or UPS to pick up the packages from your front door or you can drop them off at any shipping location, without having to stand in line to buy postage.

note

You can also print prepaid postage labels using the USPS Click-N-Ship service (www.usps.com/shipping/label.htm). This is a good choice if you're printing labels for non-eBay items.

You can access eBay's label-printing function from your Closed Auction page. Click the Print Shipping Label button, and (after a quick logon page) you're taken to a Print Your Label page on the PayPal site. You can choose to ship via USPS Priority Mail, Express Mail, Parcel Post, Media Mail, or First Class Mail; you can also select from UPS Next Day Air, Next Day Air Saver, 2nd Day Air, 2nd Day Air AM, 3 Day Select, or Ground. After you complete the shipping form, your PayPal account is billed and the label is sent to your computer's printer; affix the label to the package, and it's ready to go. The buyer is automatically informed via email that the package has shipped.

tip

When you print a prepaid postage label for USPS shipment, you get Delivery Confirmation included at no extra cost.

If you're a high-volume shipper, you can print multiple labels in a single batch using PayPal's MultiOrder Shipping Tool, shown in Figure 6.4. To open this tool, select the Auction Tools tab on the PayPal site and then click Print Multiple Shipping Labels. You can choose to import existing auction listings, or create a new list of ship-to addresses.

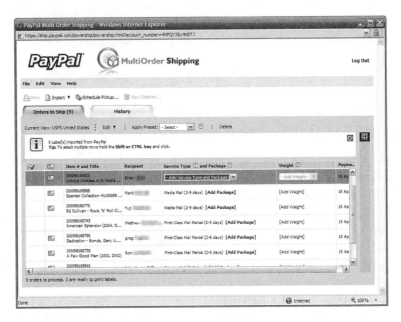

FIGURE 6.4

Print multiple labels with PayPal's MultiOrder Shipping Tool.

The eBay/PayPal combination isn't the only service that lets you print prepaid postage. For higher-volume sellers, check out the services offered by Stamps.com (www.stamps.com) and Endicia Internet Postage (www.endicia.com), both of which offer USPS postage exclusively. These sites let you print sheets of prepaid postage labels from your desktop printer, without having to go to the post office. See each individual site for more details.

Trick #56: Arrange for Daily Pick Up

The more items you sell, the more you ship. The larger and more successful your eBay business gets, the more burdensome the whole shipping process gets—and all those trips to the post office become especially time-consuming.

As you become a heavy shipper, consider setting up an account with a single shipper and arranging daily pickups from your home. This is easy enough to do if you print your own prepaid postage labels because you can have your mail person pick up all your packages when he or she makes normal rounds.

If your volume is high enough, you can also arrange regular pickup service from UPS and FedEx. (You might even get discounted shipping rates, if your pickup volume is high enough.) These carriers can also pick up single items if you arrange so in advance—but at a much higher fee.

Trick #57: Simplify Shipping Fees to Increase Sales

This next trick isn't so much about how to ship, but rather how to use shipping to your best advantage in selling your items. The trick is based on a simple fact: Customers like simplicity. The easier it is for them to understand how much they'll pay for shipping, the more likely it is that they'll bid or buy.

The simplest shipping fee, of course, is a flat one. That is, you quote a single shipping and handling charge to all customers, no matter where they live. For example, you might quote "$5.00 shipping and handling for all domestic orders." That's pretty simple.

Compare that to sellers who offer variable-rate shipping. You can do this via a table in the listing (different rates to ship to different areas of the country), or by using eBay's Shipping Calculator (to calculate exact shipping costs based on specific ZIP codes). Although these methods offer more accurate shipping rates, they're more confusing.

Think like a customer. Do you want to look up your shipping costs in a table, or enter your ZIP code to find out the shipping fee? Or would you rather just know that you'll pay a flat $5.00 (or whatever) for shipping? If you're like most consumers, you prefer the simpler flat rate.

The problem with specifying a single rate, of course, is that the shipping carriers you use seldom charge a single rate. Unless you're using a Postal Service flat-rate package, the rate you pay is predicated on how far the item has to ship (plus the weight and size of the item, of course). The farther you ship the item, the more you pay.

The challenge comes from the fact that until you sell the item, you don't know where you're going to ship it. If you live in California, it could cost several dollars more to ship an item to New York than it would to Seattle. You don't know what rate you'll pay until you sell the item and find out where the seller lives.

There are several ways to approach this problem. As noted earlier, if you're shipping something that fits in a USPS flat-rate shipping box or envelope, you can quote the flat-rate fee to all your customers. (Plus a small handling fee, perhaps.) It doesn't matter where you ship a flat-rate package, the fee is always the same.

Another approach is to calculate an average shipping cost by examining several different possible rates. Figure the shipping costs from your location to either coast (or, if you live on a coast, to Chicago and then to the other coast), and either use the highest cost or an average of the two costs. Some sellers like to quote the highest cost, knowing that they'll make a buck or two if they ship closer to home. Other sellers quote the average cost, knowing that the over and under should cancel out over time.

Whatever the case, remember that you'll attract more bidders and buyers when you quote a flat shipping/handling fee—even if that fee is slightly higher than the actual shipping rate to a given location.

Trick #58: Turn Shipping into a Profit Center

Smart sellers know that shipping can be a profit center. That's right, you can charge a little more than what you actually pay for shipping, and thus generate a small profit over time.

That said, you can generate a profit only if you cover all your costs. To that end, you need to know exactly what costs you incur to ship an item—and *all* the costs. That means the precise shipping rate charged by your shipping carrier, of course, as well as the cost of all your packing materials, including the box, Styrofoam peanuts, shipping label, packing tape, and the like. Add all your costs together, and then charge a set amount or percentage over this cost as a handling fee. Together, the shipping costs and the handling fee comprise the combined shipping and handling fee you charge your customers.

Some eBayers view any charge above and beyond the actual shipping charge as padding the shipping fee, but the charges are legitimate. You do have to pay for all those packing materials, as well as for your time and effort. So, the shipping and handling fee pays the shipping service fee, covers the cost of your supplies, and compensates you for the time involved in the packing and shipping process.

How much extra should you charge for your handling fee? That's for you to decide. Some sellers go 10% or so higher than the actual costs, whereas others tack a flat $1 or $2 onto the costs. You don't want to gouge your customers; they'll accept a reasonable handling fee, but not an outrageous one.

Whatever fee you charge above and beyond your costs is pure profit for your business. Let's say you average an extra dollar for each item you ship, and you ship out 100 items a week. That's over $5,000 in additional profit each year, which is material.

Trick #59: Always Offer Insurance

If you sell a lot of low-priced items, you can skip this trick. But if you sell higher-priced, higher-value, rare, or collectible items, you should seriously consider offering insurance with every item you ship. If you don't and an item is lost or damaged in shipment, you'll have to pay the cost to replace or refund that item from your own bank account. When insurance is purchased, the shipping carrier or insurance company pays for damages, relieving you of the responsibility.

Insurance Options

When it comes to insurance, you have three options. You can offer it as an option for your buyers; you can require that buyers purchase the insurance; or you can purchase the insurance yourself, either absorbing the cost or building it into your shipping and handling fee.

Of these options, I recommend the latter because it's the simpler option for prospective customers. Just factor insurance into your cost structure, and then bump up the shipping and handling fee to cover it. You purchase the insurance as a matter of course when you ship the item, and buyers are insured with no effort from their end.

Paying for Insurance

Every carrier offers some form of shipping insurance. Sometimes the insurance is included as part of the basic shipping fee; in other instances, the insurance has to be purchased separately.

For example, the U.S. Postal Service charges $1.65 to insure items up to $50, $2.05 for items between $50 and $100, and $2.45 for items between $100 and $200. UPS, on the other hand, includes $100 worth of insurance in its basic rates; additional insurance can be purchased for additional cost. (That's one of the important differences between shipping carriers.)

Arranging Third-Party Insurance

You can also arrange shipping insurance via a third-party firm. One of the most popular said firms is Universal Parcel Insurance Coverage (www.u-pic.com), which provides insurance for packages shipped via USPS, UPS, FedEx, and other carriers. There are two advantages to using U-PIC for your shipping insurance: It's cheaper than carrier-provided insurance, and you can do it all from your home computer. The big disadvantage is that it doesn't integrate into your auction checkout or automated end-of-auction emails. As to pricing, U-PIC's rates vary by carrier; for example, it charges $1.10 per $100 of insurance for domestic USPS orders (with Delivery Confirmation), considerably less than what the Postal Service charges.

Also worth checking out is Discount Shipping Insurance (www. dsiinsurance.com). DSI has several plans geared toward eBay sellers, and works with shipments via USPS, UPS, FedEx, and other carriers. DSI's rates also vary by carrier, and are a little lower than those of U-PIC; for example, it charges $0.75 per $100 of insurance for domestic USPS orders (with Delivery Confirmation).

Trick #60: Delight Your Customers—Provide the Unexpected

Experienced businesspeople know that packaging is a form of marketing. How your package looks reflects on you and your business.

It's no surprise, then, that many eBay sellers take special pride in their packaging and the little personal touches they add. It's not just about packaging in a professional manner; it's about going the extra mile to delight your customers when they open the boxes you shipped.

The first thing to consider is printing your own custom boxes. This is an option for only the largest sellers, of course, but if you're shipping out 1,000 items a week, it's worth examining. What you want is a box that has your logo or slogan printed on the side—that way customers will see your advertising before they even open the box.

If custom packaging is out of your league, you can still print custom labels—labels with your store's logo, address, and so forth. This is easy enough to do with any label-making software, or you can print bulk quantities of logo labels to feed into your printer.

What's inside your boxes can also make a big impact. If you have a printed catalog or brochure, include it in all your shipments. This way you use your packaging as promotion for future orders.

Other gestures can also have a big impact. Some sellers insert a business card into each box, with a short "thank you" note handwritten on the back. You can also write a personal "thank you" note on regular note paper, and include that with every order. This type of personal touch goes a long way in cementing the relationship with the customer.

Many sellers also include small gifts in their packages—logo pencils or pens, logo note pads, logo stickers or magnets, wrapped mints or candies, handmade gift tags, greeting cards, and the like. You don't have to spend a lot on these gifts, but they really make an impression on your customers.

Remember, your promotion doesn't end when you make the sale. Use your packaging to create repeat customers—and generate future sales!

Profile: Historic View Postcards

Business Profile

Business name: Historic View Postcards

eBay ID: historic_view_postcards and historic_view_postcards2

Type of business: Historical postcards

Owner: Betsy Linhares and Samuel Mudd

Location: Inverness, Florida

Earlier in this book we profiled Yia Yia's Attic, an eBay business specializing in *ephemera*, or paper-based collectibles. One of the most popular types of ephemera is postcards, which leads to our next business profile.

Betsy Linhares and Sam Mudd run Historic View Postcards, an eBay business that sells nothing but collectible postcards. It's interesting to compare how Yia Yia's Attic and Historic View Postcards are run; there are many similarities, along with a few differences. (For example: The men in both businesses are musicians. What's up with that?) Read on to get acquainted.

Downsizing for Success

Betsy Linhares was in management. Sam Mudd was a touring musician, and then ran his own construction and real estate investment business. They were tired of the rat race, and looking for a way out.

That was eight years ago. At that point, the two of them got interested in eBay, when they were looking to sell Sam's coin collection. Then they picked up an interest in and knowledge of historical postcards from Betsy's father, who was a collector. He taught Betsy and Sam all about postcards, which they applied to the skills they'd picked up selling on eBay.

It took a few years, but their eBay selling eventually grew into a full-time business—and dovetailed into a desire to simplify their lives. As Betsy explains:

Betsy Linhares of Historic View Postcards.

"Year one we decided to make a major change in our lifestyle, so we moved from a large home in the Orlando area to a cottage on a lake in Inverness, Florida. My parents live in Floral City just a stone's throw away. We downsized everything—*big time*. We own only one older model car and, other than a canoe, we have no toys! That first year, we sold our scuba gear, tools, furniture, and bowling balls on eBay. We sold anything that we could ship so we wouldn't have to 'work for the man.' In a nutshell: Goodbye rat race, *hello* simple life!"

Betsy and Sam realized that running their own business on eBay was their key to escaping the hectic corporate world. They get to live life on their terms, not somebody else's.

Today, Betsy and Sam primarily sell postcards of historical town views, dating from 1906 through the 1950s. Occasionally they buy a complete postcard collection and end up with various ephemera items—old magazines, company letterheads, and the like. But their selling revolves around those historical view postcards that give the business its name.

Most important, they're in control of their own lives. As Betsy notes, "Every single morning, we get up at 3:00 a.m. with java and jump on our computers. Sunday through Tuesday we put auctions on eBay. Wednesday through Friday we dedicate to our crafts. Saturday is yard/house cleaning day."

Betsy and Sam's success is on their terms: "We took our life experiences," Betsy says, "and asked many questions. We make just enough money to stay alive. Maybe that's all one needs."

Selling Strategies

Like Barbara and Steve of Yia Yia's Attic, Betsy and Sam sell exclusively in the eBay auction format. They don't have a separate website, and they don't run an eBay Store. They tried doing the Store thing, but then closed it up. Here was Betsy's experience:

"I opened a store last year for about eight months and then I figured out it wasn't profitable for us. In fact, we lost money and it was too much work."

So, it's all auctions, all the time for Historic View Postcards. On average, they list about 100 auctions a week. They have a very high close rate, with 60%–75% of their listings selling through. That's a pretty good sell-through percentage.

Finding and Managing Inventory

Where do Betsy and Sam find the postcards they sell? "Collectibles, antique, and postcard shows," Betsy says, along with "antique stores, auctions, flea markets, and garage sales."

They do most of their buying December through February, when the "snowbirds" come to Florida for the postcard shows. (Location *does* matter!) They sell that inventory during the summer months and start all over the following December.

When it comes to inventory management, simpler is better. They keep their postcards in a closet, organized alphabetically, topically, and by state.

Managing the Business

I asked Betsy how they manage their business on a day-to-day basis. Here's how she replied:

"I guess you could say we manage our auction activity the old-fashioned way, mixed with a tad of technology. As the auctions are listed, the item (mostly postcards) is put in an envelope with the last four numbers of the *very long* eBay auction number written on it, in a chronological order. We put the postcard in a box (Sam uses a shoe box) and then store it on a shelf in our office until the auction closes.

"Once the auction closes (seven days later), we process: send invoices via eBay, print out addresses, package, and ship. If the item is paid with PayPal, we give feedback and email the buyer to let them know their item is being shipped ASAP. This is usually the next day or two."

They ship their postcards in well-protected packaging, in most cases as soon as they receive payment. Betsy notes that they go to the post office every other day or so.

Approximately 80% of their payments come through PayPal. Betsy and Sam like PayPal because it's "virtually goof-proof." PayPal's process also helps them keep track of their buyers and orders.

Communicating Is Key

Betsy and Sam pride themselves in their prompt and copious communications with customers. As they say, "Answer all emails and communicate with your buyers—when you receive their payment and when you ship let them know via email."

They do this via a series of draft emails they send out at various times in the post-sale process. By using precomposed emails, they save a lot of time and still keep in touch with their buyers. For example, when an auction closes they send out the following email:

> *Thank you for your address/update.*
>
> *When I receive your payment, I will email you, ship your lot and at that time, you will receive positive feedback. When you receive your item, we hope you will return the favor.*
>
> *Packaging: FOR EXTRA PROTECTION ADD $1.00 (EACH) IF YOU WOULD LIKE YOUR POSTCARD IN AN ARCHIVAL SAFE HARD PLASTIC SLEEVE.*
>
> *I offer the Hard Sleeves as Extra protection for FUTURE storage. When shipped, all Items mailed securely packaged in a Poly Sleeve & cardboard with a Sturdy Padded Mailer (Stamped "DO NOT BEND"). The sleeves the postcards arrive in are polypropylene sleeves, and are archivally safe, are chemically stable, and have a neutral pH.*

When they receive payment, the next email is sent:

> *Thank you for your prompt payment! Your lot is on the way & you have positive feedback!*
>
> *Please email me when you receive your lot and when convenient—we always appreciate feedback.*
>
> *Keep an eye on our AUCTIONS as we are always buying historic postcards & paper.*
>
> *It has been a pleasure doing business with you.*

They even send out an email after a customer leaves feedback, which is a very nice touch. Here's that final bit of positive communication, which serves as positive branding and promotion for future sales:

> *Thank you for your email and the exchange of Feedback. I am glad you are happy with your purchase.*
>
> *It has been a pleasure doing business with you and I look forward to our next transaction.*
>
> *Keep an eye on our AUCTIONS as we are always buying historic paper and postcards.*

Keys to Success

When it comes to auction success, Sam and Betsy know that, in their product category, it's the pictures that are the most important detail. In each listing, they show clear, precise pictures or scans that show every flaw and detail. As they note, "Always show the front and back of everything—no matter what."

I asked Betsy and Sam for any advice they might give to aspiring eBay businesspeople. Here's how they replied:

"Check out like auctions. It's best to start by listing just a few items—and then add more auctions as you feel comfortable. Always ship the items timely and in appropriate containers so they arrive undamaged."

Finally, Betsy returns to the idea that eBay can help you simplify your life. Here are her parting words:

Condition of cards is as seen in photo. Front and back of cards are both shown. If additional information on condition or publishers name is needed, please feel free to email me.

A typical auction listing from Historic View Postcards—big front and back scans.

"If I can pass on any words of wisdom to America, it is to live a simple life. I am living proof that you can do it in four easy steps. Be nice, eat right, exercise, and burn those credit cards! NOW!"

And, of course, turn to eBay to help you take control of your new life.

7

Tricks for Promoting Your eBay Business

You can put 1,000 listings on eBay and not get a single bite—especially if nobody knows about them. Yes, your auction listings show up in eBay's search results when customers go searching, but that's not very proactive marketing. (And you can't rely on eBay's search results if you have an eBay Store because Store listings don't normally show up in eBay's search results.)

To establish your eBay business and drive customers to your listings, you need to promote your business. That means employing advertising, publicity, and other marketing devices—just like the pros do!

Trick #61: Brand Your Business—And Market It

You have a choice. You can promote individual item listings or you can promote your business as a whole. (Or, of course, you can do both; they're not mutually exclusive.)

This is an important point. Many sellers have the initiative to promote the items they sell, but don't have the foresight to promote their businesses. Naturally, promoting an item listing can help that item sell, but it doesn't do much good for you in the long term. When you promote your business, however, you create long-term awareness—and help to promote your short-term item listings.

The first step toward promoting your business is to create a business identity—that is, you brand your business. A brand identity defines your business, tells the world what business you're in, and how your

business is unique. Without a brand identity, you're just another anonymous eBay seller. With proper branding, you stand out from the crowd
with a unique and memorable identity.

The ABCs of Branding

What's involved in establishing your brand? There are a lot of separate
steps to take, but I like to think of them collectively as the ABCs of
branding:

A: **Tell 'em who you are**—Give your business a name. You're not just
JoeSmith014; you're Joe's Discount Aardvark Accessories, or
Aardvarks 'R' Us, or Aardvark Emporium, or International Aardvark
Supplies, or Aardvark Super Warehouse, or Aardvark Boutique, or
the like. Your business needs a unique name that conveys what you
sell and how you sell it (Discount? Warehouse? Boutique?), along
with a little bit of your personality.

B: **Tell 'em what you do**—Tell your customers what you sell. That can
(and probably should) be part of your brand name; if not, it can be
conveyed in a tag line or as part of your logo. And it pays to be specific—you don't want retail shoe customers calling you up if you're a
footwear wholesaler.

C: **Tell 'em what you can do for them**—Now we move beyond the
name and logo to your brand's positioning. It's important that customers know what your business can do for them. You might be Joe's
Discount Aardvark Accessories, but what does that mean? The
unique benefit offered by your business becomes clearer when you
say "Lowest prices on the Web" or "Biggest selection of custom accessories" or "We provide custom solutions" or something similar. Why
should a customer buy from your business? That is the question you
have to answer.

Establishing the Brand

Theory aside, what concrete steps do you need to take to establish your
brand? Here's the short list:

- **Business philosophy**—Before you do anything else, stop and think
about what it is that makes your business unique. Use the ABCs of
marketing to help define what type of business you want to run.
Are you the lowest-priced retailer? Or the one with the biggest selection? Or the one with the best customer service? (It's difficult, if not

impossible, to be all these things simultaneously.) Equally important is to define who your customer is; you don't sell to everyone, but rather a targeted segment of the overall market. Determine what it is that makes your business what it is, and then define your business's philosophy based on this.

- **Name**—After you know who you are, you need to give your business a name. Make it short yet memorable; you want customers to easily remember who you are.

- **Slogan**—Many businesses have a slogan or tagline that accompanies their business name. This slogan should express your business philosophy, and further define what it is you do.

- **Logo**—People remember pictures. That's why a visual logo is important to a business. When you see a big block "M" with the smaller scribbled "TV," you know you're seeing the MTV logo. When you see a lowercase "ups" in the middle of a brown shield or the purple and orange "FedEx," you know you're seeing the UPS or FedEx logos. A logo should be distinctive and easily recognizable. It can be as simple as your business name in a specific font, or as fancy as a stylized graphic. You can even incorporate your business slogan in your logo, if you want.

Reinforcing the Brand

The previous steps establish your brand. Now you need to reinforce and promote the brand. How do you do this?

The first thing you want to do is make the logo the dominant part of your business presence. That means plastering your logo on everything you do—your website, your eBay Store, and every single item listing. You also want to put your logo and slogan on your shipping labels, invoices, business cards, boxes, and envelopes. And, of course, if you create printed brochures or catalogs, as well as print or online advertisements, your logo should be prominently displayed.

tip

Whatever promotion you do, make it consistent. The key to effective branding is consistency. Use the same logo and slogan in everything you do; don't switch things up.

You want your customers to know that they're dealing with your particular business. Yes, they're buying a specific item, but they're buying it from *you*. It's the *you* they need to remember the next time they're in the market for something you sell. After all, you remember FedEx—even if you don't remember a specific visit to one of its stores.

Trick #62: Link to Your Other Listings

Although it's important to promote your overall business, you also have to promote the individual items you have for sale. With eBay, that means promoting your auctions and eBay Store listings.

Linking to Your Other Listings

The most obvious place to promote the items you're selling is through the other items you're selling. After all, if you have potential customers interested in one thing you're selling, why not show them what else you have for sale? You'd be surprised how many customers can turn into purchasers of multiple items—and those extra sales are especially profitable.

eBay helps you promote your other listings by including a View Seller's Other Items link in the Meet the Sellers section of all item listing pages, as shown in Figure 7.1; this links to a page that lists all your current listings. If you have an eBay Store, there's also a link to your Store in the same place.

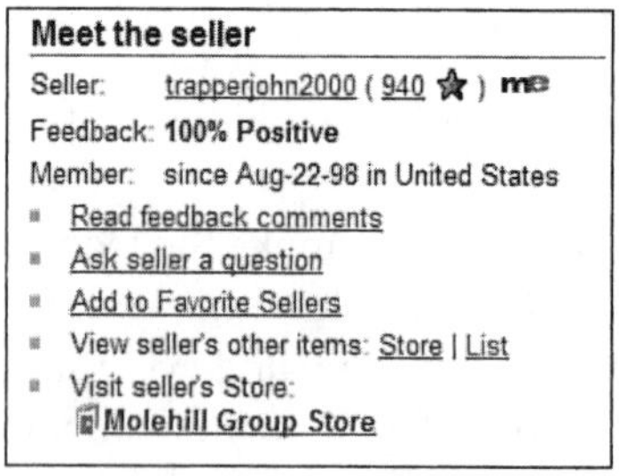

Meet the seller

Seller: trapperjohn2000 (940 ⭐) m☰

Feedback: **100% Positive**

Member: since Aug-22-98 in United States
- Read feedback comments
- Ask seller a question
- Add to Favorite Sellers
- View seller's other items: Store | List
- Visit seller's Store:
  🏠Molehill Group Store

FIGURE 7.1

Links to your other listings and eBay Store.

Unfortunately, many buyers tend to overlook these links. For this reason, you might want to emphasize your other auctions by including other, more prominent links in your item listings.

When you want to link to your active listings, insert the following HTML code in your item description:

```
<a href="http://cgi6.ebay.com/ws/eBayISAPI.dll?
➥ ViewSellersOtherItems&amp;userid=USERID&amp;include=0&amp;since=-
➥ 1&amp;sort=3&amp;rows=50&amp;sspageName=DB:OtherItems"
➥ target=_blank>
Check out my other items!
</a>
```

Naturally, you should replace USERID with your own eBay user ID. You can also replace the Check out my other items! text with any text of your choosing.

To add a link to your eBay Store to your listings, insert the following HTML code into your item description:

```
<a href="http://stores.ebay.com/StoreName" target=_blank>
Check out my eBay Store!
</a>
```

Replace StoreName with your eBay Store name. Again, you can replace the tagline with text of your own liking.

Linking from Other Sites to Your eBay Listings

You can also link to your eBay listings or eBay Store from other websites, using the same HTML code just described. You can also add an eBay button, like the one shown in Figure 7.2, to your business or personal web pages. When visitors click this button, they go to your Items for Sale page, which lists all your current auctions.

FIGURE 7.2

Add an eBay button to any web page.

To add this button to a web page, go to the Link Your Site to eBay page, located at pages.ebay.com/services/buyandsell/link-buttons.html. Check the box next to the My Listings on eBay button, enter the URL of the page where you want to display the button, scroll to the bottom of the page, and click the I Agree button. When the next page appears, copy the generated HTML code, and paste it into the code for your web page.

Linking to Your eBay Store

Building a link to your eBay Store is a bit more complicated. Start by going to the HTML Builder page (cgi6.ebay.com/ws/eBayISAPI.dll? StoreHtmlBuilderHome), shown in Figure 7.3. From there you can build links to individual items, specific Store pages (including your Store's home page), and a Store search page. Click the appropriate link and then follow the instructions to build the link.

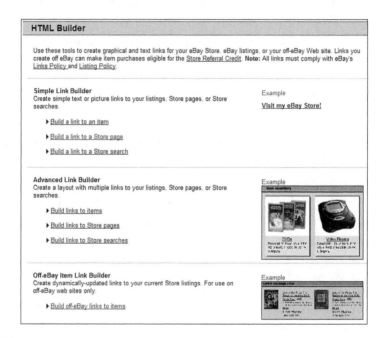

FIGURE 7.3

Build links to your eBay Store pages.

Trick #63: Set Up Product Cross-Promotions

Cross-promoting is a powerful tool to drive potential customers to the items you have for sale. If you have an eBay Store, you can scroll down to the bottom of any of your eBay listings (Store or auction) and see a cross-promotion box like the one shown in Figure 7.4. This box displays four other items you have for sale, and serves as a powerful advertisement for those items.

FIGURE 7.4

A typical eBay cross-promotion box.

This cross-promotion box is available to all eBay Store sellers, and is managed via the Cross-Promotions Tool. You use the Cross-Promotions Tool to determine which items display in which boxes—vary the items based on the types of products you're selling.

To manage your cross-promotions, go to your My eBay Summary page, scroll to the Manage My Store section, and click the Manage My Store link. When the Manage My Store page appears, go to the Marketing Tools section and click the Cross-Promotion Settings link. From there you can turn on or off cross-promotion, determine how you want to cross-promote, choose how your cross-promoted items appear, and so on.

In addition to these settings, you can configure what items display, based on product categories within your Store. To do this, click the Cross-Promotions Defaults link on the Manage My Store page. When the next page appears, click the Create New Rule link to link the display of products in a given category to the type of product viewed by a customer. For example, if you're a bookseller, you might want to display your active mystery books when someone is looking at or bidding on another book in the mystery category.

Trick #64: Encourage Add-On Sales

It costs less to sell additional items to an existing customer than it does to attract a new customer. That is, after you have someone hooked, additional profits come easily—if you can sell more items to that person.

To that end, it's in your best interest to encourage add-on sales. Instead of selling one shirt to a customer, try to sell two shirts instead—or a shirt and tie, or shirt and shoes, or whatever. Adding extra items to an existing sale doesn't cost you any more money in terms of promotion; it's a quick way to boost your profit per sale.

How do you encourage add-on sales? Here are some tricks to employ:

- Make sure to present your customers with a prominent link to your other eBay listings. This should be more than the default link that eBay creates; place a bigger link or clickable button within the body of your listing.

- Make it just as easy for the customer to view the listings in your eBay Store. Then, within your Store, make sure that you offer items that are complementary to the item the customer just purchased. If you're selling shoes, for example, your eBay Store should offer socks and shoe polish; if you're selling DVD players, offer connecting cables in your Store.

tip

Another reason to drive additional sales to your eBay Store is that eBay's Store listing fees are much lower than auction listing fees.

- Offer a combined shipping discount so that when the customer decides to purchase a second item, he doesn't pay double the shipping. Instead, offer some sort of deal, such as "$1.00 shipping for each additional item purchased."

- Offer a discount on additional items purchased. Maybe you offer a 10% discount on any items added to a purchase, or something similar—anything to encourage customers to add more items to their shopping cart.

However you accomplish it, the goal is to turn a $20 sale into a $30 one. The higher dollar value per sale, the higher your profit margin.

Trick #65: Optimize Your Listings for Search

Here's the deal: Fewer than 10% of customers find your listings by browsing. Fully 90% of eBay buyers find items by using eBay's search function. That means you need to optimize your listings so that your items show up when customers are searching for similar items.

There's another reason why you want to optimize your listings for search. You see, your listings show up not only in eBay search results, but also when web users use Google, Yahoo!, and other sites to search the Web. If your listings are heavy with the right keywords, they'll show up in Google and Yahoo! search results—which is free publicity for your items.

For eBay's search results, it's the title you need to focus on. That's because eBay's search function, by default, searches only listing titles. (There's an advanced option to search the listing description, but not all buyers use it.) So, you'll need to cram as many relevant keywords into the listing title as you can.

Web search engines, on the other hand, search your entire listing—title *and* description. So, you have more to work with there. How do you optimize your listings for web search engines? Here are a few tricks:

- **Include appropriate keywords**—What goes for the listing title is also important for the item description. You want to make sure that your item description contains the keywords that customers might use to search for your item. If you're selling a drum set, for example, make sure that your description includes words such as *drums, drum-set percussion, cymbals, snare,* and the like. Try to think through how *you* would search for this item, and work those keywords into your content.

- **Create a clear organization and hierarchy**—The crawler programs used by Google and Yahoo! can find more content on a web page if that content is in a clear hierarchical organization. You want to think of your item description as a mini-outline. The most important information should be in major headings, with lesser information in subheadings beneath the major headings. One way to do this is via standard HTML heading tags, or just normal first-, second-, and third-level headings within your listing.

- **Put the most important information first**—Think about hierarchy and think about keywords, and then think about how these two concepts work together. That's right, you want to place the most important keywords higher up on your page. Search crawlers crawl only so far, and you don't want them to give up before key information is found. In addition, search engine page rank is partially determined by content; the more important the content looks to be on a page (as determined by placement on the page), the higher the page rank will be.

- **Make the most important information look important**—Many search engines look to highlighted text to determine what's important on a page. It follows, then, that you should make an effort to format keywords in your description as bold or italic.

- **Use text instead of or in addition to images**—Here's something you might not think about. At present, search engines parse only text content; they can't figure out what a picture or graphic is about unless you describe in the text. So, if you use graphic buttons or banners (instead of plain text) to convey important information, the search engine simply won't see it. You need to put every piece of important information somewhere in the text of the page—even if it's duplicated in a banner or graphic.

tip

If you do use images in your description (and you should), make sure that you use the <ALT> tag for each image, and assign meaningful keywords to the image via this tag. Search engines will read the <ALT> tag text; they can't figure out what an image is without it.

Trick #66: Create an Email Mailing List

Savvy sellers keep good records of all their past auctions—and past buyers. Then you can create a list of buyers who want to be contacted when you have similar merchandise for sale. (Make this an opt-in list; you don't want to spam anyone.) When you have new items for sale, send out emails to interested customers, and watch the orders arrive!

The easiest way to create an email mailing list is through eBay. If you run an eBay Store, eBay offers free email marketing; it's a nice perk, and it really works. eBay lets you add a Sign Up for Store Newsletter link to all your listings, and then create up to five different mailing lists to target different types of customers or product categories. You can even use eBay's email marketing tools to measure the success of your email newsletters, which makes it easier to fine-tune your promotions in the future.

All eBay Store owners can send a total of 5,000 free emails a month to subscribers. If you want to send more than this, you'll pay an additional penny per email for each message above the base 5,000.

Creating an Email Mailing List

To create a new email mailing list, follow these instructions:

1. Go to My eBay and click the Marketing Tools link.
2. When the Marketing Tools: Summary page appears, click the Email Marketing link in the Store Marketing section.
3. When the Email Marketing: Summary page appears, as shown in Figure 7.5, click the Create Mailing List button.

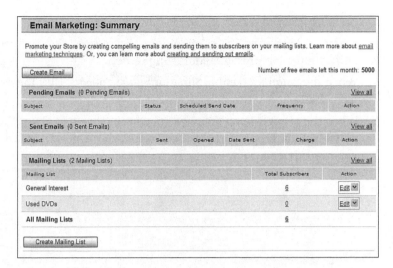

FIGURE 7.5

The Email Marketing: Summary page.

4. When the next page appears, enter a name for this mailing list, and then click the Save button.

That's it; your mailing list now appears on the Email Marketing: Summary page.

Adding Subscribers

You can't manually add subscribers to your mailing lists. Subscribers have to opt in of their own accord, which they do from your item listings and eBay Store pages. Whenever users add you to their favorite sellers list, they have the option of subscribing to your email newsletter. In addition, they can sign up when they visit your eBay Store by clicking the Sign Up for Store Newsletter link at the top of the page.

Once someone has subscribed to your newsletter, they appear in the subscriber list at the bottom of the Email Marketing: Summary page. You can manage the list of subscribers by clicking the Email Marketing Subscriber Lists link; the resulting page lets you block subscribers from receiving emails.

Sending Emails

To create an email newsletter and send it to your subscriber list, follow these steps:

1. Go to My eBay and click the Marketing Tools link.

2. When the Marketing Tools: Summary page appears, click the Email Marketing link in the Store Marketing section.

3. When the Email Marketing: Summary page appears, click the Create Email button.

4. When the Select a Template page appears, as shown in Figure 7.6, pull down the Type of Email list and select what type of newsletter you want to send.

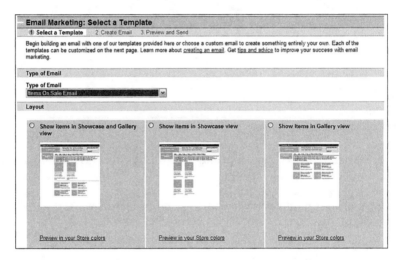

FIGURE 7.6

Selecting a template for your email newsletter.

5. Still on the Select a Template page, select a template for your email newsletter, and then click the Continue button.

6. When the Create Email page appears, as shown in Figure 7.7, enter the necessary information: which mailing list(s) you're sending to, whether to send emails on an automatic schedule, whether to display your Store header, the subject of the newsletter, the message of the newsletter, which items you want to showcase or list, and whether to display your feedback. When finished, click the Preview & Continue button.

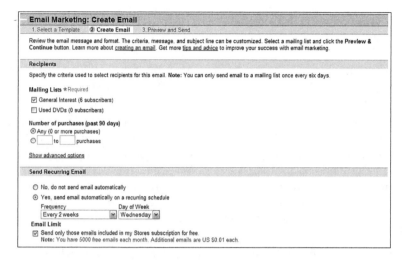

FIGURE 7.7
Creating your email newsletter.

7. The next page displays a preview of your newsletter, as shown in Figure 7.8. If you need to edit anything, click the Edit Email button. If you like what you see, click the Send Email button to send the email to your selected recipients.

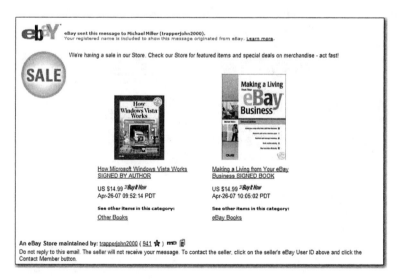

FIGURE 7.8
Your email newsletter, ready to send.

Trick #67: Gain Exposure by Writing Reviews and Guides

Here's an interesting way to promote your business and your listings. You can use eBay's Reviews and Guides to establish yourself as an expert in your field, and thus gain more exposure for your business.

You might not be familiar with the Guides and Reviews features; they're both relatively new. eBay Reviews are product reviews, written by eBay members; you can find product reviews for CDs, home audio receivers, golf clubs, and so on. Guides are more detailed how-tos that present useful information and buying advice; these are available for a number of different topics, and include both buying guides and more informational guides (Techniques for Drumset Recording, How to Plan the Perfect Vacation, and so on).

Anyone can write a Review or Guide—including you. And when users read your Reviews and Guides, they're likely to click through to your item listings or eBay Store.

Writing a Product Review

Writing a product review is quite easy. You don't have to bother supplying product details, such as model number, or dimensions, or whatever; all you have to supply is your opinion. Just follow these steps:

1. Go to the main Reviews & Guides page (reviews.ebay.com), shown in Figure 7.9.

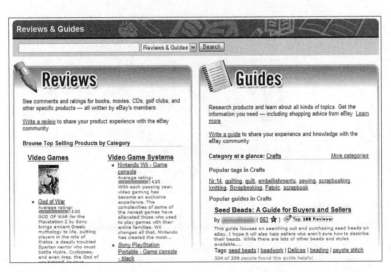

FIGURE 7.9

eBay's Reviews and Guides.

2. Use the search box at the top of the page to search for the particular product you want to review.

3. When the list of matching products appears, click the link for that product's review page.

4. When the product review page appears, select the Reviews tab and then scroll down to the bottom of the page and click the Write a Review or Be the First to Review It link.

5. When the Write a Review page appears, as shown in Figure 7.10, enter a title for your review. The title can be up to 55 characters in length.

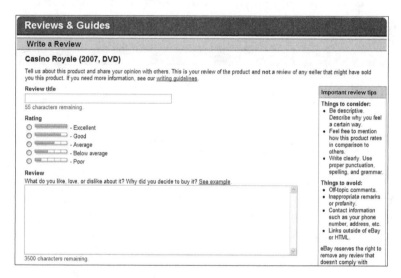

FIGURE 7.10

Writing your own product review.

6. Give the product a rating, from 1 to 5 (5 being excellent; 1 being poor).

7. Type your full review into the Review box. The review can be up to 3,500 characters long.

8. When you're done with your review, click the Submit Review button.

That's it; your review will now be listed among the other reviews for that particular product.

Creating a Guide

The process for writing a Guide is similar to writing a Review, although here it really helps if you're an expert or otherwise uniquely experienced with the topic at hand—that is, if you know enough to write a useful Guide. (Ideally, of course, you will be an expert in what you're selling.) Follow these steps:

1. Go to the main Reviews & Guides page (reviews.ebay.com).

2. Click the Write a Guide link.

3. When the Write a Guide page appears, as shown in Figure 7.11, enter a title for your Guide. The title can be up to 55 characters in length.

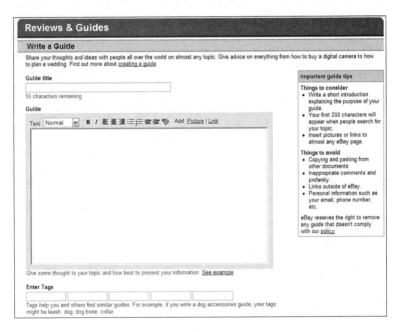

FIGURE 7.11

Creating a new Guide.

4. Type the text for your Guide into the Guide box. Remember that the first 200 characters of your Guide will be all that appears when people search for Guides by topic.

tip

Use the formatting controls at the top of the Guide box to make your Guide more readable and visually appealing. You can also use these controls to add pictures and links to your Guide. Click the Preview button at the bottom of the page to see how your formatted Guide looks.

5. Enter up to five "tags" that other members can use as keywords to search for your Guide.

6. When you're done with your Guide, click the Save and Continue button.

Fairly easy, although I recommend composing and editing your guide offline (in Microsoft Word, perhaps), and then cutting and pasting the completed text into the Guide box. This way you can take your time writing and researching, and just paste the final result into the eBay page.

Trick #68: Use Google AdWords

There's nothing to stop you from advertising your eBay listings on other websites outside of eBay. Perhaps the best way to do this is with a web placement service, such as Google AdWords. The AdWords program lets you "buy" keywords, and then display a "sponsored link" on the search results pages for that keyword. For example, if you buy the word *Hummel*, your sponsored link will appear on the results page anytime a Google user searches for the word *Hummel*. (Figure 7.12 shows some typical sponsored links.)

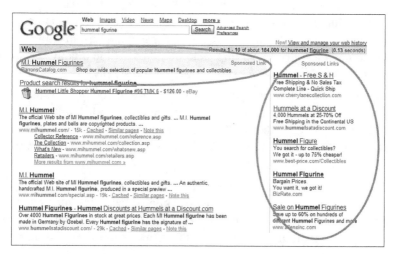

FIGURE 7.12

Sponsored links on a Google search results page—at the top and on the side.

In addition to the sponsored links on its own website, the AdWords program also places ads on third-party websites that feature similar content. (Figure 7.13 shows a typical AdWords ad.) This ensures that your advertising reaches qualified consumers who are interested in what you're offering; you're not blanketing the market blind, you're targeting specific consumers.

FIGURE 7.13

A typical Google AdWords website ad.

You can purchase ads for your eBay Store or for individual item listings. To do so, you first have to sign up for the AdWords program, which you do at adwords.google.com.

Determining Your Costs—And Choosing a Payment Option

Advertising with Google AdWords isn't like a traditional advertising buy; there are no contracts and deadlines and such. You pay a one-time $5.00 activation fee, and then are charged either on a cost-per-click (CPC) or cost-per-thousand-impressions (CPM) basis. (You can choose either payment method.) You control your costs by specifying how much you're willing to pay (per click or per impression) and by setting a daily spending budget. Google will never exceed the costs you specify.

How much does AdWords cost? It's your choice. If you go with the cost-per-click method, you can choose a maximum CPC click price from $0.01 to $100. If you go with the CPM method, there is a minimum cost of $0.25 per 1,000 impressions. Your daily budget can be as low as a penny, up to whatever you're willing to pay.

If you go the CPC route, Google uses AdWords Discounter technology to match the price you pay with the price offered by competing advertisers for a given keyword. The AdWords Discounter automatically monitors your competition and lowers your CPC to one cent above what they're willing to pay.

You can opt to prepay your advertising costs or to pay after your ads start running. With this last option, Google charges you after 30 days or when you reach your initial credit limit of $50, whichever comes first. Google accepts payment via credit card, debit card, direct debit, or bank transfer.

Creating an AdWords Ad

It's surprisingly easy to create and activate an AdWords ad. You need to determine which keywords you want to buy upfront, of course, but from there it's a simple matter of filling in the appropriate web forms. Here's how it works:

1. From the Google AdWords home page (adwords.google.com), click the Start Now button.

2. When the next page appears, as shown in Figure 7.14, choose either the Starter Edition or Standard Edition option. (If this is your first time listing, I recommend going the Starter Edition route—which is what I'll discuss throughout the rest of these numbered steps.) Also check the I Have a Webpage option, and then click Continue.

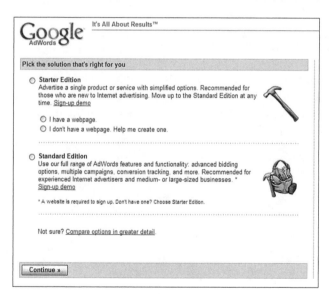

FIGURE 7.14

Choosing either the Starter Edition or Standard Edition solutions.

3. When the next page appears, enter your location and language.

4. Scroll to the Write Your Ad section, shown in Figure 7.15, and enter the following information: the URL of the website you want to add to

link to, your ad's title (25 characters max), and two lines of text (35 characters max each).

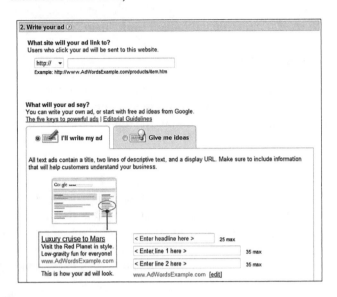

FIGURE 7.15

Entering information about your ad.

5. Scroll to the Choose Keywords section, shown in Figure 7.16, and enter up to 20 keywords that you want your ad linked to. (Enter one keyword or phrase per line; a "keyword" can actually be a multiple-word phrase.)

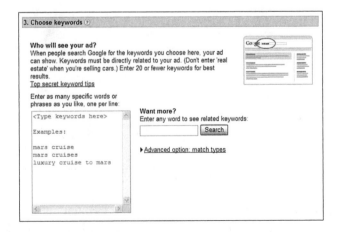

FIGURE 7.16

Entering the keywords you want to purchase.

6. Scroll to the Choose Your Currency section and enter the currency you'll be paying in.

7. Scroll to the Set Your Budget section and select your monthly AdWords budget—$50, $100, $250, or a custom amount.

8. If you want to, scroll to the Future Contact section to sign up to receive Google promotional materials.

9. When you finish entering information on this page, click the Continue button.

10. Google now prompts you to sign in to your Google account or to create a new AdWords-specific account. Follow the onscreen instructions to proceed.

11. Google will now email you with instructions on how to set up billing information for your account. Follow the instructions in this email to activate your account and launch your ads.

If you chose a Standard Edition campaign, you have a few more options to consider. In contrast to the Starter Edition, the Standard Edition lets you:

- Create multiple ads (instead of the Starter Edition's single ad)
- Choose from a variety of pricing options, including keyword-specific bidding, content bidding, ad position preference, and so on
- Target specific websites for ad placement
- Utilize a variety of advanced planning and reporting tools, including the AdWords traffic estimator, conversion tracking, and a variety of sophisticated statistics and reports

As I said earlier, the Starter Edition is probably the best way for most eBay sellers to get started. After you have a few ad campaigns under your belt, you can graduate to the advanced options available with the Standard Edition.

Monitoring Your Ads' Performance

When your ad campaign is underway, you can monitor performance from the main AdWords page. After signing in to this page, select the My Ad Campaign tab, shown in Figure 7.17. You can view the performance of each keyword you selected, in terms of impressions, clicks, and total cost to-date.

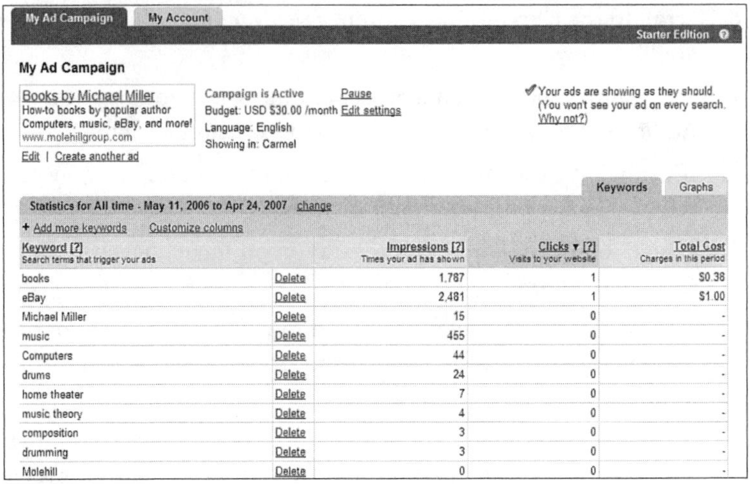

FIGURE 7.17

Viewing the performance of your ad campaign.

This page also lets you change the parameters of your campaign. You can add more keywords (by clicking the Add More Keywords link) or delete existing keywords (by clicking the Delete link next to an individual keyword). You can also upgrade to the Standard Edition option at any time by clicking the Graduate to Standard Edition link.

If you buy the right keywords, you should be able to drive significant traffic to your eBay Store or individual listings. That said, the cost of this advertising is such that you probably want to use it only with higher-priced items—or to advertise entire categories within your Store.

Trick #69: Feed Your Store Listings to Google Product Search

Google Product Search (formerly known as Froogle) is Google's search engine for online shopping. Shoppers can use Google Product Search (www.google.com/products), shown in Figure 7.18, to find specific items online and to compare prices between different retailers.

If you're an eBay Store seller, you want your items to appear in Google Product Search results. This way anyone searching Google Product Search for your type of item will see your listing, and be able to link to eBay to make a bid or purchase.

FIGURE 7.18

Google Product Search—a search engine for online shoppers.

How do you list your items with Google Product Search? You could wait for Google's crawler program to find all the items in your store and feed that information to the Google Product Search database, but that's a hit-or-miss proposition. (This method also takes too long.) A better approach is to manually submit your product listings to Google.

To do this, go to My eBay, click the Marketing Tools link, then click the Listing Feeds link. This displays the Listing Feeds page; check the option to Make a File of Your Store Inventory Listings Available.

You upload this file to Google by going to the Google Base page (base.google.com) and clicking the Bulk Upload link. You'll need to select an item type for your product upload, register the upload with Google, and then perform the upload.

The items you upload are submitted both to Google Product Search and to Google Base, which is Google's version of online classified ads. And the best thing is that both submissions are totally free!

Trick #70: Promote Your eBay Listings in the Real World

Finally, let's not neglect all the traditional means of advertising available offline, in the real world. Although these methods are probably better suited for advertising an eBay Store (or individual categories within your Store), they can be low-cost ways to drive more business online.

The key to advertising in the real world is to use your eBay Store URL.
Take that URL and plaster it everywhere:

- On business cards
- On letterhead
- In flyers you post locally
- On promotional materials you hand out to customers and col-
  leagues—hats, pens, notepads, and the like
- In classified advertisements in your local newspaper
- In small display ads in your local newspaper
- In classified or display ads in hobbyist and trade magazines and
  periodicals
- On the packing slips you send out with the items you sell
- If you have a bricks-and-mortar location, on your store invoices and
  shopping bags

The key is to put that URL *everywhere* you can. The more people who see
the URL, the more people who go online to check out your eBay Store.
And, as you know, the more Store visitors you have, the more sales
you'll make!

tip

Don't forget non-eBay online advertising. You can include your eBay Store URL
in all your personal and business email messages (as part of your signature), in
newsgroup and forum postings, in blog postings, and so forth.

eBAY BUSINESS PROFILE

Profile: Balkowitsch Enterprises, Inc.

Business Profile

Business name: Balkowitsch Enterprises, Inc.

eBay ID: balkowitsch

eBay Store: stores.ebay.com/Balkowitsch-Enterprises-Inc

Website: www.balkowtisch.com

Type of business: Medical, health, wellness, fitness, and beauty items

Owner: Shane Balkowitsch

Location: Bismarck, North Dakota

Would you believe that one of the largest businesses on eBay is located in Bismarck, North Dakota? Or that it started by listing three items normally sold from a booth at a local antique mall? Or that it's grown from $65 in sales its first month to more than $500,000 in sales a month today—fewer than 10 years later? Or that just six employees handle all those sales?

It's true. Balkowitsch Enterprises started small, like most eBay sellers, but has grown into one of eBay's true superstars—a Titanium PowerSeller profiled in *Time, Reader's Digest*, and other national magazines.

A Rags to Riches Story

Balkowitsch Enterprises started as Sharon's Collectibles, an antiques and collectibles business run by Sharon Balkowitsch. The business was a part-time one; Sharon's day job with the Federal Bureau of Reclamation paid the bills.

Sharon's Collectibles was run from a 10' × 10' booth Sharon rented at a local antique mall. It was a very small business in a very small town (Bismarck, ND; population 55,000). There were few buyers for Sharon's wares, which kept her selling prices low. In her biggest month at the antique mall, she sold just 15 items, for a total of $300.

Sharon was looking for a way to increase her sales, and heard about this new online auction site called eBay. She asked her son Shane if he could help her put some items on eBay.

Shane had a business degree, was in the process of getting a nursing degree, and had worked in the computer field. His computer background proved useful, and he helped his mother list three items on eBay.

Shane and Sharon Balkowitsch.

That was November 11th, 1998. The three items Shane listed sold within 24 hours, and the Balkowitsches were hooked. Shane started listing more of Sharon's items, and in their first year on eBay, managed to sell more than 2,000 items.

The business kept growing from there. Within a year and a half, the Balkowitsches reached PowerSeller status and were recognized as one of the most successful small businesses in the upper Midwest. Their eBay business (then named Sharonscollectables) was named Super PowerSeller of the Month in April 2002, with more than 12,000 items sold to that date. They reached Platinum PowerSeller status in September 2003, averaging more than $25,000 in sales a month.

Today, Sharon's Collectibles is Balkowitsch Enterprises. The business has morphed from selling antiques and collectibles to selling medical and health-related items. (That's Shane's nursing background showing.) Shane is now running the business; Sharon is partially retired, and works just part-time.

How to Grow a Business

From its humble beginnings, Balkowitsch Enterprises has become a very big small business. The business hit $1 million in sales in 2004, doubled that to $2.2 million in 2005, and doubled again to $5 million in 2006; it's on track to hit $6 million in sales in 2007. That's remarkable growth for any business, let alone an eBay business.

How did Shane and Sharon achieve this level of growth? By "focusing on sales and creating the systems to handle the volume we currently do. We plan every day for the future and we are always looking for new exciting and quality products to sell."

When you're moving $500,000 worth of merchandise every month, efficient merchandise management is important. Balkowitsch Enterprises represents more than 165 different brands, and the company's sales growth has been fueled by adding new products to its mix. "Finding new product is the key," Shane says, "and not only finding product that sells, but finding product that has profit in it."

Fortunately, as the business has grown, Shane has found suppliers eager to work with him: "As we have been become more of a name in the market place, you would be surprised at how many companies come to us now to ask us to sell and promote their products."

Rapid growth required an investment in systems to manage that growth. Shane notes that before he went into nursing, he was an MIS director and credit manager for a microfilm company in California for nearly 20 years. "This experience has given me the knowledge to develop systems and grow the company," he says.

Growing a business also requires a commitment on the part of its principles. Here's how Shane tells the story:

"I do not want you to think this was part of some master plan of mine, that I had any idea that we would take $50 in inventory that Sharon found at a garage sale and turn it into what we are today. I would be totally dishonest if I told you I once thought that.

"But at one point in the past eight years, I did identify that we could do much better. What we had to do is quit our jobs, and a charge nurse job here in Bismarck is a very good job, pays about $40,000 a year, which is a nice salary. But we decided to build the building, quit our day jobs, and focus full-time on what we needed to do to become independent.

"That gamble has paid off in spades. The company has grown three times in the past two years and the future is very bright. We have our struggles, but so far we have been able to adapt, change, and work our way through any problems. My family and I have won the lottery with this company."

Managing the Business

Just because Balkowitsch Enterprises is doing big business doesn't mean that Shane has it easy. He puts in long hours to make sure that everything runs smoothly—70 hours a week on average.

Of course, Shane isn't the company's only employee. Shane's two brothers, Chad and Loren, work full-time in the business; his sister-in-law works part-time; they have a full-time invoicer/receptionist; and Sharon still works part-time in the business. That's $5 million in annual sales, managed by three full-time and three part-time employees—a very efficient operation.

Shane uses eBay's selling tools to manage his listings. He uses an outside accountant, although most of the day-to-day work (invoicing, shipping, payroll, and the like) is handled with QuickBooks Enterprise Solutions software. The company's inventory is also managed via QuickBooks. Everything is stored in the 5,400–square foot facility the business built several years ago.

The Balkowitsch office and warehouse facility.

Selling Strategies

eBay isn't Shane's sole selling venue. In addition to traditional eBay listings, Balkowitsch Enterprises also runs an eBay store, has its own e-commerce website (www.balkowitsch.com), and lists some items on Amazon.com. As Shane puts it, "We do not want to be one-dimensional and only rely on eBay."

The eBay Store for Balkowitsch Enterprises.

The company's e-commerce website.

As to eBay, Shane has approximately 1,000 listings going at any given time. He runs all items as fixed-price Buy It Now listings. Here's why:

"When you are selling new items, you cannot sell things for less than cost, so using Buy It Now is the only way to go. Waiting around for seven days for an item to sell, then for the buyer to come way under cost is a waste of our time and their time. With Buy It Now I can sell 10 of the same item in the same day, which is not the case with the auction format."

Keys to Success

What has made Balkowitsch Enterprises so successful? Shane responds that it's important to "Be honest, deliver the product that is mentioned, and do your best with customer service."

He has this advice for new sellers:

"Start small, do your research, do not get yourself into a large amount of product that you will end up giving away down the road. It is not an easy proposition and we have evolved over eight years to get where we are. Our knowledge and trade secrets would be priceless."

More specifically, Shane recommends that sellers "always let the buyer know who you are—phone number, address, contact information. The biggest pitfall with eBay is that eBay has allowed people to be anonymous, which is the main reason they have so much fraud. If everyone had to tell everyone who they were, eBay would be much better for it."

Shane also notes that selling on eBay has gotten harder over time. "Profit margins are very low on some items because there are so many sellers trying to get a piece of the pie. Many of these sellers have no business sense and they will give items away and profits are not something that they worry about. It is a big problem."

That said, Shane has been able to overcome these and other obstacles to create a large and profitable online business. Shane says he was driven by "a determined willpower to never work for anyone else again. My entire family, including my children, wife, brothers, mother, and extended family all rely solely on our company and what we are able to do."

Shane and Sharon have succeeded in building a business that can more than support their family. Balkowitsch Enterprises is a true American success story, and it all started with three little eBay listings.

8

Tricks for Running a Successful Trading Assistant Business

There's a relatively new type of eBay business that might be of interest. It's consignment selling—where you sell items on consignment for other people. It's not quite the same as buying merchandise for resale; it's really a different business model.

When you sell merchandise on consignment, you're what eBay calls a Trading Assistant (TA). It works this way: The owner of the merchandise contracts with you to manage the entire auction process, which you proceed to do. You take possession of the merchandise, research it, photograph it, write up an item description, and create and launch the auction listing. You manage the auction and collect the buyer's payment when it sells; then you pack it and ship it out to the buyer. You also pay all applicable eBay fees (although you pass them on to the client as part of your fees to him or her). Your client, the owner of the merchandise, doesn't have to do a thing.

Sounds simple enough, but it's not. To be successful as a TA, you have to know the tricks—which is what this chapter is about.

Trick #71: Build a Professional Business Presence

Although it's important for any eBay business to create a professional business presence (see Trick #61), it's doubly so for a Trading Assistant business. That's because you're marketing not just to potential buyers, but also to sellers—that is, those clients who want you to sell their stuff on consignment.

Think about it. If you want someone to sell your stuff on eBay, you don't want to hand your items over to any old Joe Shmoe. No, you'll entrust your precious goods only to someone you trust—someone who seems professional in what he or she does.

Professionalism is even more important when you realize that you're competing with a lot of real businesses, in the form of franchise stores. You probably have several of them in your city already, stores like iSold It and QuikDrop that compete against you for consignment clients.

When you're competing against well-marketed franchises with visible drop-off locations, you have to do something to distinguish yourself from that competition. What competitive advantages do you offer your consignment clients?

Perhaps you have a higher success rate. Perhaps you create better-looking auction listings. Perhaps you charge lower fees. Whatever it is that makes your TA business unique, you need to play it up.

And, whatever your brand identity, you have to come off as highly professional—the independent equivalent of a franchise company store. A successful TA business is not built on selling a few items for friends and family; you have to attract real customers, strangers to you, and convince them that you can best sell their goods. If you can't do that, the TA business is not for you.

Trick #72: Establish a Competitive Fee Schedule

In the TA business, fees matter. You want higher fees to compensate you for your time and effort. Your clients want lower fees so that they don't have to pay as much to sell their stuff. Whatever fee schedule you arrange will be a compromise.

Unfortunately, when it comes to setting consignment fees, there are no set guidelines. You can charge pretty much whatever you want, or whatever the market will bear. And that last point is important: Your fees have to be competitive with the other eBay drop-off stores in your area.

tip

If you don't use a flat fee, consider selling only items with a minimum bid price of $9.99 or higher. The goal is to discourage clients with lower-priced items so that you can concentrate on selling more-profitable higher-priced merchandise.

How should you structure your fees? TAs charge a wide range of fees, anywhere from 10% to 50% of the final selling price. In the early days of the

TA experience, lower fees, in the 10%–20% range, seemed to be the order of the day. Today, however, fees seem to be inching higher, with most successful sellers charging in the 25%–35% range.

Interestingly, some sellers offer a sliding fee schedule, with varying percentages for different price points. For example, you might charge a 40% fee for items that sell for less than $50, a 30% fee for items that sell for more than $500, and a 20% fee for items that sell for more than $5,000. The goal here is to maximize the dollar amount of your commission; you charge a higher percentage on lower-priced items (which generates a higher dollar fee), and a lower percentage on higher-priced items.

Whatever fee schedule you concoct, remember to find out what your competitors are charging. Your fees need to be in the same ballpark, or you'll lose business.

tip

In addition to the commission you charge, you also need to pass through to the client all the various eBay and PayPal fees you incur. Make sure you keep good track of these fees so that they can be included on the final customer invoice.

Trick #73: Create an Iron-Clad Consignment Contract

Here's something different about running a TA business—you'll probably need a lawyer. Not because you're likely to get sued, but because you need to create an iron-clad contract for your clients to sign. I'm not a lawyer, and you probably aren't either, which is why it pays to engage an attorney to make sure all the i's are dotted and the t's are crossed.

Why do you need a contract? It's simple. Your consignment contract spells out exactly what it is you are and are not responsible for, and clarifies your legal position in terms of ownership of the product. Your contract should include the following items:

- The names and contact information for both parties (you and your client)
- The purpose of the contract—that you will offer the items owned by the client for sale on eBay
- The services you, the reseller, will offer—writing the listing, taking photos, listing the item, managing the auction, handling payment, packing the item, shipping the item, and so on

- Who takes possession of the merchandise during the transaction (typically you) and who retains ownership of the merchandise (typically the client)
- How and when the client can cancel the transaction
- What happens if the item doesn't sell (relist, return the merchandise to the client, whatever)
- Who handles buyer complaints and returns (probably you, but not necessarily)
- How and when the client receives payment for sold items
- Fees

All nice in theory, but how does all this translate into practice? Well, here's an example of a consignment contract that serves as a good starting point:

Parties: The parties to this agreement are _____ representative for *YourBusiness* and _____ , Client.

Services: *YourBusiness* will offer item(s) owned by Client for auction on eBay. As part of this process, *YourBusiness* will provide the following services on behalf of the client: Take temporary possession of the item, clean or refurbish the item as necessary, research item history and price, write description of the item, photograph the item, create the eBay listing, post the listing on eBay, communicate with potential bidders during the course of the auction, receive payment from the high bidder, process the payment, package the item for shipment, ship the item to the buyer, pay fees due from eBay and PayPal, and pay Client at the completion of the transaction.

Fees: Client agrees to pay to *YourBusiness* a commission of 25% of the item's final selling price, not including shipping/handling fees and taxes. In addition, Client agrees to pay all eBay and PayPal fees incurred for listing and selling the item.

Term: This agreement has a term of one year and may be terminated by either party by 10-day written notice to other party.

Right of refusal: *YourBusiness* may decline listing any item for any reason.

Ownership and possession: Client attests that they have legal title to and are in legal possession of all items consigned to *YourBusiness*. On signing this agreement, *YourBusiness* will retain possession of Client item(s) for the duration of the transaction process. If the item is unsold, possession will revert to Client within 10 days of the end of the auction.

Auction cancellation: If Client chooses to withdraw the item from being listed on eBay, Client must notify *YourBusiness* by phone or email at least 24 hours prior to the scheduled start of the auction. If an item is withdrawn from sale, any fees already paid to *YourBusiness* will not be refunded. In addition, Client will pay an auction cancellation fee of $10 to *YourBusiness* on return of the item to the Client. Once the item is listed on eBay, the auction will run its full course and the item must be sold to the highest bidder. If the Client demands the auction be cancelled before its scheduled end time, Client will pay to *YourBusiness* an auction cancellation fee of $100 on return of item to Client.

Client bidding: Client will not bid directly or indirectly on item(s) consigned to *YourBusiness*. Client will inform his family and associates they are also not to bid on these items.

Unsold items: Should the item not sell in the course of the eBay auction, Client has the option of relisting the item for sale for one additional auction cycle. If Client opts not to relist the item, or if the item does not sell during the second auction cycle, *YourBusiness* will return the item to the possession of Client within 30 days of the end of the auction.

Returns: *YourBusiness* permits buyers to return items for a full refund if *YourBusiness* is notified within five days of the buyer's receipt of item. If the item is returned by the buyer, Client will be contacted to approve the relist of item on eBay or return of the item to Client.

Accounting and payment: *YourBusiness* will furnish a report of sales and commissions to Client within 21 days of confirmed payment from the buyer. At that time, *YourBusiness* will provide a check for the proceeds of the sale, less all fees due to *YourBusiness*.

Loss or damage: Client will keep any items consigned to *YourBusiness* fully insured while in possession of *YourBusiness*. *YourBusiness* will make every effort to safeguard consigned item(s) and will reimburse Client for damage caused by *YourBusiness*, calculated at the average eBay sale price during the previous three months, less *YourBusiness* commission of item(s). Items lost or damaged due to fire, theft, flood, and other events beyond the control of *YourBusiness* will not be reimbursed by *YourBusiness*.

Obviously, both you and your client need to sign this contract before you can begin the selling process. This not only informs the client what to expect, but also protects you in case disgruntlement ensues. If you've both signed a contract laying out the pertinent details, an unhappy client won't have a legal leg to stand on.

Trick #74: Offer a Pickup Service

When you agree to sell an item for a client, you need to take that item into your possession. You're in the consignment business, after all; you need to have the item in your possession in order to sell it. Plus, if you don't have it, you don't know for sure that it exists—or that your client hasn't disposed of it elsewhere. Remember, it's your name on the eBay auction; you'll be held responsible if the item isn't actually available for sale.

If you're running your consignment business out of your home, or if you have a drop-off retail location, your clients can drop off their merchandise at your location. However, you can set yourself apart from your franchise competition by also offering a pickup service. This is a great time-saver for your clients, and justifies (perhaps) any higher fees you may charge. Alternatively, you can charge a separate fee for the pickup service; a $10 pickup fee will cover your gas and time, discourages clients with low-priced items, and might even put a little extra money in your pocket.

Know, however, that offering a pickup service comes with its own issues. First, you have to have some means of transporting the items you pick up back to your house or store. For small items, an SUV or minivan might do the trick, but if you plan to sell bigger items, you might need a pickup truck or full-size van. (That's an added business expense for most sellers.) In addition, consider the manpower necessary to lift and carry bigger items; it may take a two-person crew to pick up some items.

There's also the safety issue. Going to a stranger's home can get a little dicey, so you'll want to play it as safe as you can. Taking a big, burly guy along with you is always good. Otherwise, judge the location carefully, and if you're at all nervous, arrange to meet the client at a neutral (and safer) location, like a local coffeehouse or fast-food joint. Just use common sense.

Trick #75: You Don't Have to Sell Everything

Just because you're in the consignment business doesn't mean that you have to sell everything that comes your way. In fact, many TAs specialize in reselling specific types of merchandise; for example, you might specialize in selling consignment clothing, or maybe collectibles.

Some Trading Assistants won't take low-priced items on consignment for the simple reason that there's not enough money in these transactions to make them worth their while. eBay recommends using a Trading Assistant for items over $50 only; other TAs set their lower limit at $100. Still others let the starting bid price be their guide, stating a minimum $9.99 starting bid for all items sold. However you do it, you don't want to waste your time selling a lot of $5 and $10 items, when you could be reselling items for $100 or more.

In addition, it's okay to turn away goods that you think you'll have a hard time selling or that you think are worth considerably less than the client does—or that you think might have been obtained illegally. Focus your attention on items that will be easy to sell, and that will sell for a high price.

> **tip**
> Make sure that you include a clause in your consignment contract that you retain the right to refuse to accept any item for resale.

Trick #76: Let Your Clients Track Their Auctions

When you launch an auction for an item you took on consignment, chances are your client is going to be curious about how the auction is going. For this reason, you want to provide some mechanism for the client to check his current auctions.

If it's just one or two auctions, the easiest approach is simply to email the client the URL for the auction. But if you're auctioning off a dozen or more items for a single client, this can be a bit burdensome.

Although you could simply direct the client to your Items for Sale page (search.ebay.com/_W0QQsassZUSERIDQQhtZ-1), that's not a great idea if you have other items from other clients for auction at the same time. A better approach is to create a custom search for the client's specific items.

The key to this approach is to create some sort of unique identifier in the auction listing description. For example, you can include the text Client ID: XYZ12345, where XYZ are the client's initials and 12345 is the client's ZIP code. Insert this code somewhere in the description; it can be in small type at the bottom of the listing.

After you've launched the auction, click the Advanced Search on the eBay home page. When the next page appears, check the Search Title and Description option and enter the client ID you created into the Enter Keyword or Item Number box. Then scroll down to the From Sellers section, check the From Specific Sellers option, and enter your eBay ID. Now you can click the Search button.

When the search results page appears, copy the URL of this page and paste that URL into an email that you send to your client. When your client clicks the link in the email, he goes to the search results page containing his items that are up for auction.

tip

Alternatively, you can link to the search results page URL from your own web page, with link or button text specific to that client. Then the client can go to your website, click the link or button, and see the search results page for his auctions.

Trick #77: Open a Storefront Location

Most smaller TAs work out of their homes, which is fine. However, if you want to establish a professional business presence, you'll want to open your own retail storefront for merchandise drop-offs and customer interaction.

Opening a drop-off location not only says that you're running a real business, it helps you attract more clients. In part, that's because your signage provides added visibility; a retail sign is great advertising, day or night. But it's also because many people are more comfortable dealing with a storefront business than they are with a stranger over the phone.

---

note

eBay calls a Trading Assistant with a drop-off location a *Trading Post*. To qualify for official Trading Post status, you must offer a staffed drop-off location with regular hours, have a feedback rating of 500 or higher (with at least 98% positive), and have monthly sales of at least $25,000.

After all, a client can walk right in your front door, get a feel for your business, see your rates, sign a contract, and leave her merchandise for you to sell. That's in contrast to dealing with a non-storefront TA, where the client has to hand over her merchandise to a stranger who shows up at her front door—or, even less comfortable, drive to that stranger's house or apartment to leave her merchandise. A storefront location offers much greater peace of mind.

In addition, a storefront location gives you added space to store your consigned merchandise. You also have office space to conduct your business, and the feeling of a real 9–5 (or 9–9) business that you can leave behind at the end of the working day.

The downside of opening a drop-off location, of course, is that you have additional costs—the rent and utilities for your store, plus signage and so on. And you'll pay those bills every month, no matter how much auction business you do. But you don't need a *big* store, and it doesn't have to be in a high-rent location. All you need is a visible storefront in a shopping center that has adequate traffic.

Of course, just putting up a sign and unlocking your front door doesn't mean that you'll have a steady stream of customers through that door. A drop-off location is just a storefront; you still have to advertise to make customers aware of your business. Yes, a storefront itself is a form of advertising, but it's not the only advertising you need to do. You'll still want to distribute flyers, place newspaper ads, and other advertising to draw customers into your store. Then you're in business.

Trick #78: Focus on Customer Service

When you're running a TA business, you need to please both your clients and the buyers of your clients' merchandise. The trick is to offer superior customer service—for both types of customers.

If you have a drop-off location, customer service starts when you unlock the front door in the morning. Your store needs to be neat and clean; if it looks like a cluttered pawn shop, you'll drive away potential clients. And you have to look professional, too; wear a nice shirt and pair of slacks, not shorts and dirty T-shirt.

Drop-off location or not, customer service extends to how you handle client phone calls. Answer the phone in a professional manner, and within three rings. If you can't get to the phone, make sure that you have a phone machine or voice mail with a professional message. Return all calls promptly.

If you need to arrange merchandise pickup or drop-off at a different location, show up as promised—or even a few minutes early. Make sure that your vehicle is clean and presentable; the same goes for you and your helpers. No one wants to open their door and hand over their items to someone who looks like a bum.

Let's hope that sales take off and you get busy. Don't get so busy, however, that you make your clients wait. You need to prepare all contracts and paperwork within a reasonable period of time (days, not weeks), which means doing your research and preparation in a prompt fashion.

During the course of an auction, clients want to know how things are going. Some clients will be interested to the point of becoming pests. Don't let that bother you. Handle all customer questions promptly and politely, no matter how many times that same customer calls. It's human nature for them to be curious; some will even be anxious about the process. Do everything you can to answer their questions and reassure them. You're doing this for them, after all. It's your job to make them feel comfortable.

Of course, your customer service extends beyond your consignment clients to the buyers of the consigned products. You need to provide the same level of customer service to your buyers as you would expect when you buy an item on eBay. Promptly answer any questions from potential buyers, communicate clearly and promptly with winning bidders, and promptly ship purchased products. When you're a Trading Assistant, any negative feedback you receive also reflects poorly on your clients; it's your responsibility to make sure that all parties are satisfied with the experience.

Trick #79: Promote Your TA Business

As noted previously, in order to attract clients, you have to promote your Trading Assistant business. There are many ways to do this.

Advertise Locally

First, realize that a Trading Assistant business is a local business. When you want to attract customers, you need to advertise locally; it doesn't do any good to attract would-be customers in Maine if you're located in Oregon.

Next, make sure that you've created a professional business presence. That means having a business name and logo, and putting that name and logo on everything you do. Print up business cards, company letterhead, envelopes, and invoices. Make sure that everything looks professional and has the same look and feel.

Now you need to make your business known to other members of your community. Pass out those business cards, and don't forget to tack them up on any bulletin board you find. Consider advertising in local newspapers, if the rates are affordable. (Community newspapers or weekly papers are more affordable than big-city dailies.) And remember to talk yourself up to everyone you meet—word-of-mouth is often the best promotion.

You'll also need to do some targeted hunting for clients. Make up some flyers and hand them out to anyone running a garage sale or yard sale; there's always something left at the end of the sale that you could sell on eBay.

Beyond advertising is the concept of publicity—any mention of your business that you don't have to pay for. Because the concept of selling items for consignment on eBay is still relatively new, it might be newsworthy—especially in a small community or on a slow news day. You need to get the word out about what you're doing to all your local media outlets: your local newspaper, radio stations, television stations, you name it. Work up some sample stories, send out a few press releases, make a few phone calls—whatever it takes to get noticed.

In other words, be aggressive and be creative—do anything you can to attract people with stuff you can sell!

Advertise Online

Even though your TA business is local, you can still attract new customers online. Many clients find TAs to sell their items by searching eBay's Trading Assistant Directory. For this reason, you want to make sure that you're a registered member of the Trading Assistant program; all registered TAs are listed in the directory, by location and specialty. If you're not listed, you'll miss out on business.

---

tip

To join eBay's Trading Assistant program, go to pages.ebay.com/ tradingassistants/becoming-trading-assistant.html and click the Create/ Edit Your Profile link.

You should also advertise your consignment business in all your regular eBay auctions. You can do this by adding eBay's Trading Assistant button, as shown in Figure 8.1, and linking it back to your eBay Trading Assistant page. To do this, you'll need to know your Trading Assistant number (found at the end of the URL for your TA listing) and a little bit of HTML. Here's the code:

```
<a href="http://contact.ebay.com/ws1/eBayISAPI.dll?
➥ TradingAssistant&page=profile&profileId =XXXXX">
<img src=" http://pics.ebaystatic.com/aw/pics/tradingAssistant/
➥ imgTA_88x33.gif">
</a>
```

FIGURE 8.1

Add a Trading Assistant button to all your eBay auction listings.

Replace *xxxxx* with your Trading Assistant number, and the button will be added. Anyone clicking the button goes directly to your eBay TA page.

Trick #80: Solicit Local Businesses

One of the keys to becoming a successful Trading Assistant is continually finding merchandise that you can sell on consignment. Advertising is important for this, but it isn't the only way to find new clients.

Many TAs find success in soliciting local businesses for merchandise to resell. Many small businesses and manufacturers have liquidated, refurbished, or returned products they need to somehow dispose of—and you can help them with this problem. You'd be surprised how eager these companies might be to get rid of old merchandise just taking up space in their warehouses.

Working with a local business can be one of the best and most lucrative ways to quickly build up your Trading Assistant business. Many businesses would love to sell on eBay, but don't have the time, skill, or personnel to handle this task. When they partner with you, their problem is solved—and you get a steady stream of merchandise to sell.

So, print up some fancy brochures and business cards and start making some calls. It might take a lot of cold calls before you find your first interested business, but once you get it lined up, it's steady money in your pocket.

eBAY BUSINESS PROFILE

Profile: Twin Cities Online Depot

Business Profile

Business name: Twin Cities Online Depot

eBay ID: chinookmn

eBay Store: stores.ebay.com/Twin-Cities-Online-Depot

Website: www.TwinCitiesOnlineDepot.com

Type of business: Trading Assistant

Owner: Patrick Windus

Location: Apple Valley, Minnesota

Most Trading Assistants didn't start out as Trading Assistants. No, the typical TA started selling his or her own stuff on eBay, and then eased into selling items on consignment for others.

That scenario describes the genesis of this chapter's profile business, Twin Cities Online Depot. This Minnesota-based TA started out selling hockey pucks!

It Started with Hockey Pucks. . .

Patrick Windus got his start on eBay selling Minnesota Wild hockey pucks. Hockey is big in the Twin Cities, and Patrick figured he could make a little money to pay for the next season's hockey ticket.

That was back in August 2000. After getting the hang of hockey puck selling, Patrick started selling other hockey-related items, in addition to hockey pucks—specifically, programs and fan memorabilia. He tinkered around on eBay for three or four years, getting the feel for buying and selling, before he decided to move into the Trading Assistant business.

Today, Twin Cities Online Depot is a real business, on track to hit $100,000 in gross sales for calendar year 2007. His business is a mix of consignment sales and sales of hockey memorabilia.

Selling Strategies

How many items Patrick lists each week depends on the number of clients he is currently working with; on average, he has about 100 items listed on eBay in any given week. Most items are in the auction-style format. For about 90% of his auctions, Patrick offers the Buy It Now option. Here's why:

"As a buyer on eBay, I am one who does not want to wait for an item. I don't like the fact I might get 'sniped' out of an item at the last second, as an auction closes. I like to be able to browse and then buy. I carry this philosophy over to my Trading Assistant business. I would have to say that nearly all auctions end with a Buy It Now."

Patrick has tried selling items on other sites (Yahoo! Auctions and Craigslist), but with little success. "The traffic volume just wasn't there," he says, "as compared to eBay."

What Patrick does do is run an eBay Store. Items in the Store are usually duplicate items for buyers who want to get the item now—"at a premium price, of course."

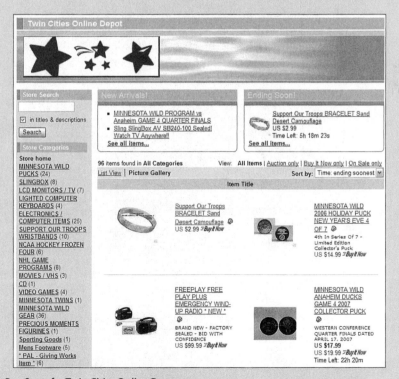

The eBay Store for Twin Cities Online Depot.

Patrick notes that lower listing costs were a big factor in his decision to open his eBay Store:

"The benefit of having a store is that seasonal items, such as NHL hockey pucks, can be on eBay all year long, but not at the cost of auction prices. By placing items in a Store on eBay, items have an insert fee as low as 6–11 cents, which includes a gallery photo. Items are in the store for 30 days, and automatically renew at the rate of just 6–11 cents."

Being a Trading Assistant

Being a Trading Assistant isn't as profitable as you might think. Patrick says his profit margin varies from 10% to 25% per item. It's not like regular selling, where you might buy an item for $10 and sell it for $20, doubling your investment. But then again, you also don't have any of your own money invested in inventory.

Like many TAs, Patrick doesn't specialize in reselling any particular type of products. However, he does try to shy away from certain items, such as furniture, clothing, and artwork.

Patrick finds most of his TA clients—or, rather, they find him—via eBay's Trading Assistant Directory. He includes his TA info in all his normal auction listings, of course, and he uses the Google AdWords program. All that said and done, Patrick says that word of mouth is his best form of advertising:

"Current and past customers tell their friends and family, and the next thing you know, I am selling items for them, too."

The Twin Cities Online Depot website.

The initial contact is typically by email, through the eBay website, or by phone. He doesn't run a drop-off location, nor does he have to do a lot of pickups. Instead, most items he sells on consignment are sent to him via U.S. mail, FedEx, or UPS. Patrick prices according to a sliding scale, detailed in the following table.

Twin Cities Online Depot Pricing Schedule

Final Selling Price	Commission
$49.99 or less	25%
$50–$500	23%
$501–$1,000	20%
$1,001 and up	15%

The TA business is a competitive one, which explains why Patrick's commission rates are on the lower end of what some TAs charge. Patrick deducts his commission from the check he sends the client at the completion of each transaction. Unlike most TAs, he does not pass on eBay or PayPal fees; he treats those as his business costs.

Clients can choose from two types of auction listings. What Patrick calls the Standard listing has no up-front fee, sets a starting auction price of 99 cents for a seven-day listing, and includes up to two digital photos of the item and a gallery picture. His Premium listing also doesn't have an upfront fee, but charges the client $9.99 plus 1% of the opening bid if the item doesn't sell. The Premium listing also includes up to five digital photos, a gallery photo, the choice of 5-, 7-, or 10-day listing, and a one-time no-charge relisting if the item doesn't sell. If a Premium item doesn't sell after the relist, Patrick moves it into his eBay Store for 30 days at no additional charge.

I asked Patrick about what particular issues he faces with his Trading Assistant business. Here is his reply:

"Customers don't have an understanding of how much it really costs to sell items on eBay, from the initial listing fee, to the final value fee, to PayPal fees. If an item doesn't sell, I, as the seller, am still out the initial listing fee."

Fortunately, he doesn't get too many customer complaints. "I have been lucky in this category," he says. "If any, it is usually why an item didn't sell for more than what it did. I think some people have higher expectations as to what an item should go for. On the other hand, I have countless examples where an item I thought might go for $30 actually sold on eBay for over $200."

One of the reasons why Patrick doesn't get a lot of complaining customers is because he walks clients through the process before he ever signs them up. His website includes a How It Works page that describes the consignment selling process in 10 easy steps; the more informed a client is upfront, the fewer problems there will be further down the line.

Twin Cities Online Depot

Phone: 952-236-4747

↗ Home Page
↗ How It Works
↗ Types of Listings
↗ How Much Does It Cost?

How Does It Work?

HERE IS WHAT WE DO FOR YOU IN JUST 10 EASY STEPS:

1) Call The **TWIN CITIES ONLINE DEPOT** at **952-236-4747**, and set up an appointment.

2) We will stop by your home, office, or wherever is convenient for you, and offer an analysis of the item or items you want to be sold.

3) We evaluate each item's condition and potential value for an eBay auction listing, using state-of-the-art real-time, online auction software.

4) We will photograph your item using state of the art digital technolgy.

5) We will create a detailed auction listing to make sure your listing stands out from all the rest.

6) We will place the item in the best eBay category, AND start your auction at the best time.

7) We monitor the progress of your auction and will answer any questions posed from potential bidders.

8) When your item sells, we will professionally pack and ship the item, at no additional cost to you.

9) We will process the auction payment, deduct our commission, and forward the remaining auction proceeds to you directly.

10) We take care of any returns, and everything else, so that you don't even have to lift a finger.

What's more? YOU retain complete anonymity throughout the whole transaction.

PLEASE NOTE: At this time, we are not able to sell vehicles or any item that weighs more than 150lbs.

Walking potential clients through the consignment process.

Managing the Business

For the bulk of the year, Patrick runs his business by himself. But during the hockey season and over the holidays, he brings in one or two part-time people to help out.

Patrick does all his own accounting. He uses Microsoft Excel to track his finances; he says he's looked at both QuickBooks and Microsoft Accounting Professional software, but has not yet transitioned to either.

Microsoft Excel is used to manage Patrick's inventory as well. He has a dedicated room where all inventory, including consignment items, is kept. The same room houses all his packing and shipping materials.

For auction management, Patrick primarily uses eBay Selling Manager Pro. He also uses Auctiva for a few listings and has, in the past, used Mpire.

Keys to Success

To Patrick, there are three keys to creating a successful listing:

"Timing is everything. Pricing comes in as a close second. Thirdly, sell what you know; don't try to be a copy-cat."

As for running a successful TA business, Patrick says that it's all about customer service:

"Treat your clients right. Word of mouth and feedback have been my best advertising, in allowing me to be successful. Every item that I sell on eBay gets a hand written thank you note when I ship out the item. When something does go wrong, I try my hardest to make sure it is corrected. Sometimes that means refunding the shipping. Sometimes it means refunding 10% of the final price."

Patrick goes on to say that it's important to treat winning bidders "with respect and gratitude. It's all about customer service. Nearly 1/3 of all my sales on eBay are repeat buyers."

Finally, Patrick does a good job of keeping his business in perspective. His parting words are apt for sellers of any size: "It should always be fun."

Yes, it should.

9

Tricks for Cutting Costs—And Increasing Profits

After your eBay business is up and running and you've gotten the hang of creating listings that have a high completion rate, it's time to start looking at your bottom line. How much profit is your business generating—and what can you do to increase that profit?

In business, there are two ways to increase your profit margin. You can reduce your costs or you can increase your average selling price. The goal is to increase the difference between your revenues and your expenses. To that end, here are 10 tricks you can use to boost your bottom line.

Trick #81: Improve Your Time Management

One of the hidden costs of an eBay business is your time. As the old saying goes, time is money; the less time you spend running your business, the more money you make per hour.

The key to effective time management is efficiency. You want to make the best use of every minute you spend running your business. Don't spend 20 minutes doing something if you could do it in 15.

To that end, here are some tricks that many eBay sellers use to improve their time management—and get more work done in fewer hours each day.

Establish a Daily Routine

To me, the key to efficient time management is to set up a daily routine. Instead of being at the beck and call of whatever task rises to the top of the pile (or whichever customer is screaming louder), take control of what you have to do by organizing it in a way that works best for you. For example, you might follow this type of daily schedule:

8:00 a.m.	*Process customer emails*
8:30 a.m.	*Process payments for previous day sales*
9:00 a.m.	*Generate invoices and shipping labels*
10:00 a.m.	*Pack items to ship today*
12:00 noon	*Lunch*
1:00 p.m.	*Deliver items to post office*
2:00 p.m.	*Manage sold eBay listings (feedback, and so on)*
2:30 p.m.	*Manage inventory*
3:00 p.m.	*Take product photos*
4:00 p.m.	*Create new listings*

When you start doing big volume, you might want to establish different schedules for different days of the week. For example, Monday might be for managing payments and post-auction emails for items that sold on Sunday evening, Tuesday for packing all those items, Wednesday for shipping those items, Thursday for taking new product photos, Friday for writing descriptions and preparing new listings, and so forth.

Whether you do it on a daily or weekly basis, the key is to establish a routine. Every day you perform the same tasks, in the same order. A set routine is much more efficient than performing tasks in random order. You always know what you need to do and when you're going to do it.

Again, when you create a schedule, you take control over all your tasks. Without a schedule, your tasks control you and your time. And if you're not in control, you're wasting time.

Don't Get Diverted from Your Routine

You have your routine. Then you have other demands on your time. Don't let those other demands interfere with your routine.

What do you do if a friend wants to meet you for coffee at 10:00 a.m. tomorrow? Well, if that's your scheduled time to pack your eBay shipments, you should decline the offer. Or maybe it's just a beautiful day outside, and you'd really like to take a walk. Avoid the temptation, and stick to your routine.

Diversions are attractive, but they're deadly when it comes to maintaining an efficient work schedule. If you must take on other tasks, do them outside of your normal schedule, not during it. Treat coffee with your friend as a perk you can indulge in *after* you've completed your daily tasks. Whatever you do, don't let outside activities get in the way of getting done what you need to get done; when you're running a business, your business comes first.

Work on a Single Task Until It's Done

One of the biggest threats to effective time management is interruptions. You can't get into a groove when you're constantly having your attention diverted.

What this means is that when you're working through your scheduled tasks, you shouldn't do anything else. Don't answer emails. Don't answer instant messages. Don't answer phone calls. Don't answer the door. Stay focused on the task at hand until it's done, and then you can answer any of those "urgent" messages that weren't really.

Even better, set aside a specific block of time to answer all your calls and messages. Maybe you return all calls and emails after 4:00 p.m. each afternoon, for example. However you do it, you want to keep from being interrupted while you're working. If you can work straight through on a task, you'll get it done quicker. If you keep getting interrupted, you might never complete the original task.

> **tip**
>
> Just because the phone is ringing doesn't mean you have to answer it right then. Most calls can wait to be returned; take control of your communications by answering the phone on your schedule.

Work on a single task until it's done, without interruption. Save the interruptions for later, as new tasks. Do one thing at a time, and you'll get done with all things faster.

Prioritize Your Tasks

You have a lot on your plate. You have to buy new inventory, rearrange your storage space, take product photos, write new listing descriptions, go to the bank, go to the post office, buy boxes and peanuts, pack items to ship, answer questions from potential buyers . . . it's a lot to do, and it's all important.

Except that not everything is of equal importance. There are some things that are more important than others, some tasks that absolutely positively have to get done today. Which is why effective time management involves prioritization.

If you can't get everything done today, make sure that you get the most important things done. Whatever is crucial to running your business should be what you do first. Save the less important tasks for later in the day—or put them off until tomorrow.

For example, for most eBay sellers, the most important tasks on a day-to-day basis are depositing checks and money orders, packing items, and shipping items. So, organize your schedule so that the first things you do every day are packing items to ship, and then taking those items to the post office—and, while you're out, going to the bank. Then you have the rest of the day free to perform those tasks that are less time-intensive.

Bottom line? Do the most important stuff first. Everything else can wait.

Do Your Most Energy-Intensive Tasks Earlier in the Day

Here's one exception to that task prioritization trick. Some things you do take more energy. Those tasks are harder to do (or take more time) when you do them late in the day.

So, when you have an energy-intensive task, do it earlier in the day, when you have more energy. Maybe that means doing your packing (energy intensive) in the morning, and saving your computer work (less energy intensive) for the afternoon. When you have more energy, you'll get those energy-intensive tasks done faster. If you try to do them when you're tired, you'll drag your way through them.

---

tip

Of course, if you're not a morning person, you might want to put off you energy-intensive tasks until the afternoon, when you're perkier.

Trick #82: Create a Factory-Like Operation

Part of efficient time management is automating as much of your eBay business as you can. Your goal is to turn your operation into a factory, with repetitive tasks instead of unique ones. Repetitive tasks take less time to do, over time, than if you have to "reinvent the wheel" with every auction item you list or sell.

What this means is that you want to make every aspect of your operation as much of a no-brainer as you can. With a factory-like operation, not only is time-per-task minimized, you also make it so that any component can be done by anyone—not just you. If your packing, for example, consists of always putting the same-shaped item into the same-sized box, it's easy enough to train a part-time employee to do that task. Not so, of course, if every item you pack is completely different; new experiences are much more difficult to train for.

Benefits of Standardization

The key to creating a factory-like operation is to standardize the items you sell. Instead of selling one thing today and a different thing tomorrow, sell the same thing day after day. Standardization enables a factory-like operation, which is the most efficient way to run your business.

When you standardize on selling items of the same type and size, you gain many efficiencies. For example, you can reuse the same product photos in all your listings, which means that you can cut back on the number of individual photo shoots you need to do. You can also reuse the same item descriptions in all your listings, which means reducing the time you have to devote to researching and writing item listings.

In addition, by standardizing the type of items you ship, you gain tremendous time and cost savings in your packing and shipping operation. First, when you're always packing the same item, you get very good at it, which means you pack faster and better. Second, you see similar gains in shipping because you always know exactly how much shipping costs for the items you ship over and over again; you don't need to be constantly looking up rates and services from different carriers. Third, you save money on packing supplies; because you can standardize on one or two types of boxes, you can buy those boxes (and accompanying supplies) in higher quantities, which means lower cost per box.

Automating Other Operations

Your can enhance your factory-like operation by the use of automated auction management tools, which we discussed back in Trick #8. These tools let you automate your listing creation and post-auction management; the more automated you get, the more time you have to do other things.

Another operation to automate is your customer communications; as you're well aware, it takes time to answer all customer questions by hand, as well as to create and send all the necessary post-auction emails. You can automate the process by preparing prewritten emails to use in various situations by utilizing the email features found in many auction management tools, or by using a separate email management tool, such as ezSupport for eBay (www.hostedsupport.com).

note

ezSupport for eBay consolidates your POP email and messages sent via the eBay system into a single inbox, and then automatically answers 80% of all messages received. The service costs $39.95 per month.

Trick #83: Save Money on Supplies

I'm constantly surprised, and not in a good way, how many eBay sellers fail to account for all the supplies they use in the course of running their business. It's easy enough to factor profit-per-item (just subtract the item cost and all eBay and PayPal fees from the selling price), but that profit isn't your business's final profit. Your real bottom line consists of the individual profits you generate per item, minus the costs of all the supplies and such you use in your day-to-day operations.

What supplies am I talking about? Here's a short and not necessarily complete list:

- Shipping labels
- Other labels ("Fragile," "Do Not Bend," and so forth)
- Packing tape
- Styrofoam peanuts
- Bubble wrap
- Tissue paper

- Plastic bags
- Boxes and envelopes
- Paper (to print invoices and packing receipts)
- Ink or toner (also to print those invoices and packing receipts)
- Note paper (to write notes to yourself or to employees)
- Pens or pencils (to write on that note paper)

And that's just a general list. Your business will have its own unique list of supplies. For example, if you sell clothing, you'll need hangers; if you sell perishable items, you'll need dry ice. You get the picture.

One of the easiest ways to increase your business profits is to reduce the price you pay for all these supplies. Think about it; if you use 100 boxes a week and reduce the cost of your boxes by 10 cents apiece, you'll save more than $500 a year—which goes straight to your bottom line.

How do you save money on supplies? There are several ways.

Compare Prices

First, you should always compare prices of multiple suppliers. Don't settle on the first supplier you find; see how that supplier's prices compare to those from other suppliers. It pays to shop around.

Ask for a Discount

Second, you should always ask for a discount. That's right, sometimes lower prices can be had just by asking. Instead of ordering from a supplier's website or catalog, call them, tell them you're from your company's purchasing department, describe what you need, and ask for a quote. You'd be surprised how often you can get a better deal by going through the quote process.

Buy in Bulk

Third, buy in bulk. Lower prices come when you buy in larger quantities. Most suppliers offer price breaks for quantity purchases; check the supplier's price chart to see where the best price breaks are. Buy in the biggest quantities you can afford and that make sense based on your usage patterns. Instead of buying a month's worth of supplies, buy two or three months' worth; stock up when the prices are good.

Trick #84: Purchase Now, Sell Later

So far we've focused on cutting various operating costs. You can also increase your profits by lowering the price you pay for the merchandise you sell.

This trick is a good one that requires some foresight and patience. The theory is simple: Buy merchandise when it's available at a lower price, then hold onto it and offer it for sale at a later date when the prices go back up. How does this work in practice? Let's look at a few examples.

Exploit Seasonality

Perhaps the best example of the "purchase now, sell later" strategy involves *seasonality*—the fact that some items sell better in some seasons than in others. What you want to do is purchase your inventory during the off season, and then sell it during the hot season.

For example, let's say you're selling swimwear. You can pick up some terrific bargains by purchasing liquidated or closeout merchandise during the winter months, when no one is going swimming (unless they live in Florida, of course). You hold onto those swimsuits through the balance of the winter and early spring, finally listing them for sale in late spring and early summer, during the height of swimwear-buying season. You purchase when the prices are lowest and sell when they're highest.

A similar example is winter sporting goods—skis, snowboards, snowmobiles, and similar items. You can purchase these items quite affordably during the summer months, and then sell them for high-season going rates during the winter. All it takes is a little patience—and the upfront money to invest in inventory.

Take Advantage of Sales and Promotions

You can also take advantage of promotional pricing occasionally offered by manufacturers and distributors. The way this works is that a manufacturer plans a promotion for a specific period of time, and offers its dealers a discount on the merchandise to coincide with the promotion. When the promotion is over, the merchandise pricing returns to its normal levels.

The trick is to purchase the merchandise at the discounted price during the promotional period, but not to sell it during that period. Instead, you hold onto the merchandise until the promotion is over, and then you can sell it at its normal price—having paid the discounted price for your inventory. You end up increasing your profit margin by buying smart.

Here's an example of this strategy from Sean Kennedy of Boston Drum Center, profiled back in Chapter 5, "Tricks for Setting Prices and Handling Payments." Sean sells accessories from Pacific Drums and Percussion (PDP), including bass drum pedals. One of PDP's most popular pedals normally sells for $99.99, and Sean typically buys them for $79 or so. When PDP ran a promotion that dropped the selling price on these pedals to $79.99, the dealer price was lowered to $59. Sean bought a truckload of pedals at this price (see Figure 9.1), and then sat on them. The promotion ended, the selling price returned to $99.99, and then Sean put his pedals on sale. Instead of making the normal $20 per pedal, he made $40 on every pedal he purchased during the promotional period. Yes, he had to devote some warehouse space to store the pedals for a few months, but it was more than worth it.

FIGURE 9.1

Drum pedals, purchased at a promotional price and sold at normal retail. (You need plenty of warehouse space for this trick!)

Profit from Supply Constraints

Sometimes the patience involves holding onto an item until it becomes rarer. The key here is to purchase discontinued products that you know will remain in demand. You hold onto the inventory until supplies run out, and then place your inventory on the market. Because you have no competition (everybody else is sold out), you can sell your items at a higher price.

An example: I once purchased a supply of Captain America model kits from a liquidator; the manufacturer (Polar Lights) had discontinued that model, and had large supplies to unload. If I had gone ahead and resold those kits immediately, I would have taken a loss because the market was flooded with the liquidated kits. But I held onto the kits for six months, until the cheap closeouts were all gone. At that time, the kits became rare, and I could sell them for a much higher markup. Patience paid off; a common item became rare, and higher priced.

Trick #85: Partner with Other Sellers for Bigger Orders

As you know, one way to increase your profits is to reduce the price you pay for the items you sell. But how do you negotiate lower prices when you're just a small individual buyer?

The answer is to join with other buyers to purchase in bulk. Two or more resellers operating as a buying group or co-op enables each member to purchase larger wholesale quantities, which translates into lower prices per item.

Where do you find such buying co-ops? I recommend contacting any trade associations or publications for your particular industry; chances are someone there will know of any existing buying groups you can join. You can also try Googling for "buying group" or "dealer co-op" plus the product name.

In addition, there are a handful of buying groups that operate within the eBay community, including the following:

- Bead Buying Group (groups.ebay.com/forum.jspa?forumID=100027768)
- Boutique Fabric Bulk Buying Group (groups.ebay.com/forum.jspa?forumID=100045431)
- Liquidation Buying Group (groups.ebay.com/forum.jspa?forumID=100010570)
- Ribbon Buying Group (groups.ebay.com/forum.jspa?forumID=100034184)

All of these groups consist of multiple sellers banded together to purchase specific products in bulk.

Trick #86: Bypass the Wholesaler—Buy Direct from the Manufacturer

Most eBay sellers purchase from some sort of wholesale distributor. That's fine and dandy, but the distributor is just a middleman—one who has to make his own profit on the merchandise. Cut out the middleman (and his profit) and you should be able to pocket some of that profit for yourself—in the form of lower prices per product.

To purchase directly from a manufacturer, you most likely have to become an authorized dealer for that manufacturer. This probably means signing some sort of dealer agreement, agreeing to meet various terms of sale and distribution, and sometimes agreeing to meet specified sales targets. Not all manufacturers are this strict, of course; in some cases, becoming an authorized dealer is no more involved than placing an order.

caution

Some manufacturers require you to advertise their goods at a set *minimum advertised price* (MAP). For dealers of these products, that means you can't use the standard auction process (where you'd be listing the items below the MAP); instead, you have to list your items with a Buy It Now price equal to the MAP or set a reserve price also equal to the MAP. When in doubt, check with your supplier as to what is and isn't allowed.

How you become a dealer varies; every supplier does it a little differently. You start out, of course, by locating and contacting the manufacturer. In some cases, the manufacturer sells direct to dealers. In many other cases, however, the manufacturer uses a two-step distribution process. That is, the manufacturer sells to a distributor that then sells to dealers. If this is the case, you'll need to contact a distributor for the product you're interested in selling. (And, as you've no doubt noted, you're back to dealing with a middleman between you and the manufacturer.)

Where do you find manufacturers? The best plan of attack is to do a Google search. This should lead you to the manufacturer's website, where you should be able to find some sort of contact information. Flex your fingers and either send an email or phone the main switchboard and pose your query.

tip

Another source for manufacturer contact information is ThomasNet (www.thomasnet.com), the home of the venerable Thomas Register.

After you set up as a dealer, you're in business—you can start ordering products and selling on eBay.

Trick #87: Reduce the Weight of What You Ship

Weight control is essential for a healthy eBay business. I'm not talking about your body weight (although, have you stepped on a scale lately?). No, I'm talking about the weight of the items you ship. The heavier your boxes, the more you pay in shipping charges. Or, looking at it another way, if you can reduce the weight of what you ship, you can reduce your shipping costs—and thus increase your business's profits.

Sell Lighter Items

One seller I know has a rule that he won't sell anything that he can't comfortably hold up at arm's length. The theory being that if you can't lift and hold it, it weighs too much.

I'm not sure that there's an absolute item weight you need to aim for; some sellers do quite well selling very large and heavy items. But in general, your life will be easier if you're handling smaller, lighter weight items, and you'll pay less to ship them, also.

Consider the difference between selling a lightweight T-shirt versus selling a bulky floorstanding speaker. The T-shirt is easy to handle, doesn't hurt your back to lift, can fit into a mid-size envelope, and can ship at basic Priority Mail rates or even less. The speaker, on the other hand, is tough to lug around, hurts your back to lift, needs a large box with lots of padding, and requires expensive ground shipping with a special carrier (UPS or FedEx). Which of these two items do you want to sell 100 of each week?

Again, many eBay sellers make a good living selling speakers and other big items. But many more retailers find it easier to manage a business selling smaller items, whether that means clothing, compact discs, postcards, or collectible stamps.

Pack Lighter Boxes

When it comes to cutting your shipping costs, weight is the number-one factor. The heavier a box is, the more it costs to ship (with the exception of the Postal Service's flat-rate boxes, of course). In this regard, it's not only the weight of the item that matters; the weight of the packaging is also crucial.

Many sellers tend to overlook the weight of their packaging materials. However, when it comes to calculating the shipping cost, your shipping carrier weighs the entire package, not just the contents. Everything you ship factors into the weight—the item you're shipping, the box you ship it in, even the cushioning and filler materials, such as Styrofoam peanuts and torn-up newspapers.

To reduce your shipping weights, it's important to know which materials are the lightest. To this end, peanuts are lighter than paper—that is, you want to use Styrofoam peanuts instead of shredded or wadded newspaper. Newspaper is actually quite heavy; you can easily save a half-pound or more in packing a large box by using peanuts instead of the heavier newsprint. Remember, every ounce you save saves you big money in shipping fees.

tip

Also light: bubble wrap and tissue paper.

Trick #88: Reduce Your Expenses During the Slow Periods

Most eBay businesses are not steady throughout the entire year. For many businesses, winter months are busier than summer months; it's typical retail seasonality.

Your busy periods might have twice as many sales as your slack periods. When you know that you're entering into a slow season, it makes sense to reduce your overhead during that period. You want to trim your expenses to a bare minimum when you know that sales will be slow and money will be tight.

For example, if you know the summer months represent slim pickings, you should cut back on all necessary expenditures from May through August. Get rid of the part-time help, cut back on advertising and promotional expenses, and don't make any unnecessary purchases. You might even want to reduce the number of listings you place on eBay, and cut back on expensive listing enhancements for the listings you do run. (That means no bold titles or gallery pictures during the slow summer months.) Run your business as slim as you can.

When business picks up again, you can ramp your expenses back up. Rehire the part-time worker, run some ads, print up those new business cards, and otherwise move back into full operational mode. You should also increase the number of items you list, and use the appropriate listing enhancements to help maximize sales.

The trick is that you have some control over your business spending. You don't have to maintain the same level of expenses throughout the entire year; it's in your power to cut expenditures during slow periods, and increase them during good times. Manage your outgoing funds to be in sync with your incoming.

Trick #89: Reduce Your eBay Fees—As Much as You Can

Cutting costs is hard work; you're often looking for nickels and dimes. But those nickels and dimes add up to real dollars, with a big impact on your bottom line.

Every eBay seller pays eBay fees. Some sellers complain about it more than others, but the fees are still a fact of life on eBay. That said, there are ways you can minimize the fees you pay; any savings you realize are pure profit for your business.

How can you cut the money you pay to eBay and PayPal? Here are a few tricks to consider:

- **Increase your volume to reduce your PayPal rate**—As you know, PayPal has a sliding merchant rate schedule, based on your average monthly sales volume. If your monthly sales are $3,000 or below, you pay a 2.9% rate. But when your sales inch above $3,001, your rate drops to 2.5%—and could go as low as 1.9%. When your monthly sales are approaching the $3,000 level, it's worth doing a little added promotion or pushing some more add-on sales; that 0.4% rate cut translates into a $120 savings at the $3,000 sales level.

- **Shift listings to your eBay Store**—You'll learn more about eBay Stores in Trick #96. For now, all you need to know is that it costs less to list an item in your Store than it does to list that same item for auction—considerably less. Although you can never do away completely with auction listings, you can run a more cost-efficient business by shifting more of your products into eBay Store listings.

- **Price under the breaks**—We discussed this in Trick #42. You can realize significant cost savings by setting your starting prices just under eBay's fee breaks: $1.00, $10.00, $25.00, $50.00, $200.00, and

$500.00. Instead of listing an item for $10, list it for $9.99 and save 20 cents in listing fees.

- **Take advantage of relisting credits**—When an item doesn't sell, you can relist it for free if you use eBay's Relist Your Item feature. When click the Relist Your Item link, eBay automatically relists your item and sets you up for a credit of the second insertion fee if the item sells. If you don't use the Relist Your Item feature but instead create a new listing, you're out two insertion fees instead of one. (You're also out that second insertion fee if the item doesn't sell the second time, either.)

- **Reclaim fees for nonpaying bidders**—If a buyer doesn't pay, you can file for a refund of eBay's final value fee for that item. Just use eBay's Unpaid Item Process (pages.ebay.com/help/tp/unpaid-item-process.html) to file a claim; there's no reason why you should have to pay fees for sales where the buyer backs out.

- **Use listing enhancements judiciously**—As discussed in Trick #32, it's easy to spend a small fortune on listing enhancements—gallery photo, bold title, highlighted title, and the like. Most of these enhancements don't do a thing for your sales; one of the easiest ways to cut eBay fees is to cut your use of these worthless enhancements.

- **Use non-eBay photo hosting**—eBay charges you for every photo you use in your listings past the first free photo. There are better deals around. As discussed in Trick #34, shop for a photo hosting service that offers lower hosting rates than you get with eBay. The savings could be considerable.

- **Make Second Chance Offers**—eBay's Second Chance Offer feature is a great way to make additional sales without additional costs. If you have multiple quantities of an item for sale—and had more than one bidder on the first item—then you can use Second Chance Offer to sell those additional quantities to losing bidders. When you sell via Second Chance Offer, you don't have to pay an additional listing fee. (You still pay the final value fee, of course.) That's a sale without a listing fee, which is more profitable for you.

- **Use Dutch auctions**—Similarly, if you have multiple quantities of an item, you can sell them in a Dutch auction, paying a single listing fee for multiple items. A Dutch auction is simply an auction for multiple quantities; the listing fee for a single Dutch auction is considerably less than the fees for multiple single auctions.

Trick #90: Re-Evaluate Your Suppliers at Least Once a Year

Even when you shop around for the lowest-cost supplier, that supplier might not always remain your best buy. Supplier prices go up and down over time; a supplier who was overpriced last year might have readjusted its prices and become a much better bargain today.

To that end, it's important that you constantly re-evaluate your suppliers. Do a yearly review (at least), comparing prices among your current suppliers and their competitors. If a new supplier offers a better deal, go for it.

Loyalty is fine, but you're in business to make money. If yesterday's supplier doesn't offer the lowest costs today, it's time to switch. Even if you only save a penny a piece, those pennies add up over time. And when it comes to making a profit on eBay, every penny counts.

eBAY BUSINESS PROFILE

Profile: Dedicated Fool Store

Business Profile

Business name: The Dedicated Fool

eBay ID: RatherRuss

eBay Store: stores.ebay.com/THE-DEDICATED-FOOL

Website: www.dedicatedfool.com

Type of business: CDs, vinyl, and cassettes

Owner: Russ Ketter

Location: Middlesex, North Carolina

Russ Ketter is an interesting guy. He started in the music retail business in 1970, in Berkeley, California. Russ's record store in Berkeley was a happening place; Patti Smith's first west coast gig was just upstairs, and The Police, Blondie, Genesis, and tons of other bands came through his store for autograph parties.

That Berkeley store is long gone, unfortunately, and today Russ lives in North Carolina and sells music online via his eBay Store. It's not like it was in the old days (what is?), but Russ has adapted—and become one of eBay's premier sellers of CDs, records, and tapes.

Moving Online

Russ was a fixture on the Berkeley scene throughout the 1970s and most of the 1980s, until a fire and flood in one year put him out of business. He tried again in the early 2000s, in North Carolina, but despite the fact that his store was two blocks from a college, it ended up not working. Part of this was because "competition from beer was pretty heavy," as Russ jokes, but it was also a sign of the changing retail environment for music.

Between the end of the 1980s and the beginning of the 2000s, the music business had gone through a major change. eBay, Amazon, and other online retailers adversely affected bricks and mortar record sales, as had digital music downloading. As a veteran of the independent record store scene, Russ doesn't think this is a change for the good; as he puts it, "People seem to prefer sitting on their asses, letting search engines do the work instead of their curiosity and ears."

I can sympathize. I used to love hanging out in funky independent record stores, listening to whatever album the staff was hipped on that day, exploring new and unusual sounds. You can't do that anymore; the independent record store has pretty much ceased to exist in most areas. Today, like it or not, I buy most of my music online.

To compete in this changing environment, Russ started selling on eBay about four years ago. He didn't have to do a lot of planning because his businesses have been computerized since the late 1970s. "It came pretty easy to me," he says.

Store Selling

Russ's first years online were good ones—but then it got more difficult. His business grew quite well from 2003 through the mid-summer of 2006. That's when eBay instituted the first of a series of price increases for eBay Store listings that adversely affected Russ's profits.

Even with the higher costs, however, it's still a lot cheaper to list an item in an eBay Store than it is to launch an auction listing. In fact, Russ says that Store listings are the only way to go on eBay:

"With a store, consumers can browse (if they so choose) your other listings, you can offer shipping discounts, free items and get somewhat of an identity, which helps, as most branding is for eBay, not the seller."

The Dedicated Fool's eBay Store.

Selling Strategies

Russ sells via both auctions and Store listings. What Russ posts for auctions are rarities. He avoids placing items for auction where there might be dozens (or hundreds) of the same title listed.

Unfortunately, in the music category, auctions have a very low success rate. Whether Russ posts 100 items or 500 for auction, the completion rate is "10%–20%, mostly toward the 10%."

So, Russ uses auctions sparingly, instead concentrating on stocking his eBay Store. He lists 100–200 items a week in his Store:

"Naturally the return is even less in the Store, but once in there, I have nothing else to do with it, except dust it off once in a while until I sell it."

In addition to selling on eBay, Russ has also tried selling on Amazon.com, but with minimal response. As Russ notes, Amazon is "a terrible place for sellers, as you first compete with them, then you can't offer any discounts or free shipping to get multiple sales."

When it comes to creating a successful eBay item listing, Russ offers this advice:

"Give information, as much as you can. Tell the customer why it is unique or worth what you are buying. Take good pictures and do some research. Do not believe all the 'you can do it too' books that tell you to start your auction at a penny, as you have then pegged what you think it is worth, and you just get to feed the beast. Make yourself as unique as possible."

Finding and Managing Inventory

Because Russ has been collecting records and CDs for more than 50 years, he has a large supply network to feed his business's inventory. These include thrift stores, record stores, flea markets, and the like.

All of Russ's inventory is listed on eBay. That's 11,000 items and growing. Why so large an inventory? "Any less and I don't make a living," Russ says. "Since everything is one-of-a kind, I don't have to replace inventory with the same item. If I sold at the rate I am selling now, I probably can die with a pretty good inventory."

Vintage vinyl for sale at the Dedicated Fool Store.

Managing the Business

Even with all that inventory, Russ's business is still pretty much a family affair. His wife does the shipping, and Russ does the rest. As Russ notes, "If we did not work from home, this would not be a business."

Russ uses Quicken for accounting and eBay Turbo Lister for bulk listings. That said, he's not a big fan of Turbo Lister, which he calls "the biggest memory hog and slowest software I have ever seen used on a large scale. It works, barely."

Keys to Success

I asked Russ what he did to make his business successful. Here's how he replied:

"At this point, any edge, however small, gets to stay home. Make yourself unique in stock, pricing, shipping, answering questions for your market."

He also had this advice for potential eBay sellers:

"Make sure you love what you are going to do. It is a monster of work to find unique items at good prices, and then work to list, picture it, etc. And then, unless it is unique, you are going to waste a lot of your time. Remember, eBay is just like a job now. Yet you compete with garage cleaners who don't care what they make, as it is a hobby for them. And they don't have to open up every day unless they want to. If you are planning to make this a business, be as unique as you can."

Challenges

You've probably noticed a tinge of bitterness in Russ's comments. It's true; although he's a genuinely fun guy, Russ is not one of the cheeriest eBay sellers I've met. I can understand why, though—the online music business is tough and getting tougher. And it's not helped any by changes eBay has made over the years.

Probably the biggest impact on the business has been eBay's fee increases for its Store listings. These fee increases have had a definite impact on Russ's bottom line. "When the items were 2 cents to list," he says, "it was a pleasure and the business grew. At 5 cents, you can see what happened to profitability."

Around the same time eBay increased its Store listing fees, revenues also took a hit, as part of the overall slowdown in physical music sales.

Before mid-2006, Russ averaged about $5,000 a month in sales. Today, he says, he struggles to get to $4,000 a month. Sales are down for music retailers across the board. Lower sales combined with higher costs is not a good equation.

"I find the whole online experience lousy as hell for retailers," Russ says, "whether online or off. It's a huge waste of time and energy for miniscule sales and a pretty obfuscated view of the music world."

The situation is made worse by eBay's moves regarding its Stores—not just the fee increases, but also poor marketing and the removal of Store listings from eBay search results. Russ doesn't have a lot of good to say about eBay's approach to things: "I don't think anyone on eBay's team has retail or direct mail experience, as every move they make seems to kill sales for long term sellers."

I wanted to include Russ's comments not to discourage you, but rather to inject some reality into the discussion. Many sellers get interested in eBay thinking that it's some sort of magic printing press for profits; in reality, eBay is just another marketplace, subject to the factors that affect any business. Sales don't always go up; sometimes the market shrinks, and an individual retailer can't do much about it. Sales and profits are often hard to come by, even on a good day. You have to learn how to adapt and roll with the punches—which is something Russ has done, over and over again in his retailing career.

Russ offers these parting words to those eager to start building an eBay business:

"Wish everyone good luck. I don't mean to be too negative, but it is a real job if you plan to make money at it. You can be lucky for awhile or once in awhile, but persistence and uniqueness are all that you have as your weapons."

eBay isn't a guaranteed money train. As Russ knows, it's a lot of hard work. All you can do is try to create a unique business model, and do the best job you can in selling your merchandise. The skilled sellers will come out on top, no matter what happens in the ever-changing eBay marketplace.

10

Tricks for Expanding Your eBay Business

As you gain experience selling on eBay, you want to grow your business. How do you turn a $100 per week business into one generating $1,000 per week? It's all about selling more items to make more money—and there are lots of ways to do that.

Trick #91: Differentiate Your Business

It's not that difficult to sell $100 worth of stuff a week on eBay. Anybody can do it, just by selling junk out of their basement or attic (of course, your sales drop when you run out of junk to sell. . .).

It's a lot harder to sell $1,000 a week. You can't do this by selling your old and unwanted stuff; you need a real business model to achieve this level of sales. And it isn't just about locating a source for inventory, writing powerful item descriptions, and placing lots of listings. That'll get you only so far before your business plateaus. To move beyond that level, you need to do something different—and make your business different.

The key to long-term success is to somehow differentiate your business. It's not good enough to say that you're a CD retailer or a reseller of women's clothing; you have to become a *unique* CD retailer or clothing reseller. Something about your business needs to be distinctive or you blend into the rest of the competition in your market segment. Only the most unique retailers rise to the top; the middle of the pack are filled with perfectly competent "me too" retailers, businesses that in no way stand out from all the others.

Why do you need to be unique? It's simple: If your business looks like all the others in your category, why should a customer do business with you? The answer is, they shouldn't—unless your products are substantially lower priced than the competition. And, with few exceptions, it's difficult to get rich by being the lowest-cost supplier; there's not a lot of profit in it.

It's far better to set yourself up as somehow different or better than the competition. When you run a unique business, it's difficult for customers to do a head-to-head comparison between you and your competitors; you can get away with charging a slightly higher price because of the unique things you offer.

So, how do you differentiate your business? There are three keys to doing just that.

Learn What Your Customers Want

Before you set off to make your business unique, find out in what ways it pays to be unique. That means talking to your customers and finding out what they want—and what your competitors don't offer. To differentiate your business, you have to understand your customers, both present and future. Look at your business from your customer's shoes, and use this knowledge to establish your unique features.

Analyze Your Competition

To be distinct from your competition, you have to know what they offer— and then do something different. Who are your competitors—both online and off? What products do they offer? What are their prices? What services do they offer? What are their particular strengths and weaknesses?

Only by analyzing what your competitors do and don't do can you differentiate *your* business. Learn about your competitors, and learn from them.

Offer Something Unique

After you understand your customers and your competitors, you can work toward building your own unique competitive advantage. What can that advantage be? There are a number of approaches to take, including

- Superior customer service
- Higher-quality product
- Greater product availability
- Wider selection

- More information

- Increased reliability

- Technology leadership

- Faster shipping

- Better packaging

- Satisfaction guarantee

- Extra value

- Experience

---

tip

You can also differentiate your business by the merchandise you offer. As discussed in Trick #15, it's tough to differentiate your business when you're selling commodity products. It's much better to pick out a profitable niche and make it yours.

The key is to offer one or more features that translate into distinct and valuable customer benefits. Maybe it's 24-hour customer service, next day shipping, or a huge catalog. Find a differentiating factor, and use that difference to make your business stand out from the competition.

Trick #92: Be Professional—Not Homey

I know there will be some eBay sellers who don't agree with this trick, but trust me—it separates the big boys from the little people. With few exceptions, the biggest players in any industry are recognizable pros, not "mom and pop" operations.

Now, you might actually be a "mom and pop" operation, but that's not the image you want to present to your customers. You want to come off as a professional, highly reliable operation, someone they can trust. Not that you can't trust a "mom and pop" store, but a lot of potential customers will be wary of a seller who looks like he operates out of his garage. They want to do business with a pro, someone who'll be around tomorrow and the day after, a real business that offers real service.

Think about it. Let's say you're looking at buying an item, and have the choice of buying it from one of two merchants. The first merchant has a very clean, detailed item listing, complete with a handful of well-lit, clearly focused pictures; this merchant also offers payment via PayPal, a money-back guarantee, and next-day shipping. The second merchant, on the other hand, has an item description that's short and full of misspellings, along with a single poorly focused photo; this merchant doesn't accept PayPal, offers no guarantee, and doesn't say anything about how or how fast it ships. If the price is the same between these two merchants, which would you buy from?

It pays to be professional in everything you say and do. You have to offer professional-quality merchandise for sale, create professional-looking listings (with professional-looking photos), accept a variety of payment types, pack and ship professionally, and communicate with your customers in a professional manner. If you're unprofessional in any of these areas, you'll lose business to more-professional sellers.

Of course, the first step to creating a professional image is your item listing. Your item listing *is* your business, at least for those customers interested in that item. You inspire more customer confidence (and more sales) when your image is more like IBM than it is Ma and Pa Kettle. Eschew homey fonts, "aw shucks" descriptions, and pictures of cute animals in favor of solid Arial or Times Roman text, grammatically correct third-person descriptions, and high-quality logos and graphics. The more professional your business looks, the more customers you'll attract.

But it's not just about looking professional; it's also about *being* professional. Image isn't everything; you have to deliver on your professional promise. That means cleaning up your communications so that your email appears almost corporate-like; it also means packing in new boxes, not used ones, and padding with peanuts and bubble wrap, instead of old newspapers and toilet paper.

To build a successful eBay business, you have to become a professional businessperson. Even if it's just you operating out of your garage, you can still be professional about what you do—and how you appear.

Trick #93: List More to Make More

This trick isn't much of a trick, I admit. If you want to increase your sales volume on eBay, you have to increase your number of listings. It's simple math: The more items you list, the more items you sell.

It isn't always a linear curve, however. Quite often, when you increase your listings in a given category, your overall success rate (the percentage of auctions that end with a sale) goes down. Still, you can benefit from an increase in listing volume, even if the closing percentage decreases.

Here's an example. Let's say you're currently listing 20 items a week, with a success rate of 50%—10 of those 20 items sell each week. To grow your business, you decide to double the number of weekly listings to 40, but then discover that because of market saturation (there are only so many customers out there), your success rate drops to just 40%. Well, 40% of 40 equates to 16 successful listings, which is 6 more than you had at your previous listing level. You didn't double your sales by doubling your listings, but you did affect a 60% increase. You'll need to do the math to see how much profit you generated; remember, you're paying double in listing fees.

Sellers like those profiled in this chapter and the preceding one operate in categories that require them to offer a huge catalog of items to customers. When you're selling books, CDs, videogames, and the like, you might have to keep 1,000 or more active listings in your eBay Store. The more items you list, the more likely you'll have the specific item that any particular customer might want. If you don't have the item listed, you won't make the sale. In these categories, and when selling in eBay Stores, "success rate" isn't a good metric; you might have 10,000 items listed and generate 500 sales a week. In traditional auctions, a 5% success rate would be a dismal failure; in large catalog categories, however, and when selling in eBay Stores, 5% is actually quite good.

Bottom line, if you want to grow your business's revenues, you have to increase your sales activity. *List more to sell more* is the motto of the day.

Trick #94: Expand Your Merchandise Offerings

One way to increase your number of listings is to expand your merchandise offerings—offer more and different products for sale. At first glance, this might appear to contradict the advice in Trick #14, where I urged you to specialize in a limited number of products or categories. But it's not necessarily contradictory; there are ways to expand your catalog while remaining focused.

First, make sure that you've completely filled out the offerings in your current product category. If you sell women's shoes, for example, are there additional brands or styles you could offer? Perhaps you're *too* specialized; instead of offering only women's athletic shoes, maybe you could also offer sandals and flip-flops.

Next, consider expanding into related categories. Building on our women's shoes example, perhaps you could expand into men's or children's shoes—or into other women's clothing. What goes best with shoes? Maybe hosiery, or purses, or accessory items. Think of other items that your current customers are likely to purchase; these items are good candidates for expansion.

Finally, don't rule out selling in a completely different product category. I know of many sellers who do two things and do them both well. Maybe you sell women's shoes and collectible figurines. They might have nothing in common, but maybe that's okay. Just be careful to keep your brand identities separate; consider creating a separate eBay ID and opening a separate eBay Store for the new type of merchandise. And, of course, make sure that your operation can handle the new category—try to pick a category that has some back-end similarities to what you're currently selling.

Trick #95: Sell Fixed-Price Merchandise on Other eBay Sites

Another way to expand your sales is to expand your sales territory. Don't limit your listings to traditional eBay auctions; eBay offers several other venues for selling fixed-price merchandise.

Open an eBay Store

For many (but not all) eBay businesses, opening an eBay Store is a logical growth step. In essence, an eBay Store, like the one shown in Figure 10.1, is an online outlet for fixed-price items. You operate your Store in addition to traditional eBay auctions, typically offering merchandise that is not available via the auction process.

FIGURE 10.1

The author's Molehill Group eBay Store.

There are many benefits to opening your own eBay Store. The benefits include:

- Offering more merchandise for sale at a lower cost (due to dramatically lower listing fees)
- Selling more merchandise than you can via the auction process
- Making add-on sales to your auction winners
- Generating repeat business from future sales to current purchasers

Opening an eBay Store is an especially good idea if you have a lot of fixed-price merchandise to sell or if your business includes a lot of different SKUs. You can put items in your eBay Store before you offer them for auction, and thus have more merchandise for sale than you might otherwise. An eBay Store is also a good place to "park" merchandise that hasn't sold at auction, before you choose to relist.

In addition, if you do your job right, you can use your eBay Store to sell more merchandise to your existing customers. And because eBay Store insertion fees are lower than auction listing fees, you'll decrease your costs by selling direct rather than through an auction—assuming that you have an acceptable sales rate, of course.

note

As cheap as eBay Store listing fees are, they used to be a lot cheaper. Before the mid-2006 price increase, it cost only 2 cents per month for a Store listing.

All this is made feasible—and more profitable—due to the lower listing costs associated with eBay Store listings. As you can see in Table 10.1, listing fees for eBay Store items are substantially lower than eBay's normal auction listing fees. These lower fees makes it affordable to offer more merchandise for sale—and more profitable when you sell it.

Table 10.1   eBay Store Listing Fees

Item Price	Listing Fee
$0.01–$24.99	5 cents per month
$25.00+	10 cents per month

note

eBay Stores also offer a full assortment of listing upgrades, just like the ones you can use in regular eBay auctions. These enhancements—gallery, bold, highlight, and so on—are priced according to the length of your listing.

That said, final value fees for eBay Store sales are substantially higher than for traditional eBay auctions. (These fees are detailed in Table 10.2.) You need to do some calculations to determine if selling in an eBay Store is actually more profitable than selling in an eBay auction, taking both listing and final value fees into account.

Table 10.2 eBay Store Final Value Fees

Selling Price	Final Value Fee
$0.01–$25.00	10%
$25.01–$100.00	10% of the initial $25, *plus* 7% of the remaining balance
$100.01–$1,000.00	10% of the initial $25, *plus* 7% on the portion between $25 and $100, *plus* 5% of the remaining balance
$1,000.01+	10% of the initial $25, *plus* 7% on the portion between $25 and $100, *plus* 5% of the portion between $100 and $1,000 *plus* 3% of the remaining balance

Then there are the fees to run the Store itself. An eBay Store isn't free; as you see in Table 10.3, eBay charges you for the privilege of having a virtual storefront on its site.

Table 10.3 eBay Stores Subscription Levels

Subscription Level	Basic	Featured	Advanced
Monthly fee	$15.95	$49.95	$499.95
Sales management tool (free subscription)	eBay Selling Manager	eBay Selling Manager Pro	eBay Selling Manager Pro
Custom pages	5	10	15
Reduce size of eBay header on Store page	No	Yes	Yes
Markdown Manager	250 listings per day	2,500 listings per day	5,000 listings per day
Picture Manager	1MB free	1MB free and $5 off subscription	1GB free plus free subscription
Email marketing	5,000 emails per month	5,000 emails per month	5,000 emails per month
Rotating placement on eBay Stores gateway page	None	Text link at center of page	Store logo at top of page
Store name appears in "Shop eBay Store" section of matching search results	Occasionally	Sometimes	Frequently
Traffic reports	Basic	Advanced	Advanced

Another benefit of selling merchandise in an eBay Store is that eBay will automatically advertise items from your store on the Bid Confirmation and Checkout Confirmation pages it displays to bidders in your regular auctions. These merchandising placements help you cross-sell additional merchandise to your auction customers.

In addition, eBay sends all eBay Store owners a monthly sales traffic report. This report provides a variety of data to help you track your Store activity, including total sales; average sales price; buyer counts; and metrics by category, format, and ending day or time. And all eBay Store owners can export their Store data to QuickBooks, using eBay's Accounting Assistant program, for their personal financial management.

---

note

Accounting Assistant is a software program that enables you to export eBay and PayPal data directly into the QuickBooks accounting program. The program is free to download and use, although to generate the necessary data you also need a subscription to either eBay Stores or Selling Manager (Basic or Pro). Find out more at pages.ebay.com/help/sell/accounting-assistant-ov.html.

Finally, all eBay Store owners get a free subscription to eBay Selling Manager or Selling Manager Pro. If you planned to use one of these tools anyway, getting them free helps to defray the costs of running your eBay Store.

Of course, it isn't all milk and honey in the land of eBay Stores. According to eBay, items listed in eBay Stores take 14 times longer to sell than do items listed in normal eBay auctions, on average—and, in some media categories (books, CDs, DVDs, and so on) up to *40 times* longer. But that's part and parcel with the strategy of using an eBay Store to list catalog merchandise; you don't expect the same sales rate when you offer a large number of SKUs for sale.

---

caution

One reason that eBay Store sell-through is lower than traditional auction sell-through is that eBay Store listings do not, by default, appear on eBay's search results pages. Store results appear only when there are 30 or fewer auction items returned. In other words, it might be difficult for searchers to find the items you have for sale in your eBay Store.

To open an eBay Store, start at the eBay Stores main page (stores.ebay.com), and click the Open a Store button. When you accept the user agreement, the Store creation process begins. You'll start by choosing a name for your Store. Then, on the subsequent Quick Store Setup page, you'll get to choose a Store design, select a color and theme, enter your Store description, select your item layout, insert promotion boxes, and select various marketing options. Click the Apply Settings button to launch your newly created store.

After you create your eBay Store, you add merchandise to it by clicking the Sell link at the top of any eBay listing page; the normal Sell page now includes an option for Store Inventory, which is what you want to select. Go through the normal Sell Your Item listing creation process, and your new listing will be added to your eBay Store. That's one of the nice things about having an eBay Store; it's well integrated with your other eBay activities.

Should you open an eBay Store? It depends on the type of merchandise you're selling. Stores are good for commodity-type products that are available day in and day out; categories that require a huge catalog of merchandise, such as books and CDs; and products that have a large number of variations on a basic theme, such as clothing with different sizes, styles, and colors. If you're selling more unique merchandise, however, such as collectibles, it might not be a good fit with your business. It's always a good idea to check out competitors in your category and see what they're doing, Store-wise.

Sell on Half.com

If you sell books, audiobooks, CDs, DVDs, videotapes, video games, or game systems, you should consider listing your items on eBay's Half.com site, shown in Figure 10.2. Half.com (www.half.com) lets you sell these types of products in a fixed-price format; it looks and works a lot like the competing Amazon Marketplace.

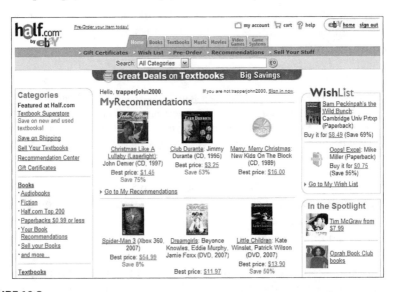

FIGURE 10.2

A fixed-price marketplace for books, CDs, DVDs, and other media—Half.com.

One drawback to Half.com is that customers don't shop by seller; instead, they search for particular items. The search results page, like the one shown in Figure 10.3, includes a list of sellers that have that item for sale. This makes Half.com more of a price-competitive marketplace than you get with eBay Stores, for example.

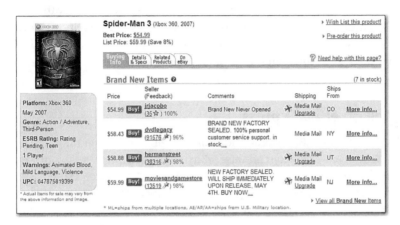

FIGURE 10.3

A typical product listing on Half.com.

One of the nice things about Half.com is that you don't pay any listing fees. Instead, you pay a higher-than-normal commission on all sold items, as detailed in Table 10.4.

Table 10.4   Half.com Commission Rates

Selling Price	Commission
<$50.00	15%
$50.01–$100.00	12.5%
$100.01–$250.00	10%
$250.01–$500.00	7.5%
>$500.00	5%

Instead of a buyer paying you directly, Half.com collects the payment as part of the checkout process. The site sends you your payment every two weeks, typically via direct deposit to your bank account.

Listing on Half.com is easy because all you need to enter is the item's UPC, ISBN, or model number, along with your selling price. Just click the Sell Your Stuff link at the top of the Half.com home page; when the Sell Your Items on Half.com page appears, click a category link or enter the item's number, and then click the Continue button. When you've entered the appropriate identifying information, Half.com then inserts prefilled item information from a massive product database. (It's the same database that feeds eBay's prefilled information in the same categories.)

Should you sell on Half.com? Given the total lack of listing fees, there's no reason not to if you sell the types of media-related items that Half.com specializes in. Many sellers like to use Half.com for those products that have market demand but won't necessarily sell in the normal seven-day auction period. Know, however, that many sellers are disappointed with Half.com sell-through rates; it's not the most popular retail site on the Web.

Sell on eBay Express

In addition to eBay Stores and Half.com, eBay offers yet another site for selling fixed-price merchandise. eBay Express (express.ebay.com), however, is an odd bird. As you can see in Figure 10.4, eBay Express is eBay's attempt to provide a fixed-priced marketplace for buyers intimidated or otherwise put off by the online auction process. eBay Express offers consumers the capability to shop from multiple sellers yet pay via a single shopping cart and checkout. Buyer peace of mind is enhanced by a special Buyer Protection Policy; payment is via PayPal.

For sellers, eBay Express really isn't a separate thing. That is, you don't explicitly list items for sale on the eBay Express site. Instead, any fixed-price item or auction item with the Buy It Now option that you have listed on the general eBay site or in an eBay Store is automatically made available to eBay Express shoppers. When a customer makes a purchase via the eBay Express checkout system, you're notified the same way you would be if it were an eBay or eBay Store purchase.

So, here's the thing: If you're selling fixed-price or Buy It Now items on eBay or in an eBay Store, you don't have any choice as to whether those items appear on eBay Express. As long as you meet the minimal seller and product requirements, your items will appear on both the original site and eBay Express.

In other words, if you want to sell on eBay Express, all you have to do is create a fixed-price eBay listing or an auction with the Buy It Now Option, or enter that item as fixed-price inventory in your eBay Store. You can't *not* list on eBay Express; as long as you're selling fixed-price or Buy It Now items, you're a member of the eBay Express retailer collective. (That's not entirely true; you can edit your general selling preferences on your My eBay page to opt out completely of eBay Express selling for all your listings.)

FIGURE 10.4

eBay's new fixed-price marketplace—eBay Express.

note

eBay Express isn't available for all product categories. To be specific, eBay Express doesn't include categories not covered by PayPal Buyer Protection (such as eBay Motors), those that don't have Item Condition values, or those where eBay's Category Managers have not yet worked out all the necessary details. For a list of non-Express (eBay-only) categories, see pages.ebay.com/sell/itemcondition/list/.

The good part of this is twofold. First, you get more exposure for your items. Second, you don't have to pay for this privilege; any item listed on eBay Express is subject to the standard eBay or eBay Stores listing and final value fees only.

That said, most sellers report minimal results from eBay Express listings. Because you don't have to do anything to use eBay Express, you're not out anything if nobody shops there. Still, it's another venue for the items you're selling—and it's good to know that it exists.

Trick #96: Sell on Other Websites

By the way, there are also other online sites where you can sell your merchandise. You don't have to limit your sales to eBay; many successful eBay businesses supplement their eBay sales with listings on other sites.

Many businesses eventually reach a plateau with their eBay sales; the universe of eBay buyers is only so big. However, there are other customers on other sites that you can market to, which is what many sellers do. In fact, some sites are better for selling certain types products than eBay is!

Other Auction Sites

Let's start by looking at other sites that do what eBay does—sell items in an online auction format. Although eBay is far and away the largest online auction site (more than 10 times bigger than Bidville, its closest competitor), the other sites might be worth checking out, especially because many have a lower fee structure than does eBay. So, in alphabetical order, here are eBay's online auction competitors:

- Amazon.com Auctions (auctions.amazon.com)
- Art By Us (www.artbyus.com—art auctions)
- Bidville (www.bidville.com, shown in Figure 10.5)
- eBid (uk.ebid.net—United Kingdom only)
- ePier (www.epier.com)
- StuffPals (www.stuffpals.com)
- Tazbar (www.tazbar.com)
- Wagglepop (www.wagglepop.com)

note

eBay's largest competitor used to be Yahoo! Auctions, but that site closed in June 2007.

FIGURE 10.5

Bidville, eBay's largest online auction competitor.

Other Online Marketplaces

If you want to skip the auction format and sell directly to the customer, there are several online marketplaces that let you sell your merchandise at a fixed price—kind of like selling an item with a Buy It Now price or in an eBay Store. These marketplaces include

- Amazon Marketplace (www.amazon.com)
- Blujay (www.blujay.com)
- Craigslist (www.craigslist.org)
- eCrater (www.ecrater.com)
- Google Base (base.google.com)
- iOffer (www.ioffer.com)
- LiveDeal (www.livedeal.com)

Amazon Marketplace

Of these sites, the Amazon Marketplace is perhaps the most promising for most eBay sellers. This is a subset of the Amazon.com site that lets individuals and small businesses sell all manner of new and used items; it's particularly well-suited to selling books, CDs, DVDs, videogames, consumer electronics, and the like.

Marketplace items are listed as options on normal Amazon product listing pages (to the right of the main listing) and show up when customers search for specific products. Figure 10.6 shows a typical listing of Marketplace items for sale.

FIGURE 10.6

Items for sale from different merchants in the Amazon Marketplace.

One nice thing about selling in the Amazon Marketplace is that customers can integrate their orders and payments with other Amazon merchandise. Customers place their orders with and pay Amazon; then Amazon informs you of the sale and transfers payment (less its fees and plus a reimbursement for shipping costs) to you. You ship the item to the customer.

You pay $0.99 to list an item in the Marketplace (although the fee isn't charged until the item sells) and then pay Amazon a percentage of the final selling price and a variable closing fee based on which type of shipping you choose. The fees charged vary by product category, as detailed in Table 10.5.

Table 10.5 Amazon Marketplace Fees

Product Category	Commission Rates	Closing Fee: Domestic Standard Shipping	Closing Fee: Domestic Expedited Shipping	Closing Fee: International Standard Shipping
Books	15%	$1.35	$1.35	$1.35
Music	15%	$0.80	$0.80	$0.80
Videotapes	15%	$0.80	$0.80	$0.80
DVDs	15%	$0.80	$0.80	$0.80
Videogames	15%	$1.35	$1.35	N/A
Computer software and games	15%	$1.35	$1.35	N/A
Electronics	8%	$0.45 + $0.05 per pound	$0.65 + $0.10 per pound	N/A
Camera and photo	8%	$0.45 + $0.05 per pound	$0.65 + $0.10 per pound	N/A
Tools and hardware	15%	$0.45 + $0.05 per pound	$0.65 + $0.10 per pound	N/A
Kitchen and housewares	15%	$0.45 + $0.05 per pound	$0.65 + $0.10 per pound	N/A
Outdoor living	15%	$0.45 + $0.05 per pound	$0.65 + $0.10 per pound	N/A
Computer hardware	6%	$0.45 + $0.05 per pound	$0.65 + $0.10 per pound	N/A
Sports and outdoors	15%	$0.45 + $0.05 per pound	$0.65 + $0.10 per pound	N/A
Cell phones and service	8%	$0.45 + $0.05 per pound	$0.65 + $0.10 per pound	N/A
Musical instruments	12%	$0.45 + $0.05 per pound	$0.65 + $0.10 per pound	N/A
Office products	15%	$0.45 + $0.05 per pound	$0.65 + $0.10 per pound	N/A
Toy and baby	15%	$0.45 + $0.05 per pound	$0.65 + $0.10 per pound	N/A
Everything else	10%	$0.45 + $0.05 per pound	$0.65 + $0.10 per pound	N/A

Amazon offers several levels of Marketplace selling. Individuals can sell items one at a time, small merchants can sell small volumes, and larger merchants can create a Pro Merchant account to list and sell items in bulk.

To learn more about selling on Amazon and to start up your own seller account, go to www.amazon.com/gp/seller-account/management/your-account.html/. This opens your own seller page, like the one shown in Figure 10.7. From there you can list single items for sale, upload multiple items in bulk, manage your inventory and orders, and learn more about Amazon Marketplace selling.

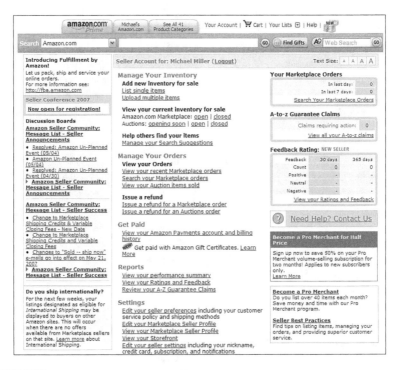

FIGURE 10.7

A seller account management page for Amazon Marketplace sellers.

> **note**
>
> High-volume sellers will want to sign up for an Amazon Pro Merchant account. For $39.99/month, you get a discount on Marketplace fees, use of volume listing tools, and your own personalized storefront. Learn more at www.amazonservices.com/promerchant/.

Trick #97: Set Up a Freestanding Online Store

Selling your goods on someone else's site is a good way to get started, but if you want to truly run your own business, you need to have your own e-commerce website. Not only can you attract non-eBay customers to your own website, you can also drive some of your eBay business to the site, thus bypassing those pesky fees that eBay charges whenever you sell something.

note

You can't link to a non-eBay website from your auctions or eBay Store. The only place you can link from is your eBay About Me page.

Fortunately, setting up your own online storefront isn't nearly as involved as you might think. Numerous services, including eBay itself, provide prepackaged storefront solutions; all you have to do is point and click (and pay some money) to get your store online. Or, if you want something really fancy, you can design your own store on your own website, complete with your own proprietary web domain.

However you do it, opening a dedicated web storefront lets you sell your merchandise 24 hours a day, 365 days of the year. You don't have to wait for an auction to end to sell an item and collect your money; you're open for business anytime your customers want to buy.

Utilizing a Prepackaged Storefront

The easiest way to set up your own online store is to use a prepackaged storefront solution. Many companies, including eBay, offer this type of service. The big advantage to using a prepackaged storefront solution is that it's extremely easy to set up; in many cases, all you have to do is fill out a series of web-based forms. On the other hand, the chief disadvantage of many prepackaged storefronts is that it's not really *your* storefront. There aren't a lot of customization options, and you have to settle for a somewhat generic look and feel, which means that your store is going to look like every other store managed by the same service—not necessarily a good thing.

Pricing on prepackaged storefronts start at around $5 per month and goes up from there. You'll probably also pay a commission or final value fee on every sale you make, typically in the 1%–5% range. The storefront service provides all necessary web hosting and storage space, as well as the tools you need to build and manage your storefront. Some of the more popular prepackaged storefront solutions include

- ChannelAdvisor Stores (www.channeladvisor.com)
- eBay ProStore (www.prostores.com)

- Homestead Storefront (storefront.homestead.com)
- Infopia (www.infopia.com)
- NetStores (www.netstores.com)
- Vendio Stores (www.vendio.com)
- Yahoo! Small Business (smallbusiness.yahoo.com/ecommerce/)
- Zoovy Storefront (www.zoovy.com)

Of these services, one of the most interesting is eBay ProStores, eBay's entry into the storefront hosting market. eBay ProStores offers much the same types of services that you find at the third-party sites, including domain hosting, real-time credit card processing, and an e-commerce shopping cart. Figure 10.8 shows a typical ProStores merchant site.

FIGURE 10.8

The ZStore ProStores site (www.zstore.com).

ProStores offers four different packages for different sizes of business (Express, Business, Advanced, and Enterprise), which range in price from

$6.95 to $249.95 per month. The different packages offer different levels of service, web storage space, and so forth.

The chief advantage to eBay ProStores over competing services is the seamless integration with regular eBay auctions and eBay Stores. You can copy your eBay listings directly to your ProStores product catalog, transfer items from your ProStores inventory to an eBay auction or eBay Stores listing, display your eBay listings in your ProStores store, and manage all your eBay listings from your ProStores store. No other e-commerce service offers this level of eBay integration.

Building Your Own Online Store from Scratch

If you want to create a truly differentiated customer experience, you might have to move beyond a prepackaged storefront to a freestanding e-commerce website. Creating your own online store from scratch can be a lot of work, and could cost a lot of money, so it's not for novice or hesitant sellers. But if you're serious about making a lot of money on the Internet, building your own e-commerce site is the only way to go.

The first step in creating your own online storefront is to contract with a professional web hosting service—a master site that will provide hundreds of megabytes of disk space, robust site-management tools, and the capability to use your own unique domain name. With your own domain name, your site's URL will read www.*yourname*.com—just like the big sites do.

After you have a host for your storefront and a domain name registered, it's time for the really hard work—creating your site. If you're handy with HTML and CSS and have a lot of free time, you can choose to do this work yourself. Or you can bite the bullet and hire a firm that specializes in designing e-commerce websites and pay it to produce the kind of site you want.

To power your new storefront, you'll have to incorporate special e-commerce software. This software will enable you to build web pages based on your current inventory, generate customer shopping carts, funnel buyers to a checkout page, and handle all customer transactions.

tip

If you're not an experienced web page designer, you'll need to hire a professional web design firm to do the job for you.

Sound like a lot of work? It is, if you do it right—which is why many small- and mid-size merchants go the prepackaged route instead. Still, if you're handy with web design and programming (or know someone who is), you can create a much more unique solution when you do it yourself.

Trick #98: Hire Additional Employees—As You Need Them

When you increase your sales, you increase the amount of work you have to do. Selling 100 items a week is a lot more work than selling 10 items a week; you not only have to create 10 times the number of listings (and shoot 10 times the number of product photos), you also have to pack and ship 10 times the number of boxes.

How do you handle the increased workload as your business grows? The solution is simple: You have to bring in more hands to help you do what needs to be done. Granted, some amount of growth can be handled just by working harder or working longer hours. But, soon enough, you'll reach the end of what you can do personally. At that point in time, you have to think about hiring additional employees.

For some small businesses, the first additional employee might be a spouse or child. If all you need is a little extra help packing and shipping, put your spouse to work in the evenings or on weekends; spousal labor is cheap labor. Beyond that, however, you'll need to look outside your family for assistance. You can hire full-time or part-time employees, depending on your business needs; it's probably best to start with part-time help so that you can adjust their hours depending on your sales trends.

Of course, before you hire an employee, you need to be clear about what it is that you want that employee to do. Most eBay sellers hire their first employee to do those activities that they either don't like to do, don't do well, or don't add any value by doing themselves. In many (but not all) instances, this translates into letting your employee handle your back-end activities: packing and shipping. That's because, when you evaluate what it is you do, you'll probably find that your talents are better suited to purchasing merchandise and creating and managing your eBay listings. It's easier, in most instances, to train someone to pack boxes and drive to the post office than it is to train him or her to create effective item listings.

After you hire your first employee, you enter into an entirely different level of recordkeeping and financial management. You have to add your employees to your accounting system, start paying employment taxes, and do all the associated paperwork. It's complicated enough that you'll probably need to bring in an accountant to manage it all for you.

If you've never managed an employee before, you have another learning curve in front of you. Being the boss is much different from working for yourself, by yourself. It's more than just managing schedules and workloads; you have to take charge and make sure that your employees do what they're supposed to do.

That's something else to consider—some part of your day will be spent managing your employees. So, if you hire an employee for four hours a day, you don't necessarily free up four hours from your schedule. Some part of that four-hour savings will be devoted to employee management.

Bottom line, you're going to need to hire an employee or two when your business reaches a certain size. You need to prepare for that eventuality, and deal with it accordingly.

Trick #99: Plan for Growth—On Your Own Terms

If you're successful with your eBay business, you'll see the sales start to grow from month to month. That's what you want, after all; the bigger your business, the more money you make.

Managing your business growth, however, can be a challenge. It's one thing to move from $50 to $500 of sales every month; it's quite another to advance to the $5,000 per month—or even $50,000 per month!—level. As your business grows, everything gets bigger. You have more auctions to manage, more photos to take, more emails to send, more items to pack and ship.

As you see growth in your business, you need to adjust your operation to manage that growth. Watch the trend lines, and estimate when you need to make additional investments—in time, inventory, and employees. Estimate your sales out several months in advance, and then plan for how to manage those sales.

Of course, one of the important things about growing your business is that you can manage the growth. When you're selling on eBay, sales growth is proportional to the number of listings you place each week. It might not be a one-to-one relationship, but in general the more auctions you list, the more sales you make.

To that end, you can manage your growth by managing the number of listings you create. For example, if you want to double the size of your business, you'll need to double (or slightly more than double) your listing volume.

That relationship between listings and sales also lets you keep your growth in check. Maybe you don't want to double your sales; if you grow too fast, you'll need to hire additional employees, rent additional warehouse space, and work twice as hard. If that doesn't sound attractive, you can limit your growth by not increasing your number of listings quite so much. Instead of doubling your listings to double your business, you might increase listings by only 20% or 30%. That kind of growth rate is easier for most people to manage.

So, maybe you plan your growth in incremental steps. Aim for a 10% or 20% growth each month so that you increase your sales and your workload at a manageable pace. Slowly ramp up your listings, and you'll be better able to manage the increase in sales.

Or maybe you don't want to grow at all. After your business reaches a certain size, it might be big enough for you—big enough to provide a decent income without unduly taxing your time. If you don't want to hire employees and don't want to rent warehouse space, cap your listings (and your sales) at just the right level.

The key concept here is taking control of your business, and not letting it control you. When you're running your own business, you don't have to keep growing sales month after month. You can grow your business to a comfortable level, and then let it stay at that level month in, month out. Unlike publicly traded corporations that require constant growth to create an acceptable return for their stockholders, the only stockholder you have to please is yourself. Control your business's growth to match your lifestyle; resist the urge to grow faster than you're comfortable with.

Trick #100: Prepare for Change

When you're selling on eBay, the only constant is change. Just as you get comfortable running your business a certain way, something changes and all your best-laid plans are torn asunder. Don't think it won't happen to you; every long-term eBay seller has had to adjust to change.

What type of change can you expect? Here's a short and common list:

- eBay fee increases
- eBay category changes
- Changes to eBay's search and browse functions (which affect how people find your merchandise)
- Changes in customer demand
- Changes in product seasonality

- New competitors in your category
- Postage increases
- Changes in shipping services
- Changes in suppliers
- Discontinued merchandise
- General economic downturns

Concerned yet? You should be; one or more of these changes can have a major impact on your business.

Consider the single issue of eBay fee increases. As you learned in last chapter's business profile, when eBay increased its Store listing fee from 2 cents per month to 5 cents per month, many businesses received a major jolt in the bottom line. How would you like it if your listing fees more than doubled overnight—with no corresponding increase in sales? This would be a shock to any business; how do you deal with it?

I can't answer that question because every change you might encounter is unique. What do you do if your main supplier of inventory goes out of business? How do you handle a new competitor coming in and undercutting your prices? What happens if the economy goes into a recession and people just stop spending money?

Whatever issues you might face in the future, you have to figure out some way to adapt. The most important part of adapting, of course, is recognizing that something has changed. You can't be blindsided by change; you have to stay on top of economic and marketplace trends, and then be quick to adjust. If you know a fee increase is coming, figure out how it affects your business and how you can adapt. If you know a supplier is shutting down, start searching for a new supplier. If you know postal rates are going up, adjust your shipping and handling fees accordingly.

The point is to be both aware and agile—aware of any possible changes in your business environment, and agile enough to deal with them appropriately. The most successful businesspeople are those who deal well with change and, whenever possible, use it to their advantage.

If your business can't adapt to change, it will die. Don't be a dinosaur; learn to evolve in the ever-changing business environment that is eBay.

Profile: BookIT Enterprises

Business Profile

Business name: BookIT Enterprises

eBay ID: bookitlbr

eBay Store: stores.ebay.com/Bookit-Inc

Website: www.bookitinc.com

Type of business: Books

Owner: Grant Thiessen

Location: Neche, North Dakota

eBay has been a good venue for used bookstores. Being able to offer vintage inventory to collectors across the country has helped many booksellers grow well beyond what they could have done locally.

One such used bookseller who's benefited from the eBay experience is Grant Thiessen, owner of BookIT Enterprises. This is his story.

Bookselling Evolves

Grant has been selling books for more than 40 years, mainly via mail order. To him, eBay is just the latest venue for his bookselling business. He started selling on eBay in 2000 as a means of reaching a different audience than the usual customers he reached through traditional bookselling venues and catalogs.

Actually, Grant's embrace of online book selling evolved out of his use of computers for his existing business. Grant bought his first Apple computer in 1979, and taught himself how to program as a means of managing his inventory and creating book catalogs:

"I entered several hundred thousand unique book titles, and produced catalogs from my computer as early as 1980. When the Internet was opened up to commerce in late 1994, I designed my own website and had it operational in fall of 1995."

As new online venues became available, such as eBay, Grant began to list his books on those sites. Being an experienced businessperson, Grant did his homework before jumping into the eBay waters:

"Before listing on eBay, I studied previous sales for similar items, then went through my entire inventory, marking items which were too common to bother listing. I monitor all of my eBay activity constantly, and I use a combination of my feedback, sales, unsold items, and price ranges to continually fine-tune the items I offer, and the prices I offer them at."

Today, Grant has more than 100,000 items in stock, although not all are listed on eBay—the cost and workload of doing so would be prohibitive. Instead, he monitors his sales and tries to maintain an inventory of 3,000–5,000 items on eBay at any one time, primarily through his eBay Store.

By the way, Grant does more than just sell books—he's also a writer and publisher. His publishing includes *The Science Fiction Collector/Megavore* magazine; he's written articles about books and book collecting for a number of other magazines and price guides.

Selling on eBay—And Elsewhere

BookIT is a bronze PowerSeller, selling between $1,000–$3,000 of books each month. He sells primarily through his eBay Store—although eBay is not his most significant source of revenue.

Grant prefers to drive customers to his website at www.bookitinc.com. "This is the best for me," he says, "since then I don't have to pay any third parties a portion of my selling price."

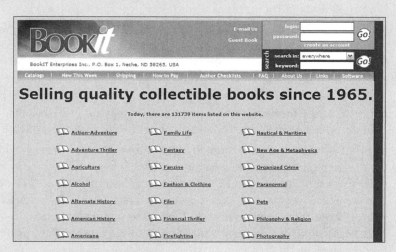

The home page for BookIT's retail website.

How does Grant drive customers to his retail website? Here's how:

"In order to convert customers to using my website, I try to provide excellent communication, new shipping materials, packing with the collector in mind, and links to similar items on my website, all of which with high-quality service in mind. I have thought in the past to offer other incentives, or lower prices on my website, but have decided that is not fair to the other venues where I do my selling. I believe that if you treat customers with integrity, you not only get to sleep really well, but you create many lasting good relationships."

Grant also sells on a number of other third-party sites, including Advanced Book Exchange, Alibris, Amazon, Amazon.ca (Canada), Australian Books & Collectibles, Biblio.com, Half.com, Auction Specialties, and several smaller sites. He also maintains an exclusively Canadian website (www.grant-thiessen.com), where he lists only books with Canadian content.

Why list on all these sites? Here's how Grant views it:

"For books these days, eBay is no longer the very best venue. In some ways, the market has become saturated, as anyone with a computer can now sell, and sell easily. As well, prior to the Internet, it was difficult to match a book with someone who wanted it, creating a large pent-up demand. When venues like eBay first started selling, competition was fierce for collectible items. A large portion of that demand has now been met, so booksellers are now selling into a less active market than before. It is not uncommon, therefore, to receive only one or no bids on a book offered for auction."

That's why, when selling on eBay, Grant's eBay Store is more important than traditional auction listings. Grant only does auctions these days when eBay runs a listing sale; the bulk of his activity is in his eBay Store.

"When eBay Stores became available," Grant says, "I thought it was an ideal way to have a large number of items available, for a longer period of time. Rather than undercut my prices, and hope for bidding action, the Store lets me set a fair, fixed price for my items, and I use the quality of the items as the primary draw to the buyer. In general, I feel that for bookstores, the eBay Store is currently a better way to sell than auctions."

Not that selling in his eBay Store is a bed of roses. As Russ Ketter noted in the previous business profile, eBay has made life more difficult for Store sellers over the past few years. "It's now harder," Grant admits. "Listing fees have gone up for eBay Stores, and search results only show store's items if fewer than 30 items are available in response to a search. In addition, many more dealers have added Stores, so the competition has become stronger."

BookIT's eBay Store.

It's not surprising, therefore, that even with his successful eBay Store, eBay is not Grant's largest bookselling venue. That honor goes to Amazon.com, where BookIT has a strong presence. Why Amazon? Because Grant can list his entire inventory for a single $39.99 charge. Here's how Grant explains it:

"I can buy a $39.99/month package which allows me unlimited listings, as opposed to eBay's 5–10 cent charge for every eBay Store item. So, for the price of 800 items on eBay, I can list 120,000 items on Amazon."

Grant goes on to note, however, that each venue has its own merits. "On Amazon, competition is very direct, as all listings for the item are on a page, and there is a lot of downward pressure on prices. On eBay, if they find your listing, no other dealer's listing appears on that page."

Creating the Perfect Listing

Wherever Grant sells, one of the keys to success is a powerful listing. Here's what Grant says is important in a listing:

"Accuracy, and a nice image. Too many sellers over-grade their material, do not disclose all flaws, and have insufficient experience in the book business to be able to properly identify the edition and publication information of their material. For example, someone will list an Ace paperback as being published in 1929. The company did not exist before 1952, and the seller is using the copyright date as if it were a printing date. Failure to identify book club and book of the month editions is another pet peeve of mine."

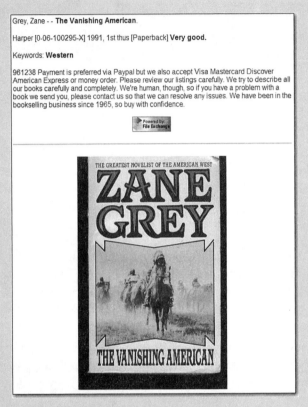

Grey, Zane - - **The Vanishing American**.

Harper [0-06-100295-X] 1991, 1st thus [Paperback] **Very good.**

Keywords: **Western**

961238 Payment is preferred via Paypal but we also accept Visa Mastercard Discover American Express or money order. Please review our listings carefully. We try to describe all our books carefully and completely. We're human, though, so if you have a problem with a book we send you, please contact us so that we can resolve any issues. We have been in the bookselling business since 1965, so buy with confidence.

A typical book listing from BookIT.

Finding and Managing Inventory

With approximately 120,000 titles in inventory, where does Grant find the books he sells? It's a lot of work, as Grant relates:

"I sell out-of-print books exclusively. I do not have primary suppliers, as such. I hunt for my items in flea markets, garage sales, thrift shops, other bookstores, etc. Over the years, I have developed extensive contacts among book collectors and sellers, and these also aid me in finding products."

To manage all that inventory, Grant uses the proprietary BookIT software that he developed. The BookIT program manages all aspects of inventory control, save for the physical filing of the books. For that, the inventory in Grant's warehouse is organized alphabetically and by size:

"For example, all paperbacks, regardless of subject matter, are filed in one continuous shelving system, alphabetically by author, then by title. As we are not open to the public, we don't have to sort our books by subject matter, we let the BookIT software look after that. Then, for hardcovers, we have another set of shelves, another for digest magazines, another for pulp magazines, and another for everything oversize. We have about 250 4×8 shelving units specially designed to fit books of the appropriate category."

Grant Thiessen, managing his business by computer with his BookIT software.

Managing the Business

BookIT Enterprises is a big business with surprisingly low overhead. Grant and his wife run the business exclusively, with the exception of some inventory held at a friend's warehouse; the friend does fulfillment for those items. Grant's BookIT software enables him to keep his personnel costs down; the software lets him list and process hundreds of items a day.

The BookIT software handles every aspect of the bookselling business, including customer management, inventory management, invoicing, accounting, receivables, and payables. It interfaces with every venue on which Grant sells, with automated file building. (Grant also sells this software to other book dealers.)

The software also serves as a front end into the eBay system; Grant has built an eBay interface into the software. "This interface allows me to quickly prepare files, at the touch of a button, for eBay auctions, eBay Stores, and Half.com, all of which I send to eBay using File Exchange. I could, if I wanted to, send 10,000 or more items to eBay in minutes."

Keys to Success

I asked Grant what it is that he does to make his business successful. His answer was short and simple:

"I treat every customer in the same way that I would want to be treated if I were the customer."

That's good advice, as is this advice Grant has for prospective eBay sellers:

"Deal in something you care about, and that you know about. If you're going to be selling on eBay, it should be fun."

This is advice echoed by many of the other businesspeople profiled in this book, and by other successful sellers. If you want to be both successful and happy, you have to know what you sell and like what you do. Trying to do it any other way can lead to failure—and a very unhappy experience. It's better to sell something you know and love, and make eBay a positive part of that experience.

11

The Ultimate Trick for eBay Business Success

We'll end this book with the one single trick that trumps all the other tricks presented so far. This is the one trick that every successful eBay businessperson knows, the trick that can spell the difference between spectacular success and dismal failure. Ignore this trick at your peril; it will make or break your eBay business.

What, then, is the ultimate eBay business trick? Make sure you're sitting down because it will knock you off your feet.

Trick #101: The Ultimate Trick

This is the point in the book where I pull the cord and reveal the man behind the curtain, where I show you that the rabbit was really at the bottom of the hat all along, where I point out the trap door beneath the table that held the disappearing girl. That's right: The ultimate trick is the ultimate reveal.

The trick is, there are no tricks.

The eBay business masters know that there are some little things they can do to make their lives easier, but in general there's no magic to being successful. The only trick to creating a successful business is that you have to work hard at it. Making money is hard work, and there are no shortcuts to success.

Go back and reread the business profiles presented throughout this book. The one common denominator for each business profiled is that the owner of that business works hard at it—very hard. These eBay masters get up early every morning, work hard every day, and take very little time off. They devote all their energies to making their businesses successful; that hard work is what propels them to the top of their class.

So, take advantage of the first 100 tricks presented in this book because they will help you become more efficient and effective. But pay closest attention to this 101st trick, and prepare to work hard to get your business off the ground. Every successful business, big or small, is built on a foundation of blood, sweat, and tears—the long hours and hard work of the business's owner and founder.

You can be successful on eBay, but you'll have to work hard to get there. That's my advice to you. Be smart, be thrifty, but ultimately be dedicated to the task at hand. There's a lot of hard work ahead, but you'll be rewarded for your efforts.

Index

N

O

T

Y-Z

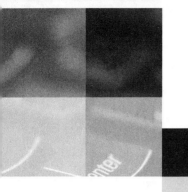

Safari®
BOOKS ONLINE
ENABLED

THIS BOOK IS SAFARI ENABLED

INCLUDES FREE 45-DAY ACCESS TO THE ONLINE EDITION

The Safari® Enabled icon on the cover of your favorite technology book means the book is available through Safari Bookshelf. When you buy this book, you get free access to the online edition for 45 days.

Safari Bookshelf is an electronic reference library that lets you easily search thousands of technical books, find code samples, download chapters, and access technical information whenever and wherever you need it.

TO GAIN 45-DAY SAFARI ENABLED ACCESS TO THIS BOOK:

- Go to **http://www.quepublishing.com/safarienabled**
- Complete the brief registration form
- Enter the coupon code found in the front of this book on the "Copyright" page

If you have difficulty registering on Safari Bookshelf or accessing the online edition, please e-mail customer-service@safaribooksonline.com.